MW01133836

German Grammar For Beginners

The Most Complete Textbook and Workbook for German Learners By My Daily German

Frédéric BIBARD (Mydailygerman.com)

Also available:

German Short Stories for Beginners

https://mydailygerman.com/product/stories-beginners-vol-1/

TABLE OF CONTENTS

INTRODUCTION

When learning any language, grammar definitely comes up as the most challenging--and boring--part. German is no different. Unfortunately, grammar is not something that can just be brushed off as an afterthought.

You simply cannot skip learning grammar if you truly want to become proficient. It doesn't work that way, and there are no shortcuts. If you want to be able to express yourself in German using clear and precise language, you need to build a strong and solid foundation in German grammar.

This book is here to help you. In the lessons in this book, we will lay down the rules in German grammar and provide you with lots of examples, clarifications, and exercises.

Practice Your German Listening Skills and Pronunciation

A key to succeed in language learning is to get a good grasp of pronunciation at the beginning of your lessons. This requires constant listening practice. With this book's audio accompaniment, you will get a headstart in your listening comprehension as well as hone your pronunciation straight off the bat.

Each lesson and exercise contains audio narrated by a native German speaker. By listening to the audio and reading the written text at the same time, you will be able to connect how a word and sentence looks versus how it sounds when spoken in actual German conversations.

Embedded Grammar Workbook

There is no need to buy a separate workbook to help you practice the grammar points you learn. We have integrated hundreds of different types of exercises into the book. This way, you will be able to cement your learning through taking the quizzes after each grammar lesson and you will be able to assess your progress as you go along.

Build a Learning Habit

This book also aims to help you build a learning habit that will help you sustain learning German even if your motivation wanes as you go along. You'll find that the book is divided into 30 lessons with each lesson meant to be tackled each day. After 30 days of studying consistently everyday, you will be able to form a learning habit that will ultimately help you achieve your learning goals.

German Grammar, Simplified

German grammar is already complicated, we don't need to make it even more complex. So in this book, you'll notice that we use the simplest yet thorough explanations. We do not want to burden you with wordy explanations and unnecessary jargons, and instead, in this book we explain German grammar in a way that makes it easily digestible and easy to grasp.

We have put a lot of effort in this book so it will come out in a way that will be most useful to your German language learning journey. We certainly hope that it will help you build the strong grammar foundation you need to eventually reach fluency in German.

Danke schön. Thank you very much.

My Daily German Team

ADVICE ON HOW TO USE THIS BOOK EFFECTIVELY

This book is divided into 30 lessons and it is designed for you to take one lesson of around 30 minutes to an hour every day.

If a lesson seems too long for you, you can split the lesson into two days. The important thing is that you work every day for 30 days (or more) so that it helps you build an effective learning habit.

LESSON 1: HOW TO INTRODUCE YOURSELF IN GERMAN 50 USEFUL PHRASES AND EXPRESSIONS

IMPORTANT: You can download the audio at page 239.

Do you ever feel lost for words, or worried you might be too familiar or formal when introducing yourself in German? Whether you are meeting new people at work, study, travel, first dates or just want to begin a casual conversation, it is always nice to start off properly.

In this lesson I will provide you with some basic phrases and expressions to use at first introductions, so you will never feel tongue-tied again and be able to start your first conversations with ease.

But first I will explain the difference between the formal and casual *you* in German. If you are already familiar with this concept, just go straight to the list of phrases.

Sie or du?

In the German language, just as in many other languages, you have two ways of addressing a person directly.

The *second person singular* **du** is the more casual way, which is reserved for friends, family and children. It goes together with addressing people by their first name, which is also considered quite familiar in Germany.

Note: In writing (except between young people or on social media) "Du" is usually capitalized.

The *third person plural* **Sie** is used to formally address individuals and groups of people. It is always capitalized and goes together with using the first or last name of a person.

In most circumstances you would address a stranger or casual acquaintance with **Sie**. There might be occasions or environments where **du** is appropriate, e.g. a music festival, party, meeting friends of a close friend. But even native speakers are sometimes unsure about which form to use. If in doubt, always use **Sie**.

In recent years Germans have become far more relaxed about this formality, but some people can be offended if addressed with **du**. Other people will offer you to use the more casual form by saying: *Wir können auch **du** sagen.* - We can say **du** as well.

And do not use the term **Fräulein**. It is not only antiquated, but also considered a bit sexist today. Use **Frau** plus the *last Name* instead.

In the following list of phrases I will provide the formal and casual options of *you*.

Listen to Track 1 (don't forget. You can find the link to download the audio page 239)

50 Basic Phrases and Expressions

Basic introduction:

Wie heißen Sie? (polite)	What is your name?
Wie heißt du? (casual)	
Wie ist Ihr Name? (polite)	
Wie ist dein Name? (casual)	
Ich heiße…	My name is…
Ich heiße Tina.	My name is Tina.
Ich heiße Tina Schmidt.	My name is Tina Schmidt.
Mein Name ist…	
Mein Name ist Tina Schmidt.	My name is…
Mein Name ist Schmidt.	My name is Tina Schmidt.
Mein Name ist Markus Bauer.	My name is Schmidt.
Mein Name ist Bauer.	My name is Markus Bauer.
	My name is Bauer.
	Note: Using just the first name, would be a casual introduction.
	Using first and last name, or just the last name, or adding Mrs or Mr would all be considered formal.
Ich bin … (Name)	I am… (Name)
Ich bin Markus.	I am Markus.
Ich bin Markus Bauer.	I am Markus Bauer.
Freut mich (Sie/dich kennenzulernen).	Pleasure (to meet you).
Nett Sie/dich kennenzulernen.	Nice to meet you.
Wie geht es Ihnen/dir?	How are you?
Gut, danke. Und (wie geht es) Ihnen/dir?	Good, thanks. And (how are) you?
Das ist …	This is …
… meine Freundin	… my girlfriend/female friend
… meine Freundin Tina.	… my (girl)friend Tina.
… mein Freund	… my boyfriend/male friend
… mein Freund Markus Bauer.	… my (boy)friend Markus Bauer.
… meine Frau	… my wife
… mein Mann	… my husband

… mein Partner/meine Partnerin	… my partner
Das sind …	These are …
… meine Eltern	… my parents
… meine Kinder	… my children

Asking questions and talking about yourself:

Listen to Track 2

Woher kommen Sie? (polite) Woher kommst du? (casual)	Where are you from?
Ich komme aus Berlin/Toronto/Japan…	I am from Berlin/Toronto/Japan…
Ich wohne in München.	I live in München.
Ich bin Deutsche und wohne in Hamburg. Ich bin italienisch und wohne in Köln. Ich bin britisch und wohne in Manchester.	I am German and live in Hamburg. I am Italian and live in Cologne. I am British and live in Manchester.
Wie lange sind Sie schon hier? Wie lange bist du schon hier in München?	How long have you been here? How long have you been here in Munich?
(Ich bin hier) seit Montag/zwei Wochen/einem Monat/…	(I am here) since Monday/two weeks/one month…
Was machen Sie? (polite) Was machst du? (casual)	What do you do?
Ich mache hier Urlaub.	I am here on holiday.
Ich besuche einen Freund/eine Freundin/meine Familie…	I visit a friend/my family…
Ich gehe zur Schule.	I am going to school.
Ich mache eine Lehre/Ausbildung.	I am doing an apprenticeship/a qualification.
Ich studiere… Ich studiere Kunst. Ich studiere Wirtschaft in Köln Ich studiere Chemie in Hamburg.	I am studying… I am studying Art. I am studying Business in Cologne. I am studying Chemistry in Hamburg.
Ich arbeite als… Ich arbeite als Designer(in). Ich arbeite als Buchhalter(in). Ich arbeite als Elektrotechniker(in).	I work as a… I work as a designer. I work as an accountant. I work as an electrical engineer. Note: In German way of making the profession female -in is added at the end.

Ich arbeite als Designer(in) bei der Agentur...	I work as a designer at the agency...
Ich arbeite als Buchhalter(in) bei der Firma...	I work as an accountant at the company...
Ich arbeite als Elektrotechniker(in) bei Siemens in Hamburg.	I work as an electrical engineer at Siemens in Hamburg.
Ich spreche (ein wenig) deutsch.	I speak (a little) German.
Ich lerne seit ... deutsch.	I have been learning German for...
Ich lerne seit sechs Wochen deutsch.	... six weeks.
Ich lerne seit drei Monaten deutsch.	... three months.
Ich lerne seit einem Jahr deutsch.	... one year.
bitte (schön)	please
danke (schön)	thank you
Entschuldigen Sie bitte.	Excuse me please. /My apologies.
Entschuldigung	Sorry
Es tut mir leid.	I am sorry.

Personal details

Whether you are at an administrative office, car rental, doctor's surgery or just like to go more into detail about yourself, you might need some of the following phrases:

Listen to Track 3

Wie alt sind Sie? Wie alt bist du?	How old are you?
Ich bin ... (Jahre alt).	I am ... (years old).
Was ist Ihr Geburtsdatum? Was ist dein Geburtsdatum?	What is your date of birth?
Ich bin am vierten zehnten neunzehnhundertvierundachtzig geboren.	I was born on the fourth of the 10th 1984.
Sind Sie verheiratet/geschieden? Bist du verheiratet/geschieden?	Are you married/divorced?
Ich bin (seit ... Jahren) verheiratet.	I am married (for ... years).
Haben Sie Kinder? Hast du Kinder?	Do you have children?
Ich habe ein Kind/eine Tochter/einen Sohn. Ich habe zwei Kinder/Töchter/Söhne.	I have one child/daughter/son. I have two children/daughters/sons.
Ich habe keine Kinder.	I have no children.
Haben Sie Geschwister? Hast du Geschwister?	Do you have siblings?

Ich habe eine Schwester/einen Bruder.	I have one sister/brother.
Ich habe zwei Schwestern/Brüder.	I have two sisters/brothers.
Ich habe keine Geschwister.	I have no siblings.

Ending the conversation

Listen to Track 4

(Ich wünsche Ihnen/dir) noch einen schönen Tag!	Have a nice day!
auf Wiedersehen	good bye (formal)
Tschüss	good bye (casual)
bis bald	see you soon

QUICK RECAP

It is not difficult to start a conversation in German. Remember to use the formal *Sie* with strangers, officials and really anybody you don't know very well. German speakers will usually let you know if they are happy to be addressed with *du*.

Memorize a few basic words and phrases to boost your confidence and start you off smoothly; you will be able to introduce yourself with ease and make a great first impression, whatever the circumstances.

TIME TO PRACTICE!

Workbook Lesson 1. How to Introduce Yourself in German

Exercise 1. Translate the following questions from English to German

English	German
1. What is your name? ((polite)	
2. What is your date of birth?	
3. Do you have children?	
4. How long have you been here?	

Exercise 2. Translate the following sentences from German to English

German	English
1. Ich mache hier Urlaub.	
2. Ich gehe zur Schule.	
3. Ich spreche (ein wenig) deutsch.	
4. Ich studiere Chemie in Hamburg.	

Exercise 3. Choose the right answer. (3/4 times)

Pick three sentences in german and 3 or 4 english translation

1. Ich _____ Markus.
   a. bin   b. ist   c. sie

2. Ich arbeite als _____.
   a. Kunst   b. Buchhalter(in).   c. Urlaub

3. Ich lerne seit drei _____ deutsch.
   a. wenig   b. datum   c. monaten

4. I am German and live in _____.
   a. *Deutsch*   b. Italienisch   c. Hamburg

5. I am _____ Art.
   a. studiere   b. deutsch   c. arbeite

6. I visit a _____
   a. freund   b. urlaub   c. jahr

Exercise 4. Match the difference sentences together

1. Haben Sie Geschwister?	a. Nett Sie/dich kennenzulernen.
2. Freut mich (Sie/dich kennenzulernen).	b. Hast du Geschwister?
3. Das ist meine Freundin	c. Ich habe zwei Schwestern.
4. Haben Sie Geschwister?	d. Das ist mein Freund

Answers:

Exercise 1:

1. Wie heißen Sie? / 2. Was ist Ihr Geburtsdatum? / 3. Haben Sie Kinder? / 4. Wie lange sind Sie schon hier?

Exercise 2:

1. I am here on holiday. / 2. I am going to school. / 3. I speak (a little) German. / 4. I am studying Chemistry in Hamburg.

Exercise 3:

1. a / 2. b / 3. c / 4. c (Hamburg) / 5. a (studying) / 6. a (friend)

Exercise 4:

1. c / 2. a / 3. d / 4. b

LESSON 2: GERMAN ALPHABET AND PRONUNCIATION

There is no shortage of myths and prejudices about the German language. People talk about how hard it is, how bad it sounds, and how different it is from English, from other European languages - and from world languages as a whole.

Did you know German and English used to be one language? They started separating off after the first century AD, but before that, it was a language Germanic tribes shared, hence the term "German languages"; a language group that includes German, English, and the Scandinavian languages.

This explains so many of the similarities. We have *Brot* – bread, *Wasser* – water, *Mann* – man, etc.

German pronunciation is a lot easier than English pronunciation. You could never fit all the pronunciation rules for English in an article of the length you're about to read!

Getting pronunciation right is easier than you think. You just need to learn the rules and patterns.

I will walk you through some of the most common (and more difficult) German sounds and provide you with some tips to help you sound more similar to how a native would. To learn all you need to know about the German alphabet and pronunciation, read on!

Listen to Track 5

Letter	Pronunciation	Example
a	[ah]	As in the first "a" of amaze
ä	This letter is called the a-umlaut.	The two dots above the letter are called umlaut. It is pronounced [ae], as in apple.
b	[be]	As in "beer"
c	[tse]	Before "a", "o", and "u", the pronunciation of c is similar to the English "k." Before "i", "e", "ö", "ä", and "ü", it sounds like "ts": Imagine the sound of a water drop falling on a hot stove.
		'ts' rarely used on its own, but it is part of the extremely commonly used consonant clusters below.
Ch		Corresponds to the English "h" as in "hard"
Sch		Corresponds to the English "sh" as in "sheet"
Tsch		Corresponds to the English "ch" as in "chair"
d	[de]	As in "Dora"

e	[eh]	As in "egg". There is no such thing as a silent e at the end of a word in German, like there is in English. These are very common, ex. cake, make, fake, take. In German, Karte, Lampe, etc. are pronounced exactly as written.
Ei	[ai]	The diphthong is very common and sounds like the pronoun "I" in English
Eu/äu	[oi]	The diphthong is very common and sounds like the one in "oil"
f	[ef]	As in "four"
g	[ge]	As in "great"
Ng		Pronounced as "ŋ" like in English (e.g., in the word "spring").
Ig		Pronounced as "ig" like in English (e.g., in the word "richtig").
h	[ha:]	As in "hair" when it's at the beginning of the word. Silent after vowels, but lengthens them. Also silent at the end of words.
i	[i:]	As in "Ida"
ie	[eeh]	The long "e" as in "teeth'
j	[jot]	As in "yo-yo"
k	[ka:]	As in "kind"
l	[ɛl]	As in "lick"
m	[ɛm]	As in "man"
n	[ɛn]	As in "man"
o	[o:]	As in "Otto"
ö	This letter is called the o-umlaut.	It sounds like the i in girl.
p	[pe:]	As in "Paul"
q	[ku:]	As in "quick", but there is an important difference to English: In German, "qu" are almost always found at the beginning of words and q and u go together, pronounced "kw"
r	[ɛr:]	As in "radio" or "red". At the beginning of a word, 'r' makes a rolling sound in the back of your throat. Pretend you are gurgling while you say 'r'. This is only when the r is at the beginning. Everywhere else, its sound is softer, like an "uh" or "ah". Ex. Mutter, Messer (mutah, messuh)
s	[ɛs]	Pronounced like the z in zoo when it's before a vowel, like the sh in sheet before p and t at the beginning of words, and as 'es' in all other cases. Ex. Sommer (pronounced "zomah") – summer Stark (pronounced shtark) – strong Spiel (pron. shpeel) – game Post – same as in English but with short "o"

t	[te:]	As in "tea" Some words begin with "th", like Theater, Theke, etc. Only the "t" is pronounced. The "th" sound in English (theta) does not exist in German.
u	[u:]	As in "Ulrich"
ü	This letter is called the u-umlaut.	It sounds like the u in "dude".
v	[fau:]	Pronounced as "fau" / "f" if it is <u>not the first letter</u> of the word (i.e. Klavier which means piano in English) It is pronounced like an English "v" if it is <u>the first letter</u> of the word. (i.e. Veronika, Verifizierung, Van)
w	[ve:]	Pronounced like the English "v" as in "van"
x	[iks]	As in "xylophone"
y	[ypsilɛn]	Very rarely used. Pronounced like the short "i" in "window".
z	[tsɛt]	Corresponds to "ts" or "tz" in English. The word 'zoo' would be pronounced "Tsoo" in German. (German "der Zoo")
ß	Eszett or scharfes S	This is like a long "s" hissing sound, "ssss." There is a movement in Germany to eliminate this letter and replace it with a double -s (ss). The word for street, "Straße", is pronounced "shtrasse"

The Umlauts – Clarification

Put simply, the umlaut shows that a hidden 'e' follows the vowel. You can read ä as ae, ö as oe, and ü as ue. Do not ignore the umlaut because it carries meaning.

Listen to Track 6

Examples:

"*fordern*" (to demand) and "*fördern*" (to promote)

"*Schon*" (already) and "*schön*" (beautiful)

Silent Letters in German and English

Silent letters are far less common in German than in English. Apart from those listed in the table above, there is only one silent letter rule; that involving the sound 'ph'. Like in English, it is pronounced 'f':

Listen to Track 7

Example:

"*philosophie*" (philosophy) – don't forget the long "i" (eeh) at the end.

Kn as in *Knoblauch* (garlic) **Rule**: say both sounds. (In English, we keep the k silent, but not in German!)

Ps as in *Psychiater* (psychiatrist) **Rule**: Pronounce both letters.

Pf as in *Pfeffer* (pepper), *Pferd* (horse) **Pronounce both letters, even if it sounds wrong to you.**

German Vowels

German vowels tend to be short and "pure," unlike English, a language dominated by diphthongs and triphthongs.

Long German Words

Listen to Track 8

You've probably noticed German has some pretty long words. Lengths such as *Höchstgeschwindigkeit* (maximum speed) and *Schwangerschaftsabbruch* (abortion) are customary. The longest word that ever existed in a human language was the German (what a surprise)

Rindfleischetikettierungsüberwachungsaufgabenübertragungsgesetz, the name of a law for proper packaging of beef. After they repealed the law, this word was dropped from the dictionary, but that didn't happen until recently.

We know compound words look scary, but here's the trick: split long words up into shorter ones and pronounce each. Then just string them together. Don't worry, natives do it too. All long words are several shorter ones put together. When you come across a long word, divide it into chunks by drawing lines between syllables on paper and work on reading each part on its own.

German Words in English

Listen to Track 9

A lot of German words have made their way into English: *Fahrenheit, Strudel, Zeppelin, Schadenfreude, Kindergarten, Hamburger, Leitmotiv, Wanderlust, Rucksack, Poltergeist, Glockenspiel, Rottweiler, and Gestalt.* Did you know any of these? Think about how they are pronounced in English.

From Exposure to Recognition

Now that you know all the rules, you need to get as much exposure to German sounds as possible. Set some time aside every day to listen to German podcasts,

German songs, and German conversations suitable to your language level. German TV shows and German movies with German subtitles. Watch Yo videos, also with German subtitles.

You can probably pronounce a lot of long and hard words in your native language. The only reason you may not be able to do that in German yet is because you're not used to the German words. With time and practice, the sounds will become familiar to you. Even the trickiest ones will become a piece of cake.

QUICK RECAP:

- The *r* (at the end of the word) sounds like "uh" or "ah"
- The *r* (at the beginning of the word) sounds like gurgling
- *v* sounds like the English and German f
- The *ch* sounds like a cat hiss
- *j* sounds like the English y
- ß is just a "ss" sound
- *w* sounds like the English v

TIME TO PRACTICE!

Workbook Lesson 2. German Alphabet and Pronunciation

Exercise 1: Fill in the blanks with the correct answer.

ss or ß?

1. Dafür wirst du mich ha___en!
2. Warum haben wir diese Ma___e?
3. Schöne Grü___e
4. An der Ka___e zahlen.
5. Bitte vergi___nicht, meine Blumen zu gie___en!
6. Kannst du auf meine Tasche aufpa___en?

The h: silent or not?

7. Stehlen ___
8. Autobahn ___
9. Lehne___
10. Ehe ___
11. Mehl ___
12. Sahne ___

13. Haar ___

14. Hitze ___

Exercise 2: What is the English equivalent of the bolded sound?

1. **ü**ber : ___   a) ue   b) u   c) o
2. brau**ch**en : ___   a) ch   b) sh   c) h
3. **sp**üren: ___   a) sp   b) p   c) sh   d) shp
4. **s**ingen: ___   a) s   b) z   c) sh
5. ungl**au**blich: ___   a) ae   b) ai   c) eu   d) none of these
6. **Ä**rger: ___   a) a   b) e   c) ae
7. **j**agen: ___   a) j   b) y   c) ae
8. **w**inkel:___   a) w   b) v   c) neither
9. h**ö**chste: ___   a) eo   b) oe   c) o   d) e
10. **Qu**atsch: ___   a) qu   b) kw   c) both   d) neither

Exercise 3: Fill in the blanks with the correct answer.

Y, i, or ü?

1. B___roklammern
2. Deb___tant
3. G___mnasium
4. Kost___m
5. Lobb___ist
6. S___mpatisch
7. K___rche

D oder t?

8. Hun___
9. ___asche
10. ___eppich

B oder p?

11. Die___
12. ___ackung

Answers:

Exercise 1:

1. ss / 2. ss / 3. ß / 4. ss / 5. ss, ß / 6. ss / 7. silent / 8. silent / 9. silent / 10. silent / 11. silent / 12. Silent / 13. not silent / 14. not silent

Exercise 2:

1. a / 2. c / 3. d / 4. b / 5. d, it is au again / 6. c / 7. b / 8. b / 9. b / 10. d, it is kv

Exercise 3:

1. ü / 2. ü / 3. y / 4. ü / 5. y / 6. y / 7. i / 8. d / 9. t / 10. t / 11. b / 12. P

LESSON 3: THE ARTICLES: DEFINITE AND INDEFINITE (BESTIMMTER UND UNBESTIMMTER ARTIKEL)

You'd be happy to know that the definitive and indefinite articles in German are used similarly to those in English. The slight difference can be seen on how it varies based on the person, case, and gender it refers to.

What are the Differences between the Definite and Indefinite Article?

Like in English, the **definite article** is used to refer to a particular place, person, or thing (the definition of a noun) in two cases:

a) When it has already been mentioned and/or we know what noun the speaker is referring to

Listen to Track 10

Example:

Ich habe eine neue Nachbarin. Die Nachbarin ist sehr nett.

I have a new neighbor. The neighbor is very nice.

In the example, 'eine' translates as 'a'. This is the indefinite article in the feminine, accusative tense. In the second sentence, 'die' means 'the', which is the definite article (again feminine, but nominative case, which is the same form as the accusative). We use 'the' in the second sentence, because the neighbor has been mentioned once already and we know who the speaker is referring to.

b) When there is only one of this place, person, or thing in the world

Listen to Track 11

Example:

Der Papst ist 81.   The Pope is 81.

Forms of the definite article

The definite article [der, die, das, die (Pl.)] is translated as 'the' in English.

Listen to Track 12

	Masculine	**Feminine**	**Neuter**	**Plural**
Nominative	*der*	*die*	*das*	*die*
Accusative	*den*	*die*	*das*	*die*

Dative	*dem*	*der*	*dem*	*den*
Genitive	*des*	*der*	*des*	*der*

Examples:

Listen to Track 13

Ich kenne einen Mann. Der Mann wohnt in der Nähe.

I know a man. The man lives around here.

If we want to connect the sentences so they sound more natural in German and English, we would still use "der" in German. Please note that the meaning of "der" would then change:

Listen to Track 14

*Ich kenne einen Mann, **der** in der Nähe wohnt.*

I know a man, **who** lives around here.

Ich habe einen Mann auf einer Party getroffen. Jetzt gehe ich mit dem Mann aus.

I met a man at a party. Now, I am going out with the man.

In the first sentence, the indefinite article *einen* is in the accusative because 'Mann' is the direct object in the sentence. We use an indefinite article because this is the first time we are mentioning the man.

In the second sentence, *der* becomes *dem* because the definite article comes after ‚mit', which always takes the dative.

To negate a noun preceded by a definite article, we just add 'nicht'.

Listen to Track 15

Example:

Ich gehe mit dem Mann nicht aus.   I don't go out with the man.

Contractions with Definite Articles

This brings us to our next section: **some prepositions bind to definite articles, forming one word.**

Examples:

An + das = ans, auf + das = aufs, an + dem = am, bei + dem = beim, für + das = fürs, durch + das = durchs, in + das = ins, in + dem = im, von + dem = vom, um + das = ums, zu + der = zur, zu + dem = zum

Listen to Track 16

Wir fahren jedes Jahr ans Meer.   We travel to the seaside every year.

We would say this if the person listening to us knew what seaside was meant, hence the use of the definite article (an + das). If they didn't, we might say:

Listen to Track 17

Wir fahren jedes Jahr ans Meer nach Bulgarien.

We go to the sea in Bulgaria every year.

(or another country) to specify the location of the seaside.

Listen to Track 18

Ich gehe zur Post.   I'm going to the post office.

We assume there is only one post office in the area because the definite article is used (zu + der = zur). *Zu* always takes the dative.

On a final note for this section, **the genitive masculine and neuter form of the definite article is des.** There is one specific thing about its use:

Listen to Track 19

Das ist das Auto des Mannes.   That's the man's car.

The genitive indicates possession. The noun order is reversed – *das Auto des Mannes* becomes *the man's car*. Notice something else? **The genitive noun takes –es at the end.** Both articles are definite because we know which car and which man are being referred to.

Listen to Track 20

Sie sind die Eltern des Schülers.   They are the student's parents.

Again, both articles are definitive because we know what parents and what student are being referred to. The genitive noun takes just **–s** at the end because it is more than a syllable.

Listen to Track 21

Das ist ein Auto der Frau.   That's (one of) the woman's cars.

Use of the indefinite article *ein* in this sentence indicates the woman has more than one car. Translated literally, it would be "That's the woman's car", the same as if the sentence were *"Das ist das Auto der Frau."* Literal translation, as you can see, can be misleading.

To mark the genitive of proper names, we add the apostrophe to mark the genitive of proper names ending in "s", "x", "z", or "ß". The name will come before the noun specified by it. It's similar to how it's use in the English language.

Listen to Track 22

Marx' Buch Marx' Book *Chris' Mutter* Chris' mother

Forms of the Indefinite Article

The indefinite article is used when the noun has not been mentioned previously and is one of many. The forms of the indefinite article in German are equivalent to "a" or "an" in English. There is no German equivalent for 'an'. It's still "ein Auto" even though Auto starts with a vowel.

Listen to Track 23

	Masculine	Feminine	Neuter
Nominative	*ein*	*eine*	*ein*
Accusative	*einen*	*eine*	*ein*
Dative	*einem*	*einer*	*einem*
Genitive	*eines*	*einer*	*eines*

There is no indefinite article in the plural because the indefinite article can only be placed before a noun in the singular. We can't say "a cars" in English. "*Einige*" (a few, some) can be used to refer to an indefinite number of objects.

Listen to Track 24

Examples:

Ich *habe einen Kollegen getroffen.*   I met a coworker.

(You have more than one coworker and we don't know which one you met).

Ich bin mit einer Freudin ins Kino gegangen.

I went to the movies with a (girl)friend.

You have more than one friend. 'Ins' comes from 'in + das', see contraction section above. Do we know which cinema you went to? Not necessarily. 'Ins Kino' and 'ins Theater' are fixed expression.

Demonstrative and Indefinite Determiners

Definite articles, indefinite articles, possessive articles, possessive determiners, indefinite determiners, and demonstrative determiners and articles are all grouped in the category of determiners. Our last section will touch upon the relevant ones.

Demonstrative determiners include *dieser, diese, dieses* (this in the masculine, feminine, and neuter, also diese for the plural) *diejenigen, derjenigen* (those), *dasselbe, demselben* (the same), etc.

Listen to Track 25

Examples:

Das gilt für diejenigen, die kein Auto besitzen.

This applies for those, who don't have a car.

This brings us to negation. **The rule is very simple.** *Ein* becomes *kein, eine* becomes *keine, einem* becomes *keinem,* etc.

Listen to Track 26

Examples:

Ich habe keine Zeit.   I don't have time.

Zeit is an uncountable noun in German like time is in English. Therefore, we can't say *Ich habe eine Zeit.* To say we have time, we'd just say *Ich habe Zeit.*

But:

Listen to Track 27

Die Zeit ist jetzt.   Now is the time.

Es ist an der Zeit.   It's high time, it's about time. (fixed expression with the dative).

Vor einiger Zeit habe ich bei einer Firma gearbeitet.

I worked for a company some time ago.

QUICK RECAP:

- The definite article is used to refer to a particular place, person, or thing (the definition of a noun) if it has already been mentioned and/or we know what noun the speaker is referring to and when there is only one of this place, person, or thing in the world.
- The indefinite article is used when the noun has not been mentioned previously and is one of many.
- Some prepositions such as *an, auf, zu, and von* bind to definite articles, forming one word with them.
- To negate a noun preceded by a definite article, we just add '*nicht*'.

- To negate a noun preceded by an indefinite article, simply an a '-k' in front of the article. Ein = kein.
- There is no indefinite article in the plural because the indefinite article can only be placed before a noun in the singular.

TIME TO PRACTICE!

Workbook Lesson 3. The Articles: Definite and Indefinite

Exercise 1. Fill in the blanks with a declined form of the definite article. Sometimes, there is more than one right answer.

1. _____ Fenster und _____ Tür stehen offen.
2. _____ Mann spricht mit _____ schönen Frau.
3. Das sind _____ Schuhe _____ Besucher.
4. Ich gehe in _____ Schule.
5. Das ist _____ Haus _____ Hundes.
6. _____ Mutter von Luis ist krank.
7. _____ Hund spielt mit _____ Katze.
8. _____ Meer ist blau und grün.
9. Ich kaufe _____ Schwester meiner Frau weiße Blumen.
10. Das ist _____ Mantel meiner Mutter.
11. Mein Schuh war _____ Garten.
12. _____ Freund meiner Schwester geht nicht mehr in _____ Schule.
13. Ich mag _____ Schwimmbad mehr als _____ Meer.
14. Wem gehört _____ Wohnung mit _____ großen Fenster?
15. Die Schule ist _____ größte Gebäude _____ Stadt.

Exercise 2. Fill in the blanks with a declined form of the indefinite article.

1. Vor unserem Haus sitzt _____ Katze, die mit _____ blauen Ball spielt.
2. In meinem Zimmer steht _____ Tisch mit _____ Computer.
3. Ich gebe _____ Kind ein Spiel.
4. Auf dem Stuhl sitzt _____ Mann und daneben sitzt _____ Kind.
5. Meine Freundin liest _____ Buch und schaut _____ Film.
6. Spiel mit _____ Oma.
7. Diese Tasse ist _____ Geschenk _____ Freundes.
8. Mein Bruder hat sich mit _____ Frau getroffen.

9. Im Garten spielen _____ Junge und _____ Mädchen.

10.   Ich pflücke im Garten _____ Rose.

Answers:

Exercise 1:

1. das/die, die / 2. der, der / 3. die, der / 4. die / 5. das, des / 6. die / 7. der, der / 8. das 9. der / 10. der / 11. im / 12. der, die / 13. das, das / 14. die, dem / 15. das, der

Exercise 2:

1. eine, einem / 2. ein, einem / 3. einem / 4. ein, ein / 5. ein, einen / 6. einer / 7. ein, eines / 8. einer / 9. ein, ein / 10. eine

LESSON 4: GERMAN NOUNS: GENDER AND NUMBER (FEMININE/MASCULINE, SINGULAR/PLURAL AND CAPITALIZATION RULES)

For English speakers the idea of grammatical gender may seem odd. Why *is a table* male, *a door* female and *a window* neutral in German? Though it might feel random and an arduous task to remember, there are some consistencies and rules to help you identify what is what. We will look at each one in detail, so you can start using grammatical gender with confidence.

The Grammatical Gender of German Nouns in brief

German nouns have a gender, including objects and abstract concepts, not just people or living creatures. This can take a bit of time to get used to, but quickly it will feel completely natural. Let us start from the beginning and review what a noun is.

What is a noun?

A noun is an identifier, it identifies what something or someone is. This can be tangible, such as **table, book, house, person** or abstract, such as **anger, idea** or **happiness.** Names are also nouns.

In written German, nouns are easy to spot, they are always capitalized.

Nouns can be preceded by a **definite (the)** or **indefinite (a) article**. Right now I would like to concentrate on the definite article, the indefinite article will come easy after that.

Now we need to look at German nouns in order to understand why gender matters.

Grammatical gender

The German language has three genders. This means, that nouns are either **masculine, feminine** or **neutral**. The gender of German nouns can be identified by the preceding definite article. The best way to learn the gender, is to learn each new noun together with the definite article.

Listen to Track 28

der (masculine)	*die* (feminine)	*das* (neutral)
der Mond	*die Katze*	*das Kind*

Whether a word is masculine, feminine or neutral is unfortunately fairly arbitrary, and sometimes seems to defy all logic. But there are a few clues that can help you learn and remember the correct gender of many words even without the article. The first clue is the word-ending.

1. Word-endings indicating grammatical gender:

Listen to Track 29

masculine

-er (mostly)	*der Spieler*	the player
-en	*der Besen*	the broom
-ig	*der Käfig*	the cage
-ismus	*der Kapitalismus*	the capitalism
-ist	*der Polizist*	the policeman
-ling	*der Frühling*	the spring
-or	*der Motor*	the motor
-mann	*der Fachmann*	the specialist (male)

Listen to Track 30

feminine:

-e	*die Blume*	the flower
-in	*die Freundin*	the friend (female)
-ei	*die Bäckerei*	the bakery
-frau	*die Fachfrau*	the specialist (female)
-keit	*die Tätigkeit*	the occupation
-heit	*die Freiheit*	the freedom
-schaft	*die Freundschaft*	the friendship
-ung	*die Überraschung*	the surprise
-ät	*die Universität*	the university
-ik	*die Kritik*	the criticism
-ion	*die Union*	the union
-ie	*die Melodie*	the melody
-ur	*die Kultur*	the culture
-enz	*die Konkurrenz*	the competition

Listen to Track 31

neutral:

-chen	*das Häuschen*	the little house
-lein	*das Mäuslein*	the little mouse
-ment	*das Dokument*	the document
-nis	*das Geheimnis*	the secret

| **-tum** | *das Eigentum* | the property |
| **-um** | *das Zentrum* | the center |

Though these rules apply to the majority of nouns, there are always exceptions. Here are some rule breakers:

Listen to Track 32

die Mauer	the wall
die Trauer	the sorrow
der Brei	the mush

2. Grammatical gender matches the person´s gender:

It also helps to know, whether you are talking about a man or woman. If the noun identifies a person, the grammatical gender usually matches the gender of the person.

Listen to Track 33

male/masculine:

der Mann	the man
der Vater	the father
der Bruder	the brother
der Sohn	the son
der Junge	the boy

Listen to Track 34

female/feminine:

die Frau	the woman
die Mutter	the mother
die Schwester	the sister
die Tochter	the daughter

exception:

| ***das* Mädchen** | the girl |

One would assume that **the girl** would be feminine, but it is neutral. But note that the word-ending is **-chen.** Nouns with this ending are always neutral**.** Adding **-chen** or **-lein** at the end of a word, emphasizes that something is small, cute or insignificant. Seems a bit sexist, but these are the rules of grammar.

3. But sometimes the grammatical gender does not relate to the personal gender. It is not an indication, whether the person is male or female:

Listen to Track 35

der Mensch	the human
der Gast	the guest
die Person	the person

4. Some words can be masculine and feminine, depending on which article you use:

The noun itself does not change. Either the male or female article is added, depending on context.

Listen to Track 36

der Reisende/die Reisende	the male/female traveler
der Schlafende/die Schafende	the male/female sleeper
der Lesende/ die Lesende	the male/female reader

5. Certain subjects or groups of words tend to be a specific gender:

Days of the week, names of the months; seasons, and many weather-related nouns are all masculine.

Listen to Track 37

der Montag	the Monday
der Januar	the January
der Frühling	the spring
der Regen	the rain
der Schnee	the snow
der Nebel	the fog

Many common names of trees and flowers are feminine.

Listen to Track 38

die Eiche	the oak
die Linde	the lime-tree
die Rose	the rose
die Kirsche	the cherry

Listen to Track 39

Verbs and adjectives that have been transformed into nouns are always neutral.

das Lesen	the reading
das Essen	the eating
das Rauchen	the smoking
das Gute	the good
das Schlechte	the bad

And because Germans love to combine words to make extra-extra-long words, let us have a quick look at thesecompound words.

6. Compound words:

Words that are put together from several words of differing genders always take the same gender as the last part of the word.

Listen to Track 40

die Tischdecke	der Tisch + <u>die</u> Decke	the tablecloth
der Türrahmen	die Tür + <u>der</u> Rahmen	the door frame
die Kirchturmuhr	die Kirche + der Turm + <u>die</u> Uhr	the clock of the church tower

QUICK RECAP:

- There are three grammatical genders in the German language, recognizable through the article in front of the noun: **masculine**, **feminine** or **neutral**.

- If you familiarize yourself with word-endings and pay attention to actual genders, you are halfway there. But there are no hard and fast rules, it can be confusing at the beginning, so try to learn each noun with the definite article right from the start.

- And if you do mix up your **der, die, das,** it´s not a disaster, you will still be understood. But if you get it right, it will be music to the German ear and make for a much smoother conversation. And it will also be relevant and useful to know the gender of your nouns when using adjectives and pronouns. But I will save this part for another time.

TIME TO PRACTICE!

Workbook Lesson 4. German Nouns: Gender and Number

Exercise 1. Choose the right article in the following sentences:

1. Das ist _____ Vater. (This is the father.)
2. Das ist _____ Frau. (This is the woman.)
3. Das ist _____ Bauer. (This is the farmer.)
4. Das ist _____ Dokument. (This is the document.)

5. Das ist _____ Strasse. (This is the street.)
6. Das ist _____ Katze. (This is the cat.)
7. Das ist _____ Kätzchen. (This is the little cat - diminutive ending!)

Exercise 2. Fill in the blanks with the correct article:

1. Anna ist ____ Freundin von Tia. (Anne is the friend of Tia.)
2. ____ Mädchen hat den Bus verpasst, deshalb kommt sie zu spät in ____ Schule. (The girl missed the bus, that's why she is late for the school)
3. ____ Hund dort drüben gehört mir. (The dog over there is mine.)
4. Mir ist ____ Freiheit, sich äußern zu können, wichtig. (The freedom to express oneself is important to me.)
5. Wie heißt ____ Künstler dieser Ausstellung? What is the artist of this exhibition called?)
6. Er findet ____ Zentrum von Berlin zu überfüllt. (He finds the center of Berlin too crowded.)
7. Geduld ist ____ beste Eigenschaft für mich. (Patience is the best quality for me.)
8. Wir glauben, dass ____ Kritik unberechtigt ist. (We believe that the criticism is unfounded.)
9. ____ Kleidchen ist für meine Schwester. (The little dress is for my sister.)
10. Das ist ____ erste Schmetterling in diesem Frühling. (This is the first butterfly this spring.)

Exercise 3. Place the right article in the following sentences:

1. Ich kenne ____ Person nicht. (I don't know the person.)
2. Sie war ____ letzte Gast. (She was the last guest.)
3. Sie war ____ erste Reisende auf dem Schiff. (She was the first traveler on the ship.)
4. Er ist ____ Reisende mit dem roten Koffer. (He is the traveler with the red suitcase)
5. Mein Mann ist ____ Sitzende dort drüben. (My husband is the sitting (person) over there.)
6. Im Garten ist ____ Rauchen erlaubt. (In the garden the smoking is allowed.)
7. ____ Singen war zu laut für mich. (The singing was too loud for me.)
8. ____ Interessante an dem Film war die Musik. (The interesting (thing) about the film was the musik.)
9. Sie glaubt an ____ Gute im Menschen. (She believes in the good of people.)

> **Fun fact:** Until 2007 a law related to beef quality control used to be the longest word in the German language: *Rindfleischetikettierungsüberwachungsaufgabenübertragungsgesetz*
>
> Thanks to changes in legislation, it doesn't exist anymore. Currently one of the contenders for the longest word is:
> *Aufmerksamkeitsdefizit-Hyperaktivitätsstörung* meaning Attention Deficit Hyperactivity Disorder

Exercise 4. Choose the correct article:

1. ____ Berufstätigkeit (the occupation)
2. ____ Motorhaube (the engine bonnet)
3. ____ Eichhörnchen (the squirrel)
4. ____ Geschwindigkeitskontrolle (the speed control)
5. ____ Springbrunnen (the water fountain)
6. ____ Staatseigentum (the government property)
7. ____ Vogelkäfig (the bird cage)
8. ____ Kurzstreckenfahrkarte (the ticket for short journeys)
9. ____ Machtverhältnis (the balance of power)

Answers:

Exercise 1

1. der / 2. die / 3. der / 4. das / 5. die / 6. die / 7. das

Exercise 2

1. die / 2. das, die / 3. der / 4. die / 5. der / 6. das / 7. die / 8. die / 9. das / 10. der

Exercise 3

1. die / 2. der / 3. die / 4. der / 5. der / 6. das / 7. das / 8. das / 9. das

Exercise 4

1. die / 2. die / 3. das / 4. die / 5. der / 6. das / 7. der / 8. die / 9. das

LESSON 5: THE FOUR CASES IN GERMAN (NOMINATIVE, ACCUSATIVE, DATIVE & GENITIVE) AND DECLENSIO (DIE DEKLINATION DER NOMEN)

German Declension: The Four Grammatical Cases in Detail

In this lesson I will explain the dreaded subject of **declension** (*Deklination der Nomen*) and **the four German grammatical cases** (*Kasus*). Feared by many, but once you understand the rules, it will be much less intimidating.

The term declension in the German language describes the inflection (change) of nouns, articles, pronouns and adjectives according to the four cases: **nominative, accusative, dative** and **genitive**. You will also have to consider the grammatical gender (*Genus*) and whether a noun is singular or plural (*Numerus*). The grammatical cases help you to identify the function of a noun within a sentence.

In the scope of this lesson I will focus on the declension of nouns and articles, as this is the foundation of all further learning. But first I will explain what the grammatical cases are and how they are used.

Understanding the Four German Cases (Kasus):

Each grammatical case determines a specific function within a sentence. These functions include the **subject (nominative)**, the **direct object (accusative)**, the **indirect object (dative)**, and the **attributive use (genitive)**.

Let's look at a simple sentence:

Listen to Track 41

Der Mann gibt	*dem Hund*	*des Nachbarn*	*einen Knochen.*
The man gives	the dog	of the neighbor	a bone.
subject → nominative	indirect object → dative	attributive use → genitive	direct object → accusative

It can also help to use questions to determine the grammatical case.

Nominative

- indicates the subject of the sentence, the one that performs the action. It is also used after the verbs: *sein, bleiben, werden*. It is the basic form you find in the dictionary.

Ask the question:

Listen to Track 42

Wer gibt dem Hund des Nachbarn einen Knochen?

Who gives the dog of the neighbor a bone?

Der Mann   The man

Accusative

- indicates the direct object of the sentence, the object which directly receives the action. It is also used after the prepositions: *durch, für, gegen, ohne, um*

Ask the question:

Listen to Track 43

Wen oder Was gibt der Mann dem Hund?

What does the man give to the dog?

Einen Knochen   A bone

Dative

- indicates the indirect object, the receiver of the direct object. It is also used after the prepositions: *aus, bei, mit, von, zu*

Ask the question:

Listen to Track 44

Wem gibt der Mann einen Knochen?

To whom does the man give a bone?

Dem Hund   To the dog

Genitive

- indicates possession by s.o./s.th. or attributes of s.o./s.th., and it is also used after certain prepositions: e.g. *wegen, trotz, infolge, dank*

Ask the question:

Listen to Track 45

Wessen Hund gibt der Mann einen Knochen?

Whose dog does the man give a bone to?

Des Nachbarn   The neighbor's.

Depending on the case, the **definite** or **indefinite article** changes, and sometimes the ending of the noun itself. The article is the most obvious indicator for German grammatical cases.

Declension with the definite/indefinite (the/a) article in singular

Listen to Track 46

	masculine	*feminine*	*neutrum*
nominative *Wer?*	**der/ein** Maler **der/ein** Nachbar **der/ein** Gedanke **der/ein** Lieferant	**die/eine** Katze	**das/ein** Zimmer **das/ein** Kind
accusative *Wen/Was?*	**den/einen** Maler **den/einen** Nachbarn **den/einen** Gedanken **den/einen** Lieferanten	**die/eine** Katze	**das/ein** Zimmer **das/ein** Kind
dative *Wem?*	**dem/einem** Maler **dem/einem** Nachbarn **dem/einem** Gedanken **dem/einem** Lieferanten	**der/einer** Katze	**dem/einem** Zimmer **dem/einem** Kind
genitive *Wessen?*	**des/eines** Malers **des/eines** Nachbarn **des/eines** Gedankens **des/eines** Lieferanten	**der/einer** Katze	**des/eines** Zimmers **des/eines** Kindes

The declension of definite and indefinite articles is straightforward, though you do have to memorize it. The only tricky bits are some of the differing endings for the masculine and neutrum. But there is some logic to this.

Types of Declension in Singular

Accusative/dative noun endings:

All feminine nouns remain the same. Most **masculine** and all **neutrum nouns** (with the exception of *das Herz*) do not change either.

Note: But there are some exceptions that have the letters **-n** or **-en** added*:

Listen to Track 47

- **Masculine living beings with the ending *-e:***

  der Junge, den Jungen, dem Jungen   the boy

der Kunde, den Kunden, dem Kunden	the customer
der Rabe, den Raben, dem Raben	the raven

Listen to Track 48

- **Masculine nationalities with the ending -e:**

der Russe, den Russen, dem Russen	the Russian
der Deutsche, den Deutschen, dem Deutschen	the German

Listen to Track 49

- **And a few more masculine nouns, mostly also living beings:**

der Bauer, den Bauern, dem Bauern	the farmer
der Nachbar, den Nachbarn, dem Nachbarn	the neighbor
der Bär, den Bären, dem Bären	the bear

Listen to Track 50

- **Masculine professions originating from other languages:**

der Fotograf, den Fotografen, dem Fotografen	the photographer
der Assistent, den Assistenten, dem Assistenten	the assistant
der Advokat, den Advokaten, dem Advokaten	the lawyer

Listen to Track 51

- **Masculine abstracts with the ending -e and one neutrum word (das Herz):**

  This last group also ends with **-s** in the **genitive** case (the others don't!):

der Buchstabe, den Buchstaben, dem Buchstaben,	the letter
des Buchstabens	
der Wille, den Willen, dem Willen, des Willens	the will
das Herz, das Herz, dem Herzen, des Herzens	the heart

Genitive noun endings:

In the Genitive the fast majority of **feminine** nouns remain the same.

Listen to Track 52

And so do **names used with article**, e.g.:

Die Leiden des jungen Werther.   The sufferings of the young Werther.

Some **masculine** and **neutrum** nouns have the letters *-es* added:

Listen to Track 53

- **Mono-syllabic words:**

  Am Rande des Weges steht eine Eiche.   At the side of the path stands an oak.

  Am Ende des Tages gehen wir zu dir.   At the end of the day we go to yours.

Listen to Track 54

- **If the last syllable is stressed:**

Aufgrund ihres Erfolges wurde sie berühmt.	Due to her success she became famous.

Listen to Track 55

- **Nouns ending in -s, -ß, -sch, -st, -z, -x:**

Am Rande des Glases war eine Fliege.	There was a fly vertically sitting on the edge of the glass
Ich habe den Sinn des Witzes nicht verstanden.	I did not understand the meaning of the joke.

Listen to Track 56

- **But:** Names of people ending with **-s, -ß, -x** have instead an **apostrophe** added:

  Lars' Auto war kaputt.   Lars's car was broken.

  Max' Freundin ist nicht zu Hause.   Max's girlfriend is not at home.

Nouns that have the letters *-s* added:

Listen to Track 57

- **Multi-syllabic words:**

  Der Griff des Hammers ist aus Holz.   The handle of the hammer is wood.

  Die Lage des Zimmers war im Obergeschoss.   The room was situated upstairs.

Listen to Track 58

- **Most nouns ending on a vowel:**

  Das Wasser des Sees war kalt.   The water of the lake was cold.

  Der Geruch des Kaffees ist angenehm.   The smell of the coffee is pleasant.

Listen to Track 59

- **Names of people and places:**

*Er hat Anna**s** Mutter getroffen.*	He met Anna's mother.
*Wir wohnen im Zentrum Hamburg**s**.*	We live in the center of Hamburg.

Nouns that have the letter **-(e)n** added:

Listen to Track 60

- ***The same nouns that have the letter -(e)n added in accusative and dative:**

*Die Ernte des Bauer**n** war mager.*	The harvest of the farmer was poor.
*Das Käfig des Aff**en** ist klein.*	The cage of the monkey is small.
*Die Arbeit des Fotograf**en** ist schön.*	The work of the photographer is beautiful.

Listen to Track 61

- **Adjectives transformed into nouns:**

*Ich glaube an die Macht des Gut**en**.*	I believe in the power of (the) good.

The genitive is more commonly used in the written language. More casually Germans often use: **von + dative**, e.g.

Listen to Track 62

Er hat die Mutter von Anna getroffen.

He met Anna's mother.

Der Käfig von des Affen ist klein.	The monkey's cage is small.

And finally we have to look at how declension affects the plural form of nouns.

Declension in Plural

Plural declension is much more simple than singular.

You only have to remember the declension of the article **die**, which **is identical for masculine, feminine and neutrum**.

If you want to refer to an unspecified amount, you just omit the article altogether, same a in English, e.g.

Listen to Track 63

Fische schwimmen im Wasser.	Fish swim in the water.
Ich kaufe Taschen.	I buy bags.

The plural nouns remain unchanged in **nominative**, **accusative** and **genitive**.

The only case they can change, is the **dative**, which always needs to end with **-n**.

Exceptions are words ending with **-s**. They remain unchanged in all four cases.

Declension with the definite (the) article in plural
Listen to Track 64

	words in plural with the following endings:				
	-e	*-en*	singular & plural are the same	*-er*	*-s*
nominative	*die* Fische	*die* Taschen	*die* Hügel	*die* Kinder	*die* Büros
accusative	*die* Fische	*die* Taschen	*die* Hügel	*die* Kinder	*die* Büros
dative	*den* Fischen	*den* Taschen	*den* Hügeln	*den* Kindern	*den* Büros
genitive	*der* Fische	*der* Taschen	*der* Hügel	*der* Kinder	*der* Büros

You have now mastered the four German cases and the basics of declension!

QUICK RECAP:

- There are four grammatical cases in German; the case you use, depends on the grammatical function of the noun in the sentence.
- It can be helpful to use the questions: *Wer? Wen oder Was? Wem? Wessen?* to verify, if the noun is in nominative, accusative, dative or genitive; certain prepositions and a few verbs also require a specific case.
- The article is another good identifier of the grammatical case. Learn which article belongs to which case by heart, there are not that many! Memorizing them will instantly demystify declension for you.
- The endings of nouns can be a bit trickier, but often the noun actually does not change at all. So don't agonize about the endings, it will take some time to get used to. But eventually you will develop a feeling for what sounds right in conjunction with which article.

TIME TO PRACTICE!

Workbook Lesson 5. The Four Cases in German and Declensio

Exercise 1. Complete the sentences with the words in parenthesis, using the correct grammatical case:

1. Die Mädchen liest _____. (das Buch)
   (The girl reads the book.)

2. Ich schenke dir _____. (ein Blumenstrauß)
    (I give you a bunch of flowers.)
3. Die Kinder gehen mit _____ spazieren. (der Hund)
    (The children take the dog for a walk.)
4. Die Jacke _____ ist rot. (die Freundin)
    (The jacket of the girlfriend is red.)
5. _____ bringt mir ein Glas Wein. (der Kellner)
    (The waiter brings me a glass of wine.)
6. Die Blüten _____ duften lieblich. (der Baum)
    (The flowers of the tree smell lovely.)
7. Die Krallen _____ können sehr scharf sein. (eine Katze)
    (The claws of a cat can be very sharp.)
8. Sie gaben _____ die Schuld dafür. (ein Kollege)
    (They blamed it on a colleague.)
9. Er lobte den _____ für seine gute Arbeit. (der Fotograf)
    He praised the photographer for his good work.)
10. Ich bewundere _____ neues Auto. (Peter)
    (I admire Peter's new car.)
11. Poesie ist die Sprache _____. (das Herz)
    (Poetry is the language of the heart.)
12. Die Frau möchte _____ essen. (ein Apfel)
    (The woman would like to eat an apple.)

Exercise 2. Determine the correct grammatical case of the underlined words :

	Wir gehen nach der Arbeit in eine Bar.	dative
1	Meine Mutter kocht eine Hühnersuppe für mich.	
2	Das Dach des Hauses musste neu gedeckt werden.	
3	Die Spielsachen der Kinder waren im Zimmer verstreut.	
4	Jedes Jahr fliegen die Vögel in den Süden.	
5	Ich freue mich schon auf die Reise.	
6	Sie wünschten dem Nachbarn viel Glück.	
7	Der Junge sitzt auf einer Schaukel.	
8	Wir interessieren uns für Thomas' Semesterarbeit.	
9	Frauen werden statistisch älter als Männer.	
10	Ich bezahle für die Einkäufe.	
11	Das Käfig des Bären wurde gereinigt.	
12	Sie beugen sich dem Willen der Mehrheit.	

> **Fun fact:** The *Tiergarten*, Berlin's most popular inner-city park, is with a size of 210 hectare larger than the area of Monaco.

Exercise 3. Fill in the blanks using the correct grammatical case:

1. Die Reise mit _____ dauert drei Stunden. (The trip on the train takes three hours.)
2. Meine Gäste warten in _____. (My guests wait in the kitchen.)
3. Deine Mutter schenkt dir _____ zum Geburtstag.
   (Your mother gives you a dog for your birthday.)
4. Wir warteten auf die Ankunft _____. (We waited for the arrival of the plane.)
5. Er freute sich Tinas ____ kennenzulernen. (He was happy to meet Tina's parents.)
6. Sie bedanken sich bei _____. (They thank the neighbor.)
7. Sie ist größer als _____. (She is taller than the boy.)
8. Ich sehe mir _____ im Kino an. (I watch a movie at the cinema.)
9. Das Auto steht vor _____. (The car stands in front of the house.)
10. Die Einrichtung _____ war sehr luxuriös.
    (The Furniture of the room was very luxurious.)
11. Am Wochenende wandern wir in _____.
    (At the weekend we walk in the mountains.)
12. Ich sehe _____ auf dem Feld arbeiten. (I see the farmer work in the field.)

Answers

Exercise 1:

1. das Buch / 2. einen Blumenstrauß / 3. dem Hund / 4. der Freundin / 5. Der Kellner / 6. des Baumes / 7. einer Katze / 8. einem Kollegen / 9. den Fotografen / 10. Peters / 11. des Herzens / 12. einen Apfel

Exercise 2:

1. accusative / 2. genitive / 3. genitive / 4. nominative / 5. accusative / 6. dative / 7. dative / 8. genitive / 9. nominative / 10. accusative / 11. genitive / 12. dative

Exercise 3:

1. dem Zug / 2. der Küche / 3. einen Hund / 4. des Flugzeuges / 5. Eltern / 6. dem Nachbarn/ 7. der Junge / 8. einen Film / 9. dem Haus / 10. des Zimmers / 11. den Bergen /12. den Bauern

LESSON 6: NUMBES IN GERMAN (KARDINALZAHLEN, ORDNUNGSZAHLEN)

Learn to Count and Much More

Learning to count might not seem appealing once you have passed primary school, but numbers are omnipresent in daily life. Whether you want to negotiate a price, arrange a meeting, find out an address or phone number, or even just reserve a table for four, without some basic knowledge of numbers, even simple transactions can be difficult. The good news is, learning German numbers is pretty easy!

In this lesson, we will mainly look at cardinal and ordinal numbers, when to use which, and different useful applications for both. The important concepts you are going to learn will help you to navigate everyday situations and instantly boost your understanding and confidence.

Let's start with cardinal ones, as these are the basis for everything else.

German Cardinal Numbers (Kardinalzahlen)

The term **cardinal numbers** or **cardinals** refers to the basic numbers, e.g. *one, two, three...*

Listen to Track 65

Numbers can be used as nouns, and as such they are capitalized and always feminine:

*Er zählte bis **Drei**.*   He counted to three.

***Die Acht** ist meine Glückszahl.* (The) eight is my lucky number.

Listen to Track 66

They can also be used as adjectives:

*Die **fünf** Freunde sitzen im Cafe.*   The five friends sit in a cafe.

*Es kostet **fünf** Euro.*   It costs five Euro.

If you use cardinal numbers as adjectives, they are, in contrast to other adjectives, not subject to declension and always stay the same.

Eins (1) cannot be used as an adjective before a noun. Instead you use the indefinite article **(ein/eine)** to refer to a single person or thing:

Listen to Track 67

*Er hat nur **einen** Freund.*   He has only one friend.

*Wir brauchen nur **eine** Zwiebel.*   We only need one onion.

Try to learn the following list by heart, because it will be the foundation for everything related to numbers:

German Cardinal Numbers from 1 to 99

Listen to Track 68

0	null	10	zehn	20	zwanzig		
1	eins	11	**elf**	21	einundzwanzig	10	zehn
2	zwei	12	**zwölf**	22	zweiundzwanzig	20	zwanzig
3	drei	13	dreizehn	23	dreiundzwanzig	30	dreißig
4	vier	14	vierzehn	24	vierundzwanzig	40	vierzig
5	fünf	15	fünfzehn	25	fünfundzwanzig	50	fünfzig
6	sechs	16	**Sech**zehn (without -s)	26	sechsundzwanzig	60	**sech**zig (without -s)
7	sieben	17	**Sieb**zehn (without -en)	27	siebenundzwanzig	70	**sieb**zig (without -en)
8	acht	18	achtzehn	28	achtundzwanzig	80	achtzig
9	neun	19	neunzehn	29	neunundzwanzig	90	neunzig

Besides some deviations in spelling of a few numbers (highlighted in bold), it is all pretty straight forward. Just remember that two-digit numbers are always spelled the other way around.

Listen to Track 69

19 *neunzehn*

35 *fünfunddreißig*

78 *achtundsiebzig*

You are now already able to count to 99! And from here on you can easily make it to a million.

Cardinals from 100 to 100 000 000

Try to remember the following three numbers:

Listen to Track 70

100	1000	1 000 000
(ein)hundert	(ein)tausend	(eine)Million

Now you only have to combine any of the one- and two-digit numbers with **hundert**, **tausend** or **Million**. Please note, that **eine Million** and above is generally not written as a numeral, but as a word.

Listen to Track 71

200	*zweihundert*
300	*dreihundert*
400	*vierhundert*
900	*neunhundert*
2000	*zweitausend*
4000	*viertausend*
10 000	*zehntausend*
20 000	*zwanzigtausend*
100 000	*(ein)hunderttausend*
200 000	*zweihunderttausend*
3 000 000	*drei Millionen*

Combinations

These might seem more complicated, but only because they can be very long words. They all follow the same rules. Here are some examples:

Listen to Track 72

420	*vierhundertzwanzig*
597	*fünfhundertsiebenundneunzig*
1005	*(ein)tausend(und)fünf*
2344	*zweitausenddreihundertvierundvierzig*
17 420	*siebzehntausendvierhundertzwanzig*
340 812	*dreihundertvierzigtausendachthundertzwölf*
1 600 000	*Eine Million sechshunderttausend*

German Ordinal Numbers (Ordnungszahlen)

The **ordinal numbers** are used to express a sequence or order. Written as numerals, they are always followed by a full stop:

Listen to Track 73

der **1. (erste)** Platz   die **2. (zweite)** Etage   das **3. (dritte)** Mal

the first place   the second floor   the third time

> **Fun facts in ordinal numbers:** Germans count the floors starting on "Ground Floor (First Floor)", "1. Etage (Second Floor)", "2. Etage (Third Floor)" and so on.

Ordinal numbers 1. to 19.

Formed by using the **cardinal number** plus **-t** (but **1.** and **3.** are irregular):

Listen to Track 74

1.	*erst-* (der *erst*e, die *erst*en, *erst*ens…)	8.	*acht- (nur ein -t)*
2.	*zweit-*	9.	*neunt-*
3.	*dritt-*	10.	*zehnt-*
4.	*viert-*	11.	*elft-*
5.	*fünft-*	12.	*zwölft-*
6.	*sechst-*	13.	*dreizehnt-*
7.	*sieb(en)t-*	14.	*vierzehnt-*

Ordinal numbers from 20. Upwards

Formed by using cardinal number plus -st:

Listen to Track 75

20.	*zwanzigst-*	30.	*dreißigst-*
21.	*einundzwanzigst-*	31.	*einunddreißigst-*
22.	*zweiundzwanzigst-*	32.	*zweiunddreißigst-*
23.	*dreiundzwanzigst-*	33.	*dreiunddreißigst-*
24.	*vierundzwanzigst-*	34.	*vierunddreißigst-*
25.	*fünfundzwanzigst-*	35.	*fünfunddreißigst-*
26.	*sechsundzwanzigst-*	36.	*sechsunddreißigst-*
27.	*siebenundzwanzigst-*	37.	*siebenunddreißigst-*
28.	*achtundzwanzigst-*	38.	*achtunddreißigst-*
29.	*neunundzwanzigst-*	39.	*neununddreißigst-*

As **adjectives**, in contrast to cardinal numbers, they follow the same rules of declension as other adjectives. They can be used with or without an article in front of a noun.

Listen to Track 76

without an article	*Dieses Angebot war* **erste** *Kasse.* This offer was first class.
with the definite article	*Er ging* **das erste** *Mal allein zur Schule.* He went for the first time alone to school.
with the indefinite article	*Es gibt immer* **eine zweite** *Chance.* There is always a second chance.
in lists (ordinal number plus -ens)	**erstens, zweitens, drittens** First, second, third
	Erstens *habe ich keine Lust,* **zweitens** *keine Zeit.* In the first place, I don't feel like it, secondly I don't have time.

Ordinal numbers can also be used as **nouns**:

Listen to Track 77

*Er will immer **Erster** sein.*	He always wants to be first.
*Heinrich der **Achte** war König von England seit 1509.*	Henry the eighth, was king of England.

They can also be used in conjunction with the word **zu:**

Listen to Track 78

*Es geht einfacher **zu zweit.***   It is easier with two.

*Wir waren **zu viert** im Urlaub.*   We were four (people) on holiday.

Using Dates in German

German dates are always in this order: **Day/Month/Year**

For the years just the cardinals are needed, same as in English:

Listen to Track 79

1412   *vierzehnhundertzwölf*

1984   *neunzehnhundertvierundachtzig*

2020   *zweitausendzwanzig*

In German there is no preposition before the year, unless the date is actually preceded by the word **year.**

Listen to Track 80

*Er ist **1992** geboren.*	He is born in 1992.
*Wir sind **2005** nach Australien gereist.*	We travelled to Australia in 2005.
*In Jahr(e) **1989** ist meine Schwester geboren.*	In the year 1989 my sister was born.

For specific dates we need the ordinals:

Listen to Track 81

***zwölfter Fünfter** neunzehnhundertzweiundsiebzig*	12.05.1972
***Der Erste (1.)** Mai ist der Tag der Arbeit*	The first of May is Workers' day.
*Ich möchte **vom ersten Dritten (1.3.)** bis **zum zehnten Vierten (10.4)** reservieren.*	I would like to reserve from 1.3. to 10.04.

And finally I would like to introduce you to a few common expressions which also use numbers.

Miscellaneous Number Words in German

Listen to Track 82

Using a cardinal number with the ending **-fach,** tells you how many of each there are:

*Das war **zweifacher** Betrug.*	That was a double scam.
*Ich brauche das in **dreifacher** Ausführung.*	I need three copies of it.

Using a cardinal number with the ending **-er** plus **-lei** tells you how many different kinds there are:

Listen to Track 83

*Das ist alles **einerlei** für mich.*	This is all one and the same to me.
*Sie kauft **zweierlei** Marmelade.*	She buys two different kinds of jam.
*Es beinhaltet **dreierlei** Zutaten.*	It contains three kinds of ingredients.

Using a Cardinal number with the ending **-mal** tells you how often something is repeated:

Listen to Track 84

*Ich habe **zweimal** angerufen.*	I called two times.
*Er geht **fünfmal** die Woche zum Sport.*	He is doing sports five times a week.

QUICK RECAP:

- The cardinal numbers are the basic numbers. As a noun they always feminine, and as an adjective they do not require declension.
- The ordinal numbers are the numerals followed by a full stop and refer to an order or sequence. These do have to follow the rules of declension as other nouns and adjectives.
- Begin by learning the cardinals from 1 to 20, then to 99, and you have already mastered the most important part. From here on, you can easily learn to count to 100, a million, learn ordinals and everything else in German language. And the rewards are instant! You will suddenly notice numbers everywhere and understand so much more.

TIME TO PRACTICE!

Workbook Lesson 6. Numbers in German

Exercise 1. Fill in the blanks using cardinal numbers:

1. Wir sind _____ Personen im Auto. (We are four people in the car.)
2. Die _____ ist meine Glückszahl. (Nine is my lucky number.)
3. Er fängt morgens um _____ Uhr an zu arbeiten.
   (He starts work at ten o'clock in the morning.)
4. Dieser Pullover kostet _____ Euros. (This sweater costs forty Euros.)
5. Sie ist _____ Jahre alt. (She is thirty-two years old.)
6. Der Bus Nummer _____ fährt zum Hauptbahnhof.
   (The bus number twelve goes to the main station.)
7. Sie reservieren einen Tisch für _____ Leute um _____ Uhr.
   (They reserve a table for six people at nineteen hours.)
8. Die _____ wurde vom Rennen disqualifiziert.
   (The forty-five was disqualified from the race.)
9. In _____ Tagen seid ihr schon im Urlaub.
   (In fourteen days you are already on holiday.)
10. Ich benötige _____ Gramm Mehl für dieses Rezept.
    I (need eighty gram of flour for this recipe.)

Exercise 2. Fill in the correct number in the blanks below:

	72	zweiundsiebzig
1	86	
2	105	
3		dreihundert
4	340	
5		fünfhundertachtundsiebzig
6	700	
7	722	
8		zweitausendvierhundert
9	2455	
10		fünfzehntausenddreihundert
11	470 711	
12	1 200 000	

> **Fun facts in numbers:** The average German has 118 Euros in their wallet, 6.70 in coins. The baggage claim conveyor belt in Frankfurt airport is with 73,8 km the longest in the world. And 38 seems to be the luckiest number in Germany, because it has come up the most in the lottery draw.

Exercise 3. Fill in the blanks using ordinal numbers:

1. Er war der_____, der das Ziel erreichte.

   (He was the first to reach the finishing line.)

2. Unser Büro befindet sich auf der _____ Etage.

   (Our office is located on the seventh floor.)

3. Mein Geburtstag ist am _____ September.

   (My birthday is on the twenty-third of September.)

4. Hör mir zu! Das sag ich dir jetzt schon zum _____ Mal.

   (Listen to me! I am telling you this already for the fifth time.)

5. Sie gingen zu _____ ins Kino.

   (The four of them went to the cinema.)

6. Der Zahnarzttermin ist am _____.

   (The dentist appointment is on the first of the tenth.)

7. Sie reist immer nur _____ Klasse. (She only travels first class.)

8. Sein Haus ist das _____ von links. (His house is the third from the left)

Exercise 4. Fill in the blanks using cardinals, ordinals or miscellaneous number words where appropriate:

1. Du hast ___ Schwestern und ___ Bruder. (You have two sisters and one brother.)

2. _____ bin ich nicht dumm und _____ kann ich das auch alleine machen. (First of all I am not stupid, and secondly I can do it by myself.)

3. Er ist jetzt zum _____ Mal verheiratet. (He is now married for the third time.)

4. Das habe ich dir schon _____ gesagt. (I told you that a hundred times already.)

5. Ob wir zu dir oder zu mir gehen, ist mir _____.

   (If we go to yours or mine is one and the same to me.)

6. Euer Abgabe-Termin ist am _____ July.

   (Your deadline is on the fifteenth of July.)

7. Sie fahren zu _____ in den Urlaub. (The three of them go on holiday.)

8. Wir sind _____ Studenten in meinem Kurs.

   (We are forty-two students on my course.)

9. Sie sind _____ zu den Olympischen Spielen gereist.

   (They travelled in two thousand and two to the Olympic games.)

10. Ich bin der _____ in meiner Familie, der ein Musikinstrument spielt.

    (I am the first one in my Family to play a musical instrument.)

Answers

Exercise 1:

1. vier / 2. Neun / 3. zehn / 4. vierzig / 5. zweiunddreißig / 6. zwölf / 7. sechs, neunzehn / 8. fünfundvierzig / 9. vierzehn / 10. achtzig

Exercise 2:

1.sechsundachtzig / 2.hundertfünf / 3.300 / 4.dreihundertvierzig / 5.578 / 6.siebenhundert / 7.siebenhundertzweiundzwanzig / 8.2400 / 9.zweitausendvierhundertfünfundfünfzig / 10. 15 300 / 11. vierhundertsiebzigtausendsiebenhundertelf / 12. eine Million zweihunderttausend

Exercise 3:

1. erste / 2. siebten / 3. dreiundzwanzigsten / 4. fünften / 5. viert / 6. dritten zehnten / 7. erster / 8. dritte

Exercise 4:

1. zwei ,einen / 2. erstens , zweitens / 3 . dritten / 4. hundertmal / 5. einerlei / 6. fünfzehnten / 7. dritt / 8. zweiundvierzig / 9. zweitausend(und) zwei / 10. erste

LESSON 7: SENTENCE STRUCTURE AND WORD ORDER IN GERMAN

In German, simple main clauses can have the same word order as English – Subject-Verb-Object or SVO.

Listen to Track 85

Ich gab dem Verkäufer das Geld.   I gave the seller the money.

However, German word order permits a great deal more variation. It can also be rearranged to draw attention to the object rather than the subject. The only thing you need to remember about this is that **the verb always comes second:**

Listen to Track 86

Dem Verkäufer gab ich das Geld.	I gave the seller (not someone else) the money.

When we use compound verbs (one conjugated and one in the infinitive, perfect tense, etc.) in German, the conjugated verb stays in second position, while the second verb goes at the end of the sentence. The conjugated verb is called the <u>auxiliary verb</u>, and the one in the infinitive is the <u>main verb</u>. In English, compound verbs usually stay together.

Listen to Track 87

Ich werde dich bald sehen.   I will see you soon.

Subordinate and Coordinate Clauses

There are three rules for coordinate and subordinate (the latter also called dependent) clauses.

1. Word order remains 'normal' with coordinating conjunctions like 'denn', 'und', 'aber', *beziehungsweise, oder,* and *sondern.*

Listen to Track 88

Ich habe einen Bruder und eine Schwester.   I have a brother and a sister.

Sentence structure is the same as in a main clause in a clause that a conjunction introduces:

Listen to Track 89

Ich trinke, denn du hast mich verlassen.   I'm drinking because you left me.

2. Word order is inverted with subordinating conjunctions like *'deshalb',* *daher, and 'trotzdem'.* **The verb comes after the conjunction:**

Listen to Track 90

Ich bin müde, deshalb will ich schlafen.   I'm tired, that's why I want to sleep.

3. The verb goes to the end of the subordinate clause with subordinating conjunctions. These are *'weil', 'obwohl', 'da', als, bevor, ob, sowie, während, dass, bis, seit, wenn, damit, wie, seitdem, and nachdem,* among others:

Listen to Track 91

Ich will schlafen, weil ich müde bin.   I want to sleep because I'm tired.

In German, subordinate clauses don't stand alone as sentences. They are always dependent on a main or independent clause. A comma separates dependent and independent clauses. The conjugated verb is placed at the end of the clause.

Listen to Track 92

Ich habe keine Ahnung, warum du das brauchst.

I have no idea why you need it.

The main clause starts with the conjugated verb when a dependent clause comes before the main clause:

Listen to Track 93

Ich habe keine Ahnung, ob ihr das nutzt.   I have no idea if you're using that.

This is also the case with infinitive constructions, relative clauses, and other dependent clauses:

Listen to Track 94

Hier ist das Geld, das wir suchen!   Here's the money we're looking for!

Standard word order is sustained with common conjunctions (und/oder/aber):

Listen to Track 95

Der Mann lächelt und die Frau singt.	The man is smiling and the woman is singing.

Questions

Listen to Track 96

In questions, **the conjugated verb can take the first or second position**. It depends on whether we have a question word or not. Without a question word, it takes first position:

Arbeitest du?   Are you working?

With a question word, it takes second position:

Was sind Sie von Beruf?   What do you (*polite form*) do?

In the perfect tense, it is analogical, except the participle goes at the end whatever the case may be:

Hast du das gesagt?   Did you say that?

Warum hast du das gesagt?   Why did you say that?

Listen to Track 97

Imperative

In a direct order (imperative statement), the conjugated verb comes first:

Sprich langsamer!   Speak more slowly!

An exception is if we use the word 'please' (*bitte*). That would go at the beginning:

Bitte sprich langsamer!   Please speak more slowly.

Negation

In German, negative sentences are formed with the words *kein* (no/none) or *nicht* (not). **We use 'kein' before nouns:**

Listen to Track 98

Examples:

Ich habe Durst. – Ich habe keinen Durst.   I'm thirsty – I'm not thirsty.

Das ist ein Hund. – Das ist kein Hund.   That is a dog – That is not a dog.

The endings for <u>kein</u> correspond to possessive article endings:

Listen to Track 99

	nominative	genitive	dative	accusative
masculine	kein	keines	keinem	keinen

feminine	keine	keiner	keiner	keine
neuter	kein	keines	keinem	kein
plural	keine	keiner	keinen	keine

In German, *nicht* is used to negate sentences. You can place this word in different places of a sentence depending on what you want to draw focus to or negate. You use *nicht*:

Before possessive pronouns or the definite article used with nouns

Listen to Track 100

Examples:

Sie haben nicht das Bier bezahlt, sondern das Essen.

You didn't pay for the beer, you paid for the food.

Sein Haus kenne ich nicht, aber eures.

I don't know his house, I know yours.

At the end of a sentence with verbs in the present, future, or past simple:

Listen to Track 101

Examples:

Er schläft nicht.	He does not sleep.
Ich werde nicht hier sein.	I will not be here.
Sie kamen nicht.	They didn't come.

Before the full verb in compound tenses, such as the perfect tense:

Listen to Track 102

Sie sind gestern nicht gekommen.	You didn't come yesterday.

Before names and proper nouns:

Listen to Track 103

Wir sind nicht in Berlin.	We are not in Berlin.

Before adjectives and adverbs:

Listen to Track 104

Das ist nicht teuer!	That is not expensive!
Kinder gehen nicht gerne schlafen.	Children don't like to go to sleep.

Before pronouns:

Listen to Track 105

Ich habe nicht ihn angerufen.   I didn't call him.

Before prepositions with indicators of time, place, and manner.

Listen to Track 106

Sie kommen nicht um 20 Uhr.   You don't come at 8pm.

Wir wohnen nicht in Deutschland.   We don't live in Germany.

Er hat die Tür nicht mit dem Schlüssel geöffnet.

He didn't open the door with the key.

Unless Nicht is negating a verb, it comes before the word it negates.

QUICK RECAP:

- This lesson covered the grammar rules for the subordinate and coordinate clauses in German, how to structure questions and the imperative, and how to express negation.

- To remember the rules more easily, spend time learning vocabulary, in particular the translations of the conjunctions in your language. Once you've done that, you'll have no problem applying the German grammar rules.

TIME TO PRACTICE!

Workbook Lesson 7. Sentence Structure and Word Order in German

Exercise 1: Put the words in the right order to form a meaningful sentence. Start with the first word.

1. Er [Kellnerin / Geld / der / gibt / das] – He gives the waitress the money.
   _____

2. Ich [Abend / nach / heute / komme / Hause] – I am coming home this evening.
   _____

3. Wir [Sommer / nach / jeden / Spanien / fliegen] – We fly to Spain every summer. _____

4. Er [möchte / die / nicht / um / Katze / sich / kümmern] – He doesn't want to take care of the cat. _____

5. Jeden [ich / Deutschunterricht / habe / Dienstag] – I have German class every Tuesday. _____

6. Ihr [geantwortet / habt / ihm / nicht] – You didn't answer him.
_____

7. Mathe [gar / mir / nicht / gefällt] – I don't like math at all.
_____

8. Warum [so / immer / die / ? / Musik / ist / laut] – Why is the music always so loud? _____

9. Das [steht / der / Auto / Park / im] / - The car is parked in the park.
_____

10. Meine [immer / zu / Hausaufgaben / vergesse / Hause / ich] – I always forget my homework at home. _____

Exercise 2: Fill in the blanks with the correct word.

1. _____meine Mutter den Strand mag, sind wir jedes Jahr am Meer.

2. Gib mir bitte den schwarzen_____den weißen Anzug. Es ist mir egal.

3. Mein Nachbar hat zwei Söhne. Sie heißen Mark _____ Silvo.

4. Mein Freund ist clever _____schön.

5. Die Flugtickets sind zu teuer, _____ fliegen wir nicht.

6. Entweder mein Vater _____ meine Freundin holt dich ab.

7. Ich habe Lust, Sie zu treffen,_____ich weiß nicht,_____ ich Zeit habe.

8. Weißt du, _____morgen das Wetter gut ist?

9. Ich weiß nicht, _____uns meine Mutter besucht.

10. Ich komme nicht in die Schule, _____ ich krank bin.

11. Der Zug fährt nicht, _____ zu hoch Schnee liegt.

12. _____ich schlafe, klingelt das Telefon.

13. _____ ich 16 war, reiste ich zum ersten Mal nach England.

14. Ich kaufe noch ein, _____ich nach Hause komme.

15. Sagst du mir, _____ du mich besuchen kommst.

Answers:

Exercise 1:

1. Er gibt der Kellnerin das Geld. / 2. Ich komme nach Hause heute Abend. / 3. Wir fliegen jeden Sommer nach Spanien. / 4. Er möchte sich um die Katze nicht kümmern. / 5. Jeden Dienstag habe ich Deutschunterricht. / 6. Ihr habt ihm nicht geantwortet. /

7. Mathe gefällt mir gar nicht. / 8. Warum ist die Musik immer so laut? / 9. Das Auto steht im Park. / 10. Meine Hausaufgaben vergesse ich immer zu Hause.

Exercise 2:

1. da / 2. oder / 3. und / 4. und / 5. deshalb / 6. oder / 7. aber, ob / 8. ob / 9. wann / 10. weil / 11. denn, wenn / 12. wenn / 13. als / 14. wenn / 15. wenn, ob

LESSON 8: PERSONAL PRONOUNS (PERSONALPRONOMEN)

The personal pronouns are the basis to form sentences, which is why they are one of the first things we learn in German! This lesson will remind you what they are, explain how to use them and how they are formed in the nominative, accusative, and dative cases.

We'll also discuss the pronoun "man" and end with a short set of exercises to practice the personal pronouns. Let's go!

What Are Personal Pronouns?

Listen to Track 107

Nominative		Accusative		Dative	
ich	I	*mich*	me	*mir*	me, to me
du	You (sg)	*dich*	you	*dir*	you, to you
er	He	*ihn*	him	*ihm*	him,to him
sie	She	*sie*	her	*ihr*	her, to her
es	It	*es*	it	*ihm*	it, to it
wir	We	*uns*	us	*uns*	us, to us
ihr	You (pl)	*euch*	you	*euch*	you, to you
sie Sie	they you (formal)	*sie Sie*	them you (formal)	*ihnen Ihnen*	to them to you (formal)

The formal you "Sie" is always capitalized. **We form the third person singular with "er" (he), "sie" (she) and "es" (it) in the nominative, "ihn", "sie" and "es" in the accusative, and "ihm", "ihr", and "ihm" again in the dative. As you know, only the masculine form changes in the accusative.**

Listen to Track 108

Examples:

Ohne dich kann ich nicht sein.   I can't be (can't exist) without you.

Mit dir bin ich auch allein.   With you, I am alone too.

These sentences were in the lyrics to one of the most beautiful ballads in history, "Ohne dich" by Rammstein. Because the preposition "ohne" always takes the accusative, "dich" follows. The dative form of the personal pronoun "dir" follows "mit", which always takes the dative.

What is "Man"?

"Man" translates roughly to "one". It is very common in German; more so than the passive voice in everyday speech. **We use it when we don't know who performs a given action or is in a given state or it is not important.**

Examples:

Listen to Track 109

Man kauft Sachen, die zu teuer sind.   One buys things that are too expensive.

It is understood in the sense of "people", something people do.

Kann man hier rauchen?   Can one smoke here?

In the sense of "is smoking allowed"?

Man is only used in the nominative singular. What happens when we have a subordinate clause? We want to say, "One buys things that are too expensive, because one has too much money." In German, it *would be:*

Listen to Track 110

Man kauft Sachen, die zu teuer sind, da hat einer zu viel Geld .

You buy things that are too expensive, because you have too much money.

It's not wrong to use "man" twice, but it sounds unnatural.

A more complicated **example**:

Listen to Track 111

Man will nicht zum Arzt (gehen), immer geben sie einem Antibiotika.

One doesn't want to go to the doctor because they always give one antibiotics.

In German, the second part has "man" in dative because of the way the verb "geben" is used. We don't repeat "man" because it wouldn't be a sentence that would make sense.

Personal Pronouns Can Reflect Number or Gender

In the third person, we use personal pronouns (er, sie, es) to replace a noun that was mentioned earlier.

Listen to Track 112

Example:

Ich habe einen Hund. Er ist sehr klein.   I have a dog. It is very small.

You should always make it clear which noun is being replaced to avoid confusion. Just repeat the noun in case of doubt.

Listen to Track 113

Example:

Mein Nachbar hatte einen Hund. Er ist weg.

My neighbor had a dog. He is gone.

Here, the dog is probably meant, but we can't be 100% sure who disappeared (the neighbor or his dog), can we?

In impersonal forms, we use pronouns in the third person neuter (es), just like in English.

Listen to Track 114

Example:

Es schneit. Es ist zu früh. It is snowing. It is too early.

Es can be used as a placeholder for a whole clause.

Example:

Es freut mich, dass sie wiederkommen. I am glad that they are coming again.

In German, **we use personal pronouns in the first person to say something about ourselves. The singular nominative is ich, accusative mich, dative mir. The plural nominative is wir, accusative and dative uns.**

Listen to Track 115

Examples:

Wir haben Durst.	We are thirsty.
Uns ist heiß.	We are hot.
Ich gehe ins Kino.	I go to the movies.
Mir ist das egal.	I do not care.

To address other people, we use personal pronouns in the second person (du, ihr) or the formal Sie, always written with a capital letter.

Listen to Track 116

Example:

Wie heißen Sie? Wie geht es Ihnen?

What's your name? How are you?

Woher kommst du? Welche Filme gefallen dir?

Where are you from? Which films do you like?

Könnt ihr bitte kommen? Darf ich euch helfen?

Can you come please? May I help you?

When do We use Pronouns in the Nominative?

The basic pronoun form is the nominative case. This is the subject of a sentence. We ask who or what is in a state or performing an action to find the subject (*Wer/Was*).

Listen to Track 117

Example:

Die Frau hat einen Freund. Sie ist in ihn verliebt.

The woman has a boyfriend. She is in love with him.

Mein Kollege hat ein Geschenk bekommen. Er mag es sehr.

My coworker got a present. He likes it a lot.

In the nominative case, personal pronouns replace a known or previously mentioned noun. "Sie" replaces "die Frau." "Er" replaces "mein Kollege."

The accusative case or direct object comes after specific prepositions and verbs. We use it for the person or thing receiving the action. In the above example, "ihn" replaces "einen Freund" and "es" replaces "das Geschenk." To find out what or who is receiving the action, we ask "wen" or "was".

Listen to Track 118

Examples:

In wen ist sie verliebt?	Who is she in love with?
Was hat er bekommen?	What did he get?
Bastian sucht seine Schuhe. Ohne sie kann er das Haus nicht verlassen.	Bastian is looking for his shoes. He can't leave the house without them (on).

The subject is "Bastian" and "er". The direct object is "die Schuhe" and "sie."

When Do We Use Pronouns in the Accusative?

We use pronouns in the accusative after verbs like "suchen" and after the prepositions ohne, durch, gegen, um, für, etc.

Listen to Track 119

Example:

Seine Mutter hat sie ihm weggenommen.

His mother took them away from him.

On this note, a pronoun comes before the indirect object if it is the direct object. "Sie" comes before "ihm."

When do We use Pronouns in the Dative?

The dative case is used to designate the indirect recipient of an action.
It is used with specific verbs like *begegnen, helfen, schmecken, antworten, danken, zuhören,* and certain prepositions like *mit, von, nach, zu,* etc. In English, pronouns like "me" and "them" and prepositions like "to" and "for" indicate the indirect object. To ask who or what the indirect recipient of the action was, we use *wem/was.*

Listen to Track 120

Example:

Ich habe Tom seine Essen gegeben, aber es schmeckt ihm nicht.

I gave Tom his meal, but it doesn't taste good to him.

Das sind meine Eltern. Ich habe ihnen geholfen.

Those are my parents. I helped them.

Das sind meine Freunde. Leider kann ich nicht mit ihnen kommen.

Those are my friends. Unfortunately, I can't come with them.

Personal pronouns can't be used with the genitive case.

QUICK RECAP:

- We form the third person singular with "er" (he), "sie" (she) and "es" (it) in the nominative, "ihn", "sie" and "es" in the accusative, and "ihm", "ihr", and "ihm" again in the dative. Only the masculine form changes in the accusative.
- We use the pronoun "man" when we don't know who performs a given action or is in a given state or if it is not important.

- In the third person, we use personal pronouns (er, sie, es) to replace a noun that was mentioned earlier.
- In impersonal forms, we use pronouns in the third person neuter (es), just like in English.
- We use personal pronouns in the first person to say something about ourselves. The singular nominative is "ich", accusative "mich", dative "mir". The plural nominative is "wir", accusative and dative "uns".
- To address other people, we use personal pronouns in the second person (du, ihr) or the formal Sie, always written with a capital letter.
- The basic pronoun form is the nominative case. This is the subject of a sentence.
- The accusative case is used to designate the direct recipient of an action.
- The dative case is used to designate the indirect recipient of an action.

TIME TO PRACTICE!

Workbook Lesson 8. Personal Pronouns

Exercise 1: Fill in the blanks with the correct personal pronoun.

1. Meine Kusine ist 11. _____ist meine jüngste Kusine.
2. Hast _____ ein Auto für sie?
3. Mein Freund und ich fahren in den Urlaub. _____wir nehmen das Flugzeug.
4. _____regnet schon den ganzen Tag.
5. _____ist das schnellste Mädchen der Schule.
6. Seit Tagen hat _____sich schon auf den Besuch seiner Mutter gefreut.
7. _____lieben uns und werden uns immer lieben.
8. _____wohnen in Japan, _____wohnen in China.
9. _____habe mich verlaufen. Könntet _____mir helfen?
10. _____ist der Bruder, _____ist die Schwester.
11. Wollt _____uns nicht besuchen kommen?
12. _____bist hübsch, _____ bin das nicht.
13. Michaela ist in ihrem Raum, _____ schläft noch.
14. Und _____, mein lieber Sohn, was möchtest du zum Frühstück?
15. Ihr Onkel ist schon weg. _____spielt gern Tennis früh am Morgen.
16. Die Mutter sagt uns: « _____könnt ans Meer fahren.»
17. Und was machen _____nach dem Abendessen?
18. Die Kinder aber möchten an den Strand fahren und _____weinen sehr laut, so laut!

19. Na ja, aber heute ist das Wetter nicht so schön. _____ ist kalt.

20. Also gut ! Dann bereite _____ eine Mahlzeit zu.

21. _____ wollen mit unseren Freunden am Meer spielen.

22. _____ gehe nach Hause.

23. _____ heißt Sandra.

24. _____ seid aus Spanien.

25. _____ wohnst in Bonn.

26. Wo ist Maria? Ich möchte _____ dieses Buch zurück geben. – (Where is Maria? I want to give her this book back.)

27. Mein armer Vater! Alle schenken _____ Socken zum Geburtstag. – (My poor dad! Everyone gives him socks for his birthday.)

28. Frau Hanke, schön dass Sie gekommen sind! Darf ich _____ eine Tasse Tee anbieten? – (Ms. Hanke, how nice of you to come! May I offer you a cup of tea?)

29. Lieber Opa, erzählst du _____ jetzt eine Geschichte? – (Dear grandpa, can you tell us a story now?)

30. Wie oft muss ich _____ noch sagen, dass ihr euer Zimmer aufräumen sollt? – (How often must I tell you that you must tidy up your room?)

Exercise 2: Multiple choice. Select the right answer.

1. Gibst du ... bitte das Buch? – Will you give him the book?
   a. ihr   b. ihm   c. dir   d. euch

2. Gebt ihr ... die Bonbons? – Will you give them the candy?
   a. uns   b. ihnen   c. ihm   d. euch

3. Sie schenkt ... einen großen Fernseher. – She's gifting him a big TV.
   a. ihr   b. ihm   c. es   d. uns

4. Gehen Sie mit Luca in den Deutschkurs? - Nein, ich gehe nicht mit ... . – No, I'm not going with him.
   a. er   b. ihm   c. dir   d. mir

5. Gibst du uns Geld? - Nein, ich gebe ... kein Geld! – Will you give us money? No, I won't give you money!
   a. euch   b. uns   c. ihnen   d. dir

6. Schenkst du ... Blumen? - Ja, ich schenke ... auch Pralinen. – Will you gift me flowers? Yes, I will gift you chocolates too.
   a. dir – uns   b. mir – euch   c. mir – dir   d. euch – uns

7. Immer, wenn er auf dem Markt einkauft, schenkt ... der Frau eine Rose. – Every time he goes shopping at the market, he gifts the woman a rose.

   a. er   b. sie   c. ihm   d. ihn

8. Die Fenster in der Küche sind schon wieder schmutzig, obwohl ich ... erst letzte Woche geputzt habe. – The kitchen windows are dirty again even though I cleaned them last week.

   a. sie   b. ihnen   c. es   d. mich

9. Es macht so großen Spaß, mit .. zu lernen. – It's so much fun learning with you.

   a. du   b. ich   c. dich   d. dir

10. Meine Tante organisiert ein großes Familienfest. Für ... gibt es nichts Schöneres, als die ganze Familie um sich zu haben. – My aunt is organizing a big family gathering. For her, there's nothing nicer than having the whole family around her.

    a. ihr   b. sie   c. Sie   d. Ihnen

Answers:

Exercise 1:

1. sie / 2. du / 3. wir / 4. es / 5. es / 6. er / 7. er / 8. sie, wir or vice versa / 9. ich, ihr / 10. er, sie / 11. ihr / 12. du, ich / 13. sie / 14. du / 15. er / 16. ihr / 17. wir, sie, sie / 18. sie / 19. es / 20. ich / 21. wir / 22. ich / 23. sie / 24. ihr / 25. du / 26. ihr / 27. ihm / 28. ihnen / 29. uns / 30. euch

Exercise 2:

1. b / 2. b / 3. b / 4. b / 5. a / 6. c / 7. a / 8. a / 9. d / 10. b

LESSON 9: PREPOSITIONS WITH DATIVE AND ACCUSATIVE (PRÄPOSITIONEN MIT DATIV UND MIT AKKUSATIV)

Prepositions are used to connect nouns, adjectives, or verbs with other nouns, adjectives, or verbs. Different prepositions go with different cases. They determine the case of nouns, pronouns, articles, and adjectives.

This lesson will explain the difference between prepositions with dative and accusative as well as mixed prepositions. It also includes pointers on how to properly use them according to context in each sentence.

German Prepositions with Dative vs. Accusative and Mixed

In German, some prepositions always go with the dative case, like *zu, von, mit,* and *nach*. Others always go with the accusative, like ohne, bis, gegen, and um. However, the vast majority of them are mixed or Wechselpräpositionen.

When there is movement, they go with the accusative. When a static verb is used, they go with the dative. The case affects the noun, pronoun, or article immediately after the preposition.

Listen to Track 121

Accusative	Accusative/Dative	Dative
gegen	auf	Zu
durch	an	ab
bis	neben	aus
für	hinter	bei
um	in	außer
ohne	vor	mit
	über	von
	unter	nach
	zwischen	seit

Prepositions with Accusative

Listen to Track 122

Durch means 'by means of' or 'through':

Wir machen eine Reise ***durch das Land.***

We're going on a trip through the country.

*Die Firma wird **durch Werbung finanziert**.*

The company is financed through advertising.

*Das Verbrechen wird **mit einer Geldstrafe geahndet.***

The crime is punished by a fine.

Bis means "until":
Listen to Track 123

*Fahren Sie **bis zum Bahnhof**.*   Drive to the train station.

*Wir feiern **bis zum Morgen**.*   We celebrate until morning.

Für - for
Listen to Track 124

*Ich interessiere mich **für dich**.*   I'm interested in you.

*Der Fernseher ist **für mein Wohnzimmer**.*   The TV is for my living room.

It would be wrong to say:

für mein Wohnzimmer, because it's *das Wohnzimmer*.

for my living room because it's the living room.

Contraction: fürs (für + das)

We can also say: *fürs Wohnzimmer*.   for the living room.

Listen to Track 125

*Ich sorge **für die Reinigung** des Hauses .*

I take care of cleaning the house.

*Mein Freund gibt **für sein Auto** viel Geld aus.*

My friend spends a lot of money on his car.

*Sie entschuldigen sich **für ihre Fehler**.*

They apologize for their mistakes.

*Du hast dich **für die falsche Lösung** entschieden.*

You chose the wrong solution.

Ohne – without
Listen to Track 126

*Ich träume von einer **Welt ohne Krieg**.*

I dream of a world without war.

*Ich kann mir mein Leben **ohne dich** nicht vorstellen.*

I can't imagine my life without you.

gegen - against
Listen to Track 127

*Die Forscher kämpfen **gegen die Krankheit.***

The researchers are fighting the disease.

*Ich bin **gegen die Wand gestoßen.***

I bumped into the wall.

*Sie protestieren **gegen die Regierung.***

They are protesting against the government.

Um – at (for time), around
Listen to Track 128

*Die Apotheke ist gleich **um die Ecke.***

The pharmacy is just around the corner.

*Ich bitte **um eine Tasse.***	I ask for a cup.
*Ich kümmere mich **um meine Eltern.***	I take care of my parents.

<u>Prepositions with Dative</u>
Aus – from, of
Listen to Track 129

*Wir kommen **aus der Stadt.***	We come from the city.
*Der Stuhl wird **aus feinem Holz** gemacht.*	The chair is made of fine wood.

*Die Familie besteht **aus meiner Mutter und mir.***

The family consists of my mother and me.

Ab - starting at/on (time), from (place)
Listen to Track 130

*Der Vertrag tritt **ab dem 04. April** in Kraft.*

The contract will come into effect on April 4th.

*Wir fliegen **ab dem Flughafen** Köln.*

We fly from Cologne Airport.

Außer – except
Listen to Track 131

*Ich brauche nichts **außer dir.***   I don't need anything but you.

*Wir haben **außer diesem Brot** nichts zu Essen.*

We have nothing to eat other than this bread.

Entgegen - against, contrary to
Listen to Track 132

Das ist entgegen allen Erwartungen passiert.

That happened against all expectations.

Bei - next to, near (for location), with (for people), for (company)
Listen to Track 133

*Die Post ist **bei dem Hotel**. (contraction – beim)*

The post office is at the hotel. (contraction - at)

*Ich wohne **bei meinen Eltern.***   I live with my parents.

*Die Schule ist **neben meinem Haus.***   The school is next to my house

*Ich arbeite **bei einem großen** Unternehmen.*   I work for a large company.

Nach - to, toward (place)
Listen to Track 134

*Wir fahren **nach Köln.***   We are driving to Cologne.

In most cases nach is used for cities or countries without an article or as in *ich gehe nach Hause* (I'm going home).

It can mean 'after':

Ich fliege nach Paris.   I'm flying / I fly to Paris.

It can also mean 'according to':

Nach den Regeln ist die Summe zu bezahlen.

The sum is to be paid according to the rules.

It is also used as in *nach links* (to the left) and *nach rechts* (to the right).

It can mean 'after' (for time)

Mein Mann trainiert *nach der Arbeit.*   My husband trains after work.

Mit – with (‚by' for vehicles)
Listen to Track 135

Die Kinder wollen *mit ihm* nicht spielen.

The children don't want to play with him.

Wir fahren *mit dem Auto.*   We go by car.

Ich fange *mit der Hausaufgabe* an.   I start with homework.

Ich rechne *mit diesem Geld.*   I count on this money.

Die Nachbarn reden *mit dem Polizisten.*

The neighbors talk to the policeman.

Meine Lehrerin spricht oft *mit meiner Mutter.*

My teacher often speaks to my mother.

Ich kann diese Daten nicht *mit ihnen* teilen.

I cannot share this data with you.

Seit - since (for time)
Listen to Track 136

Ich wohne da *seit meiner Kindheit.*   I have lived there since childhood.

Zu – to, towards
Listen to Track 137

Kommen Sie *zu mir.*   Come to me.

Ihr fahrt *zum Supermarkt.* (contraction – zu dem)

You drive to the supermarket. (contraction - to that)

Das ist der Weg *zum Gebirge.*

That is the way to the mountains.

Wie komme ich *zur Post?* (contraction – zu der)

How do I get to the post office? (contraction - to the)

Von - from, of (place, time, or thing)
Listen to Track 138

Ich hatte *von dieser Sache* nie gehört.   I had never heard of this.

Das hängt *vom Mann* ab (contraction – von dem)

It depends on the man (contraction - on that)

Ich möchte *vom Vertrag* zurücktreten.

I want to withdraw from the contract.

Mixed Prepositions

Mixed prepositions are also called "Wechselpräpositionen". **They are dative if they indicate a resting state and accusative if they indicate motion. Some verbs always indicate movement. Others always indicate a state of rest.**

Listen to Track 139

Action verbs	State verbs
legen (to place horizontally)	*liegen* (to be lying down)
stellen (to place vertically)	*stehen* (to stand)
setzen (to sit down)	*sitzen* (to be seated)
hängen (to hang)	*hängen* (to be hung)

Auf - in, about, on
Listen to Track 140

Ich lege das Buch *auf den Tisch* (Contraction: auf + der)

I put the book on the table (contraction: on + the)

Das Buch liegt *auf dem Tisch*.   The book is on the table.

Ich setze mich *auf den Stuhl*.   I sit down on the chair.

Ich sitze *auf dem Stuhl*.   I'm sitting on the chair.

Sie hängen das Bild *an die Wand*.   They hang the picture on the wall.

Das Bild hängt *an der Wand*.   The picture hangs on the wall.

Ich stelle die Vase *nebens Fenster* (Contraction: neben das)

I put the vase next to the window (contraction: next to that)

Die Vase steht *neben dem Fenster*.   The vase is next to the window

Verbs that go with fixed prepositions like 'an' and 'auf' almost always take the accusative even though in some cases, there is no motion.

Let's take *"sich freuen auf"* as an example – "to be looking forward to something, happy about something":

Listen to Track 141

Example:

Ich freue mich schon *auf meinen Urlaub.*

I'm already looking forward to my vacation.

achten auf - to pay attention to

Listen to Track 142

Example:

Bitte achte auf das Auto!   Please watch the car!

warten auf - to wait for

Nobody could claim "wait" denotes any kind of movement. Yet:

Listen to Track 143

Example:

Ich warte nicht mehr auf diese Person.

I'm not waiting for this person (*diese Person* = accusative) anymore.

denken an – think about

Listen to Track 144

Example:

Die ganze Zeit denke ich an dich.   I think about you all the time.

As always, there are exceptions to the rule:

antworten auf - to reply to

Listen to Track 145

Example:

Ich antworte auf deine Frage

I am answering / I will answer your question (*deine Frage* = dative)

An – on, in, next to

Listen to Track 146

Am Montag, am Nachmittag   Monday afternoon

Contraction: am [(an + dem Montag, dem Nachmittag), ans (an + das)]

Listen to Track 147

Example:

Meine Familie fährt jeden Sommer ans Meer.

My family goes to the sea every summer.

In this example, we have movement (which is travelling), so the noun following the preposition takes the accusative. *An* with *das Meer* becomes *ans Meer. Ans Meer* would answer the question, 'Wohin' (Where to)?

Listen to Track 148

However:

Meine Familie ist jeden Sommer am Meer.

My family is at the sea every summer.

In this example, we don't have movement (the verb ,to be' is used), so the noun following the preposition takes the dative. *An* with *dem Meer* becomes *am Meer. Am Meer* would answer the question, 'Wo' (Where)?

In some expressions, *an* always takes the dative.

Listen to Track 149

Example:

Wenn ich an deiner Stelle wäre...   If I were in your place...

Hinter – behind

Listen to Track 150

Examples:

Ich stelle die Teller hinter die Töpfe (movement).

I put the plates behind the pots.

Der Mann steht hinter dem Haus (no movement).

The man is behind the house.

Neben - next to, near

Listen to Track 151

Die Post liegt *neben der Schule*.   The post office is near the school.

Über - over, above

Listen to Track 152

Examples:

Das Flugzeug fliegt über die Stadt (movement).

The plane flies over the city.

Die Lampe hängt über dem Tisch (no movement).

The lamp hangs over the table.

In *nachdenken über* and *reden über*, the noun following *über* always takes the accusative.

Listen to Track 153

Example:

Warum redest du immer so schlecht über deine Kolleginnen?

Why do you always talk so badly about your colleagues?

Unter – under

Listen to Track 154

Examples:

Deine Schuhe liegen unter dem Tisch.   Your shoes are under the table.

Wir schwimmen im Meer.   We swim in the sea.

Dem Tisch and *im Meer* answer the question ‚Wo'. Although *schwimmen* indicates movement, it also indicates a specific location, within which the action is taking place, which is why *im Meer* is dative. You are in the water both before and after the period in time expressed by the sentence. It is the same with:

Listen to Track 155

Wir gehen unter der Brücke hindurch.   We pass under the bridge.

You are at a specific place – under the bridge – at the time expressed in the sentence. So we have dative even though there is movement which brings us to the next important rule:

The case is determined depending on where we are at the time of speaking: at, in, on, or on our way to or back from a certain place. This is where the previous grammar rules do not apply. If we are at, in, or on a certain place, we use dative. If we are moving toward or away from a certain place, we use the accusative.

One more **example with 'in' meaning 'in' or 'inside':**

Listen to Track 156

Wir gehen in den Park.   If the accusative is used, it means we are going to the park. We are not there.

Wir gehen im Park. Use of the dative indicates we are taking a walk **in** the park.

Contractions: *im (in + dem), ins (in + das)*

Ich steige ins Auto ein.   I get in the car.

But:

Ich steige aus dem Auto aus   I get out of the car

(because 'aus' always takes dative, even if there is movement.)

Vor - in front of (place) or ago (for time, always dative)

Listen to Track 157

Meine Mutter wartet auf mich vor der Schule.

My mother is waiting for me in front of the school.

Er stellte sich vor mich.   He positioned himself in front of me.

Ich bin vor zwei Monaten nach Österreich gekommen.

I came to Austria two months ago.

Zwischen – between

Listen to Track 158

Ein Vertrag zwischen den beiden Parteien wurde unterzeichnet.

A contract between the two parties has been signed.

Ich hänge die Bilder zwischen den Fernseher und den Schrank.

I hang the pictures between the TV and the closet.

QUICK RECAP:

• The case affects the noun, pronoun, or article immediately after the preposition.

- Some prepositions always go with the dative case, while others always go with the accusative. Most prepositions are mixed. When a verb of movement is used, they go with the accusative. When a static verb is used, they go with the dative.

- Verbs that go with fixed prepositions like 'an' and 'auf' almost always take the accusative even though in some cases, there is no motion.

- The case is determined depending on where we are at the time of speaking: at, in, on, or on our way to or back from a certain place, where the previous rules do not apply. If we are at, in, or on a certain place, we use dative. If we are moving toward or away from a certain place, we use the accusative.

TIME TO PRACTICE!

Workbook Lesson 9. Prepositions with Dative and Accusative

Exercise 1: Fill in the blanks with the correct case of the article or pronoun.

1. Sie hat die Flasche in _____ Kühlschrank gestellt.
2. Er legt das Buch auf _____ Schreibtisch.
3. Ich sitze zwischen _____ Freunden.
4. Er lag auf _____ Bett.
5. Jeden Tag nach der Arbeit setzte er sich in _____ Sessel.
6. Ich hänge meinen Mantel an _____ Kleiderhaken.
7. Der Schüler schreibt den Satz an _____ Tafel.
8. Sie steht vor _____ Tür.
9. Das Bild hat jahrelang an _____ Wand gehangen.
10. Liegt eine Decke auf _____ Bett?
11. Plötzlich lief das Kind auf _____ Straße.
12. Jana hat ihren Ehemann auf _____ Reise kennengelernt.
13. An _____ Stelle von Hans bliebe ich zu Hause.
14. Der Vater hängt die Hängematte zwischen _____ Bäume.
15. Die Krankenschwester legt ein Kissen unter _____ Kopf des Patienten.
16. Ich habe die Dokumente in _____ Schublade gelegt.
17. Das Unternehmen hat ein Büro in _____ Stadt eröffnet.
18. Öffne bitte das Fenster zwischen _____ Türen.

Answers:

Exercise 1

1. den / 2. den / 3. meinen / 4. dem / 5. den / 6. den / 7. der / 8. der / 9. der / 10. dem / 11. die / 12. einer / 13. der / 14. die / 15. den / 16. die / 17. der / 18. den

LESSON 10: TWO-WAY PREPOSITIONS (WECHSELPRÄPOSITION)

Rules of Usage of Two-way Prepositions in German

In German, two-way prepositions (Wechselpräpositionen) can take either the dative or the accusative case. They **take the dative when there is no movement or movement is limited to one place**:

Listen to Track 159

Dativ:

> *Die Leute bleiben im (in + dem) Haus.*
>
> The people stay / are staying in the house.
>
> (im Haus = location, answers the question "where" / 'wo').

They take the accusative when they designate motion from one place to another.

Listen to Track 160

Akkusativ:

> *Die Leute gehen in den Hof.*
>
> The people go / are going into the yard.
>
> (in den Hof = motion, answers the question "where to" / 'wohin')?

A man who studied German for many years finally decides to take a trip to Germany. He gets a taxi and the driver asks him, "Wohin?" (Where to?) He responds with confidence, "Accusative!"

Below is a list of two-way prepositions in German:

Hinter – behind

Listen to Track 161

> *Ich fahre hinter das Gebäude.*   I drive behind the building.
>
> *Ich warte auf dich hinter dem Gebäude.*
>
> I'm waiting for you behind the building.

The first is accusative because there is movement. The second sentence is dative because there is no movement (I am waiting for you behind the building.)

An – at, on, to
Listen to Track 162

Ich hänge das Bild an die Wand. Das Bild hängt an der Wand.

I am hanging the picture on the wall. The picture is hanging / hangs on the wall.

As you can see, the verb is exactly the same here. Only the case is different.

Auf – on, at, to, upon
Listen to Track 163

Ich stelle den Teller auf den Tisch. Der Teller steht auf dem Tisch.

I am putting the plate on the table. The plate is on the table.

Ich setze mich auf den Stuhl. Ich sitze auf dem Stuhl.

I sit down (seating myself) on the chair. I sit / am sitting on the chair.

Neben – next to, near, beside

Vor – in front of, before, ago (for time, always dativ = vor vielen Jahren)

In – in, into
Listen to Track 164

Ich gehe ins Büro. Ich bin im Büro.

I am going into the office. I am in the office.

Zwischen – between
Listen to Track 165

Wir laufen zwischen die Autos. Wir stehen zwischen den Autos.

We walk between the cars. We stand between the cars.

Unter – under, among, amongst

(always dativ = unter den fans "among the fans")

Über – above, across, about, over
Some Clarifications

- **Auf** is not used in connection with time, only for horizontal surfaces.
- **An** is used for vertical surfaces and dates. With dates, it always takes the dative (*an **diesem** Tag, an **diesem** Datum*).

- **Neben** is used for next to in the physical sense, but it can also be used in the sense of in addition to. In this case, it always takes the dative (*Neben **der** Tatsache* / in addition to the fact...)
- **In** means 'into' when used to designate movement and always takes the accusative in this case as with the office example above. It is also used temporally (with the dative) with months and to reference a future time (*im Juni* (in + dem), *in einigen Jahren* / in a few years).
- **Über** means above, when we speak of where something is located it can also means "over".

Listen to Track 166

Ich hänge die Lampe über das Bett. Die Lampe hängt über dem Bett.

I am hanging the lamp over the bed. The lamp is hanging / hangs over the bed.

- When used to reference a physical location, **vor** means "in front of". In a temporal phrase, it can mean "before" or "to" as in 'fünf vor rauri' (five to seven).
- **Unter** is just like "under" in English. It is often used as a phrase *unter der Woche* (during the week).

Here are a few more examples

Listen to Track 167

- *Der Mann klettert auf die Mauer. Er sitzt auf der Mauer.*
  The man climbs / is climbing onto the wall. He sits / is sitting on the wall.
- *Sie sperrt seine Tochter in einen Turm. Das Mädchen war raurig im Turm.*
  She locks his daughter in a tower. The girl was sad in the tower.
- *Der Mann steigt auf sein Pferd. Er reitet auf seinem Pferd.*
  The man climbs on his horse. He rides his horse.
- *Er ruft sie an das Fenster. Der König steht neben ihr am Fenster.*
  He calls her to the window. The king stands by her at the window.

You can combine **an** and **in** with the (masculine and neutral) articles after them:

Listen to Track 168

Neuter accusative			Masculine/neuter dative		
an + das	=>	ans	an + dem	=>	am
in + das	=>	ins	in + dem	=>	Im
She goes into the house. *Sie geht in das Haus.*			=>	*Sie geht ins Haus.*	

He calls her to the window. *Er ruft sie an das Fenster.*	=>	*Er ruft sie ans Fenster.*
The king is at the window. *Der König steht an dem Fenster.*	=>	*Der König steht am Fenster.*

Accusative articles

Listen to Track 169

	the	**a/an**	**None**	
masculine	*den Mann*	*einen Mann*	*keinen Mann*	(man)
feminine	*die Frau*	*eine Frau*	*keine Frau*	(woman)
neuter	*das Kind*	*ein Kind*	*kein Kind*	(child)
plural	*die Menschen*	*Menschen*	*keine Menschen*	(people)

Dative articles

Listen to Track 170

	the	**a/an**	**None**	
masculine	*dem Mann*	*einem Mann*	*keinem Mann*	(man)
feminine	*der Frau*	*einer Frau*	*keiner Frau*	(woman)
neuter	*dem Kind*	*einem Kind*	*keinem Kind*	(child)
plural	*den Menschen*	*Menschen*	*keinen Menschen*	(people)

We add '-n' at the end of most plural nouns in Dative in German. Kinder becomes *Kindern*, Fernseher becomes *Fernsehern*, Tische becomes *Tischen* and so on. The exception is nouns that take –s at the end in Plural. So Autos remains *Autos*, Pizzas remains *Pizzas* in dative, etc. That should be fairly obvious as how do 'Autosn' and 'Pizzasn' sound to you?

QUICK RECAP:

Two-way prepositions take the dative when there is no movement or the movement is limited to one place. They take the accusative when they designate motion from one place to another.

TIME TO PRACTICE!

Workbook Lesson 10. Two-Way Prepositions

Exercise 1: Fill in the blanks with the correct two-way preposition and the article.

1. _____ Tisch steht ein Teller und eine Tasse.

2. Ich fahre mit _____ Fahrrad in _____ Schule.

3. Die Lampe hängt _____ Tisch.

4. Heute gehe ich _____ Schule, morgen bin ich nicht _____ Schule.

5. Jetzt steht meine Tasche _____ Teller und _____ Glas.

6. Der Baum steht _____ Haus.

7. Die Uhr hängt _____ Wand.

8. Ich stehe _____ Mutter und _____ Vater.

9. _____ Haus wohnen fünf Personen.

10. Ich sende einen Brief _____ Vater.

11. Das Messer liegt _____ Gabel.

12. In _____ Haus sitzt ein alter Mann.

13. _____ Auto versteckt sich eine Katze.

14. Ich stelle meine Tasche _____ Tisch.

15. Du fährst nächste Woche _____ Urlaub.

16. Ich setzte mich _____ freien Stuhl.

17. Ich setzte mich _____ Bruder.

18. Ich springe _____ Zaun in den Garten.

Answers:

Exercise 1

1. Auf dem / 2. dem … die / 3. über dem / 4. in die … in der / 5. zwischen dem…dem / 6. vor dem , hinter dem / 7. an der / 8. zwischen meiner … meinem / 9. Im / 10. an meinen / 11. neben der / 12. dem / 13. Unter dem / 14. auf den / 15. in den / 16. auf den / 17. neben meinen / 18. über den

LESSON 11: A SIMPLE GUIDE TO THE GERMAN PRETERITE TENSE

What is the German preterite tense?

The German preterite (or *Präteritum*) is the first past tense in German. There are three different past tenses in general (*Präteritum*, *Perfekt* and *Plusquamperfekt*) and each of them is used for specific reasons.

When should we use the German preterite tense?

It is important to know, when to use the German *Präteritum* and when the *Perfekt*, since these two forms resemble the most in their use. For the German preterite, we can say that in general, it is almost used exclusively in written German.

There are a few verbs, which are frequently used in daily communication (we will mark them down below) but mainly, this tense has withdrawn into our written language. We find the preterite in telling, reports, facts, states and to describe actions that were completed in the past. This can include one single, completed event or also a series of completed actions.

The German *Perfekt*, on the other hand, has taken a lot of work off the *Präteritum*. It is much easier to build and has fewer irregularities. The *Perfekt* is our go-to language for daily, spoken communication. In written language, however, it might seem a bit clumsy to use. The *Präteritum*, however, is more elegant and defends its status as hard to learn but beautiful tense.

How do we form the preterite tense?

As you already know from, German tenses always require personal pronouns.

These are the German personal pronouns, which you have to learn by heart:

Listen to Track 171

1st person singular	*ich*	1st person plural	*wir*
2nd person singular	*du*	2nd person plural	*ihr*
3rd person singular	*er / sie / es*	3rd person plural	*sie / Sie**

*The polite form in German is the 3rd person plural *Sie*.

In order to form our verbs in the preterite tense, we need the **infinitive**. The infinitive is the basic form of our verb, so the verb that has not been conjugated yet.

The regular German verbs end on "*-en*". We take away this suffix (or ending) which leaves us with the verb's stem. To this stem we now add this suffixes to mark the preterite tense:

Listen to Track 172

1st person singular	- te	1st person plural	- ten
2nd person singular	- test	2nd person plural	- tet
3rd person singular	- te	3rd person plural	- ten

Take for example the important verb *machen* (*to do*). To the stem *mach* we now add our endings of the preterite tense.

Listen to Track 173

1st person singular	*ich mach - te*	1st person plural	*wir mach - ten*
2nd person singular	*du mach - test*	2nd person plural	*ihr mach - tet*
3rd person singular	*er/sie/es mach - te*	3rd person plural	*sie/Sie mach - ten*

With the mandatory personal pronouns, this gives us: *ich machte, du machstest er / sie / es machte, wir machten, ihr machtet, sie / Sie machten.*

Or as another example the verb *wohnen* (to live; to stay). The stem is *wohn*, which gives us the following conjugation:

Listen to Track 174

1st person singular	*ich wohn - te*	1st person plural	*wir wohn - ten*
2nd person singular	*du wohn - test*	2nd person plural	*ihr wohn - tet*
3rd person singular	*er/sie/es wohn - te*	3rd person plural	*sie/Sie wohn - ten*

Irregularities in the preterite tense

Reading a written medium in German, you will soon notice that most of the preterite forms are irregular. Unfortunately, there is no way around those irregularities and you simply have to learn them by heart. For the beginning, we can focus on the most important ones, which are necessary to know. Additionally, the verbs marked with an "!" are often used as preterite form in spoken, daily German, too.

Listen to Track 175

Sein (to be) !

1st person singular	*ich war*	1st person plural	*wir waren*
2nd person singular	*du warst*	2nd person plural	*ihr wart*
3rd person singular	*er/sie/es war*	3rd person plural	*sie/Sie waren*

Listen to Track 176

Haben (to have) **!**

1st person singular	ich hatte	1st person plural	wir hatten
2nd person singular	du hattest	2nd person plural	ihr hattet
3rd person singular	er/sie/es hatte	3rd person plural	sie/Sie hatten

Listen to Track 177

Gehen (to go)

1st person singular	ich ging	1st person plural	wir gingen
2nd person singular	du gingst	2nd person plural	ihr gingt
3rd person singular	er/sie/es ging	3rd person plural	sie/Sie gingen

Listen to Track 178

Mögen (to like) **!**

1st person singular	ich mochte	1st person plural	wir mochten
2nd person singular	du mochtest	2nd person plural	ihr mochtet
3rd person singular	er/sie/es mochte	3rd person plural	sie/Sie mochten

Here are some sentences, which contain irregular verbs in the preterite tense:

Listen to Track 179

Ich war am Samstag da.	I was there on Saturday.
Wo wart ihr gestern?*	Where have you been yesterday?
Seine Familie hatte nie einen Hund.	His family never had a dog.
Damals hatten wir noch ein großes Haus.	Back then, we still had a big house.
Sie gingen zusammen nach Hause.	They went home together.
Mochtest du die Vorstellung?*	Did you like the performance?
Ihr mochtet euch schon immer.	You have always liked each other.

*You might notice that the personal pronoun stands behind the conjugated verb when you are asking a question. This type of question we call *Inversion*.

a. Modal verbs

Let us continue with some more irregular verbs. German has modal verbs, which are used frequently in our daily communication. Also the preterite for appears daily in spoken German and should be thus learned by heart.

You might notice that the *Umlaut* in *können*, *müssen* and *dürfen* changes:

Können, *ö* -> *o*

Müssen & *dürfen*, *ü* -> *u*

Listen to Track 180

Können (to can; to know how to do sth.) **!**

1st person singular	ich konnte	1st person plural	wir konnten
2nd person singular	du konntest	2nd person plural	ihr konntet
3rd person singular	er/sie/es konnte	3rd person plural	sie/Sie konnten

Listen to Track 181

Müssen (to must; to have to) **!**

1st person singular	ich musste	1st person plural	wir mussten
2nd person singular	du musstest	2nd person plural	ihr musstet
3rd person singular	er/sie/es musste	3rd person plural	sie/Sie mussten

Listen to Track 182

Dürfen (to be allowed; to can) **!**

1st person singular	ich durfte	1st person plural	wir durften
2nd person singular	du durftest	2nd person plural	ihr durftet
3rd person singular	er/sie/es durfte	3rd person plural	sie/Sie durften

The last two modal verbs, *wollen* and *sollen*, are in fact regular! Nevertheless, we added them to the other modal verbs so that it is easier for you two learn them together.

Listen to Track 183

Wollen (to want) **!**

1st person singular	ich wollte	1st person plural	wir wollten
2nd person singular	du wolltest	2nd person plural	ihr wolltet
3rd person singular	er/sie/es wollte	3rd person plural	sie/Sie wollten

Listen to Track 184

Sollen (to be supposed to; shall) **!**

1st person singular	ich sollte	1st person plural	wir sollten
2nd person singular	du solltest	2nd person plural	ihr solltet
3rd person singular	er/sie/es sollte	3rd person plural	sie/Sie sollten

Here are some sentences which contain modal verbs in the preterite tense:

Listen to Track 185

Ich musste ihm helfen.	I had to help him.
Du konntest die Aufgabe lösen.	You could solve the task.
Wir konnten nicht kommen.	We couldn't come.
Konnte sie schon immer so gut tanzen?	Could she always dance that well?
Ihr musstet lange dort bleiben.	You had to stay there a long time.
Ich musste früher gehen.	I had to go earlier.
Er durfte nicht mit uns kommen.	He wasn't allowed to come with us.
Durften sie das essen?	Were they allowed to eat that?
Sie wollte das nicht.	She didn't want it.
Ich wollte immer Kinder.	I always wanted kids.
Ihr solltet anrufen, wenn ihr angekommen seid.	You were supposed to call when you arrived.

b. **Strong verbs**

Strong verbs change their main vocal, which makes them irregular. However, they are part of our daily communication and you will especially notice them in written German.

Here you find the most commonly used strong verbs.

Listen to Track 186

Essen   to eat

Notice that this verb also changes its *double s* to a German *ß*!

Listen to Track 187

1st person singular	ich aß	1st person plural	wir aßen
2nd person singular	du aßest	2nd person plural	ihr aßet
3rd person singular	er/sie/es aß	3rd person plural	sie/Sie aßen

Listen to Track 188

Sehen (to see)

1st person singular	ich sah	1st person plural	wir sahen
2nd person singular	du sahst	2nd person plural	ihr saht
3rd person singular	er/sie/es sah	3rd person plural	sie/Sie sahen

Listen to Track 189

Sprechen (to speak)

1st person singular	ich sprach	1st person plural	wir sprachen
2nd person singular	du sprachst	2nd person plural	ihr spracht
3rd person singular	er/sie/es sprach	3rd person plural	sie/Sie sprachen

Listen to Track 190

Helfen (to help)

1st person singular	*ich half*	1st person plural	*wir halfen*
2nd person singular	*du halfst*	2nd person plural	*ihr halft*
3rd person singular	*er/sie/es half*	3rd person plural	*sie/Sie halfen*

Listen to Track 191

Geben **(to give)**

1st person singular	*ich gab*	1st person plural	*wir gaben*
2nd person singular	*du gabst*	2nd person plural	*ihr gabt*
3rd person singular	*er/sie/es gab*	3rd person plural	*sie/Sie gaben*

Listen to Track 192

Schreiben (to write)

1st person singular	*ich schrieb*	1st person plural	*wir schrieben*
2nd person singular	*du schriebst*	2nd person plural	*ihr schriebt*
3rd person singular	*er/sie/es schrieb*	3rd person plural	*sie/Sie schrieben*

Listen to Track 193

Fahren (to drive)

1st person singular	*ich fuhr*	1st person plural	*wir fuhren*
2nd person singular	*du fuhrst*	2nd person plural	*ihr fuhrt*
3rd person singular	*er/sie/es fuhr*	3rd person plural	*sie/Sie fuhren*

Listen to Track 194

Laufen (to walk; to run) **!**

1st person singular	*ich lief*	1st person plural	*wir liefen*
2nd person singular	*du liefst*	2nd person plural	*ihr lieft*
3rd person singular	*er/sie/es lief*	3rd person plural	*sie/Sie liefen*

Listen to Track 195

Tragen (to carry, to wear)

1st person singular	*ich trug*	1st person plural	*wir trugen*
2nd person singular	*du trugst*	2nd person plural	*ihr trugt*
3rd person singular	*er/sie/es trug*	3rd person plural	*sie/Sie trugen*

Listen to Track 196

Beginnen (to begin, to start)

1st person singular	*ich begann*	1st person plural	*wir begannen*
2nd person singular	*du begannst*	2nd person plural	*ihr begannt*
3rd person singular	*er/sie/es begann*	3rd person plural	*sie/Sie begannen*

Here are some sentences, which contain strong verbs in the preterite tense. Only the sentence marked with " **!** " are likely to be used in spoken German, too.

Listen to Track 197

Am Abend aß er nur Brot.	In the evening, he only ate bread.
Wir aßen gemeinsam.	We ate together.
Er sah sie an einem Tisch sitzen.	He saw her sitting at a table.
Ihr saht müde aus.	You looked tired.
Ich sprach nicht aus, was ich dachte.	I did not say what I thought.
Sie sprachen leise.	They talked quietly.
Sie half mir.	She helped me.
Wir halfen den Jungen.	We helped the boys.
Gab es etwas zu essen? **!**	Was there something to eat?
Wir gaben alles, was wir konnten.	We gave everything we could.
Sie schrieben sich Briefe.	They wrote letters to each other.
Ich schrieb dir eine Nachricht.	I wrote you a message.
Ihr nahmt das Auto.	You took the car.
Er fuhr am Abend zu ihr.	He drove to her in the evening.
Wie lief deine Klausur? **!**	How was your exam?
Es lief gut. **!**	It went well.
Wir liefen uns über den Weg. **!**	We ran into each other.
Sie trug ein schönes Kleid.	She wore a nice dress.
Ich trug seine Tasche.	I carried his bag.
Wir trugen die gleiche Jacke.	We wore the same jackets.
Ich begann mir Sorgen zu machen. **!**	I began to worry.

QUICK RECAP:

- The simple past of regular German verbs is formed by taking away the "*-en*".
- Then, we add the suffix -te, -test, -ten, or -tet depending on the subject of the sentence. The form of the irregular verbs needs to be memorized.
- The suffix added also depends on the subject.
- For modal verbs, we drop the umlaut and add -te, -test, -ten, or -tet depending on the subject of the sentence.

TIME TO PRACTICE!

Workbook Lesson 11. A Simple Guide to the German Preterite Tense

Exercise 1. Fill in the blanks with the simple past form of the infinitive.

1. schreiben: er _____ - he wrote
2. sagen: sie _____ - they said
3. machen: ich _____ - I made / did
4. denken: er _____ - he thought
5. fragen: du _____ - you asked
6. nehmen: ihr _____ - you took
7. essen: er _____ - he ate
8. fahren: es _____ - it travelled
9. geben: Sie _____ - You gave
10. kommen: sie _____ - she came
11. kaufen: es _____ - it bought
12. sein: wir _____ - we were
13. haben: er _____ - he had
14. sehen: er _____ - he saw
15. arbeiten: es _____ - it worked
16. sprechen: sie _____ - they spoke
17. gehen: ihr_____ - you went
18. wohnen: sie _____ - she lived
19. anrufen: du_____ an – you called
20. trinken: ich _____ - I drank
21. helfen: er _____ - he helped
22. einladen: er _____ ein – he invited
23. laufen: sie _____ - they ran
24. hören: wir _____ - we heard
25. lesen: ihr _____ - you read
26. kennen: er _____ - he knew
27. fliegen: er _____ - he flew
28. finden: du _____ - you found
29. kosten: es _____ - it cost
30. warten: ich _____ - I waited
31. reisen: sie _____ - she traveled

32. schlafen: ihr _____ - you slept
33. bringen: sie _____ - they brought
34. verlieren: du _____ - you lost
35. tragen: wir _____ - we carried
36. studieren: es _____ - it studied
37. anfangen: ihr _____ an – you started

Exercise 2. Fill in the blanks

	German	English
1	Gestern Abend _____ (sitzen) wir lange auf dieser Bank.	We sat on this bench for a long time last night.
2	Der Affe _____ (sein) auf dem Baum.	The monkey was in the tree.
3	Ich _____(haben) es eilig, denn ich flog nach Paris.	I was in a hurry because I was flying to Paris.
4	Er _____ (essen) so viel Kuchen, dass ihm schlecht wurde.	He ate so much cake that he got sick.
5	Er_____ (kennen) ein gutes Restaurant im Bezirk.	He knew a good restaurant in the area.
6	_____ (lieben) du wirklich Sophie?	Did you really love Sophie?
7	_____ (arbeiten) ihr zusammen in deinem alten Unternehmen?	Did you work together at your old company?
8	Vor vier Jahren _____ (leben) wir noch hier.	Four years ago we were still living here.
9	Sie _____ (beraten) sich mit dem Bürgermeister, um diese wichtige Arbeit in Angriff zu nehmen.	You consulted the mayor to undertake this important work.
10	Wir _____ eine billige Wohnung. (suchen)	We looked for a cheap apartment.
11	Die Kinder _____ gern im Freien. (spielen)	The children liked playing outdoors.
12	Der Hund _____ die ganze Nacht. (bellen)	The dog barked all night.
13	Letzte Woche _____ ihr mehrere Kleider in der Boutique an. (anprobieren)	Last week you tried several dresses in the boutique on.
14	Du _____ das Fotoalbum aus deinem Zimmer. (holen)	You got the photo album from your room.

15	Frau Schneider _____ Kaffee in der Küche. (kochen)	Ms. Schneider made coffee in the kitchen.
16	Er _____ Klara einen schönen Blumenstrauß. (schenken)	He gave Klara a beautiful bouquet.
17	Ich _____ mein Baumhaus vor drei Monaten. (bauen)	I built my tree house three months ago.
18	Letzten Sonntag _____ ihr die Großeltern. (besuchen)	Last Sunday you visited the grandparents.
19	Die Eltern _____ viele Blaubeeren im Wald. (sammeln)	The parents gathered lots of blueberries in the forest.

Exercise 3. Haben or sein? Fill in the blanks in the past simple as appropriate.

1. Du _____ Kopfschmerzen.

2. Ihr _____ im Zoo.

3. Er _____ nicht zu Hause.

4. _____ Sie als Kind einen Hund?

5. Ich _____ nicht durstig.

Exercise 4. Enter the correct past simple form of each verb.

	German	English
1	Meine Eltern _____ (kaufen) mir eine Gitarre.	My parents bought me a guitar.
2	Wir _____ (reisen) in einem Wohnmobil durch Österreich.	We travelled through Austria in a mobile home.
3	Auf wen _____ (warten) er?	Who was he waiting for?
4	Ich _____ (tanzen) die ganze Nacht.	I danced all night.
5	Mein Opa _____ (wandern) früher viel.	My grandpa used to hike a lot in the past.
6	Unsere Freunde _____ (kommen) uns besuchen.	Our friends came to visit us.
7	Ich _____ (essen) den ganzen Kuchen.	I ate the whole cake.
8	Du _____ (laufen) ganz schnell weg.	You ran away very fast.
9	Worüber _____ (sprechen) ihr bei der Versammlung?	What did you talk about at the meeting?
10	Meine Oma _____ (kennen) einen berühmten Schauspieler.	My grandma knew a famous actor.

Answer:

Exercise 1:

1.schrieb / 2.sagten / 3.machte / 4.dachte / 5.fragtest / 6.nahmt / 7.aß / 8.fuhr / 9.gaben / 10.kam / 11.kaufte /12.waren / 13.hatte / 14.sah / 15.arbeitete / 16.sprachen / 17.gingt / 18.wohnte / 19.riefst (an) /20.trank / 21.half /22.lud (ein) /23.liefen /24. hörten /25.last / 26.kannte /27.flog / 28.fandest / 29.kostete / 30.wartete / 31.reiste / 32.schlieft / 33.brachten / 34.verlorst / 35.trugen / 36.studierte / 37.fingt (an)

Exercise 2:

1.saßen / 2.war / 3.hatte / 4.aß / 5.kannte / 6.Liebtest / 7.arbeitetet / 8.lebten / 9.berieten / 10.suchten / 11.spielten / 12.bellte / 13.probiertet / 14.holtest / 15.kochte / 16.schenkte / 17.baute / 18.besuchtet / 19.sammelten

Exercise 3:

1.hattest / 2.wart / 3.war / 4.Hatten / 5.war

Exercise 4.

1.kauften / 2.reisten / 3.wartete /4.tanzte / 5.wanderte / 6.kamen / 7.aß / 8.liefst / 9.spracht / 10.kannte

LESSON 12: PRESENT TENSE

Learn all about the present tense in German--how to use it, how to form it, the irregularities, and so much more in this lesson.

What is the German present tense?

The German *Präsens* (or *Gegenwartsform*) is the only tense to express the present. From all German tenses, the *Präsens* is the one that is used the most. This tense is always taught first because it is our most important and basic tense. It is used to express both present and future.

When should we use the German present tense?

From all German tenses, the *Präsens* is the one that is used the most.

We use the German present tense when we want to express:

- what we are doing right now

- what we do in general, our habits, our routine

- what we are planning to do or what will happen in the near future

As you can see, the German present tense is our go-to when it comes to basic and everyday communication.

How do we form the present tense?

In order to form German verbs in the present tense, we need the **infinitive**. The infinitive is the basic form of our verb, so the verb that has not been conjugated yet.

Please note: When we conjugate a verb in German, we always have to **add the personal pronoun at the beginning**. Maybe you know a language (e.g. Spanish or Italian) where it is possible to just use the conjugated verb form (without a personal pronoun) because its ending is already telling us if it is for example 1. personal singular.

However, in this case, German is like English. In the English present tense, you cannot just say "*Am from England.*" or "*Are a nice person.*" It has to be "*I am from England.*" and "***You*** *are a nice person.*" **The same rule applies for German!**

These are the German personal pronouns, which you have to learn by heart:

Listen to Track 198

1st person singular	ich	1st person plural	wir
2nd person singular	du	2nd person plural	ihr
3rd person singular	er / sie / es	3rd person plural	sie / Sie*

*The polite form in German is the 3rd person plural *Sie.*

Back to the infinitive of the verb. The regular German verbs end on "*-en*". We take away this suffix (or ending) which leaves us with the verb's stem. To this stem we now add this suffixes:

Listen to Track 199

1st person singular	- e	1st person plural	- en*
2nd person singular	- st	2nd person plural	- t
3rd person singular	- t	3rd person plural	- en*

*You might notice that 1st and 3rd person plural are similar to the infinitive. One more reason to add the personal pronoun!

Take for example the important verb *machen* (*to do*). To the stem *mach* we now add our endings of the present tense.

Listen to Track 200

1st person singular	ich mach - e	1st person plural	wir mach - en
2nd person singular	du mach - st	2nd person plural	ihr mach - t
3rd person singular	er/sie/es mach - t	3rd person plural	sie/Sie mach - en

With the mandatory personal pronouns, this gives us: *ich mache, du machst, er / sie / es macht, wir machen, ihr macht, sie / Sie machen.*

Or as another example the verb *fragen* (to ask). The stem is *frag,* which gives us the following conjugation:

Listen to Track 201

1st person singular	ich frage	1st person plural	wir fragen
2nd person singular	du fragst	2nd person plural	ihr fragt
3rd person singular	er/sie/es fragt	3rd person plural	sie/Sie fragen

And also the important verb *gehen* (to go). The stem is *geh,* which gives us the following conjugation:

Listen to Track 202

1st person singular	ich gehe	1st person plural	wir gehen
2nd person singular	du gehst	2nd person plural	ihr geht
3rd person singular	er/sie/es geht	3rd person plural	sie/Sie gehen

Irregularities in the present tense

As almost every other language, German too has its irregularities. But don't worry, here you find a list of the most frequently used verbs in our daily communication.

Listen to Track 203

Sein (to be)

1st person singular	ich bin	1st person plural	wir sind
2nd person singular	du bist	2nd person plural	ihr seid
3rd person singular	er/sie/es ist	3rd person plural	sie/Sie sind

Listen to Track 204

Haben (to have (got))

1st person singular	ich habe	1st person plural	wir haben
2nd person singular	du hast	2nd person plural	ihr habt
3rd person singular	er/sie/es hat*	3rd person plural	sie/Sie haben

*The only irregularity in this verb are the 2nd and 3rd person singular.

Listen to Track 205

Heißen

When you present yourself, you can use the verb *heißen*. There is no correct translation into English, it would be *to be called* but there is just no real equivalent. But maybe you know the French *s'appeler*, Spanish *llamarse* or Italine *chiamarsi*, they are equal to the verb's sense in German!

1st person singular	ich heiße	1st person plural	wir heißen
2nd person singular	du heißt*	2nd person plural	ihr heißt
3rd person singular	er/sie/es heißt	3rd person plural	sie/Sie heißen

*The only irregularity in this verb is the 2nd person singular.

Here are some sentences, which contain irregular verbs in the present tense:

Listen to Track 206

Ich bin hier.	I am here.
Wo seid ihr?*	Where are you?
Er hat einen Hund.	He has got a dog
Wir haben ein großes Haus.	We have a big house.
Sie heißt Lisa.	Her name is Lisa.
Wie heißt du?*	What is you name?

*You might notice that the personal pronoun stands behind the conjugated verb when you are asking a question. This type of question we call *Inversion*.

a) Modal verbs

Let us continue with more irregular verbs. German has modal verbs, which are used frequently in our daily communication.

Maybe you can recognize a pattern concerning the (ir)regularity in the conjugation... If not, don't despair! We will give you the solution at the end of this paragraph.

Listen to Track 207

Wollen   to want

1st person singular	ich will	1st person plural	wir wollen
2nd person singular	du willst	2nd person plural	ihr wollt
3rd person singular	er/sie/es will	3rd person plural	sie/Sie wollen

Listen to Track 208

Können (to can; to know how to do sth.)

1st person singular	ich kann	1st person plural	wir können
2nd person singular	du kannst	2nd person plural	ihr könnt
3rd person singular	er/sie/es kann	3rd person plural	sie/Sie können

Listen to Track 209

Müssen (to must; to have to)

1st person singular	ich muss	1st person plural	wir müssen
2nd person singular	du musst	2nd person plural	ihr müsst
3rd person singular	er/sie/es muss	3rd person plural	sie/Sie müssen

Listen to Track 210

Dürfen (to be allowed; to can)

1st person singular	ich darf	1st person plural	wir dürfen
2nd person singular	du darfst	2nd person plural	ihr dürft
3rd person singular	er/sie/es darf	3rd person plural	sie/Sie dürfen

Listen to Track 211

Sollen (to be supposed to; shall)

1st person singular	ich soll	1st person plural	wir sollen
2nd person singular	du sollst	2nd person plural	ihr sollt
3rd person singular	er/sie/es soll	3rd person plural	sie/Sie sollen

There is a pattern with these modal verbs in the present tense, which facilitates your studying! Just have a look at the three plural forms. They still follow the rule from above: stem + regular suffix. Only the singular forms are irregular!

Here are some sentences, which contain modal verbs in the present tense:

Listen to Track 212

Du musst mir helfen.	You have to help me.
Ich will dich wiedersehen.	I want to see you again.
Wir können das schaffen.	We can manage it.
Kannst du tanzen?	Can you dance?
Was wollt ihr tun?	What do you want to do?
Ihr sollt das nicht essen.	You are not supposed to eat that.
Er darf mich nicht stören.	He is not allowed to disturb me.
Sie müssen ihr Zimmer aufräumen.	They have to tidy up their room.
Darfst du heute ausgehen?	Can you go out tonight? (Are you allowed to go out tonight?)
Sie soll es ihm sagen.	She is supposed to tell him.

b) Strong verbs

Strong verbs change their vocal in the 2nd and 3rd person singular.

    a -> ä ("Umlaut")   *e -> i* or *ie*

Here you find the most commonly used strong verbs.

    a -> ä

Listen to Track 213

Fahren (to drive)

1st person singular	ich fahre	1st person plural	wir fahren
2nd person singular	du fährst	2nd person plural	ihr fahrt
3rd person singular	er/sie/es fährt	3rd person plural	sie/Sie fahren

Listen to Track 214

Laufen (to walk; to run)

1st person singular	ich laufe	1st person plural	wir laufen
2nd person singular	du läufst	2nd person plural	ihr lauft
3rd person singular	er/sie/es läuft	3rd person plural	sie/Sie laufen

Listen to Track 215

Tragen (to carry; to wear)

1st person singular	ich trage	1st person plural	wir tragen
2nd person singular	du trägst	2nd person plural	ihr tragt
3rd person singular	er/sie/es trägt	3rd person plural	sie/Sie tragen

e -> ie

Listen to Track 216

Lesen (to read)

1st person singular	ich lese	1st person plural	wir lesen
2nd person singular	du liest	2nd person plural	ihr lest
3rd person singular	er/sie/es liest	3rd person plural	sie/Sie lesen

Listen to Track 217

Sehen (to see)

1st person singular	ich sehe	1st person plural	wir sehen
2nd person singular	du siehst	2nd person plural	ihr seht
3rd person singular	er/sie/es sieht	3rd person plural	sie/Sie sehen

e -> i

Listen to Track 218

Brechen (to break)

1st person singular	*ich breche*	1st person plural	*wir brechen*
2nd person singular	*du brichst*	2nd person plural	*ihr brecht*
3rd person singular	*er/sie/es bricht*	3rd person plural	*sie/Sie brechen*

Listen to Track 219

Essen (to eat)

1st person singular	*ich esse*	1st person plural	*wir essen*
2nd person singular	*du isst*	2nd person plural	*ihr esst*
3rd person singular	*er/sie/es isst*	3rd person plural	*sie/Sie essen*

Listen to Track 220

Sprechen (to speak)

1st person singular	*ich spreche*	1st person plural	*wir sprechen*
2nd person singular	*du sprichst*	2nd person plural	*ihr sprecht*
3rd person singular	*er/sie/es spricht*	3rd person plural	*sie/Sie sprechen*

Listen to Track 221

Geben (to give)

1st person singular	*ich gebe*	1st person plural	*wir geben*
2nd person singular	*du gibst*	2nd person plural	*ihr gebt*
3rd person singular	*er/sie/es gibt*	3rd person plural	*sie/Sie geben*

Here are some sentences, which contain strong verbs in the present tense:

Listen to Track 222

Ich fahre dich nach Hause.	I will drive you home.
Er fährt einen BMW.	He drives a BMW.
Fährst du mit dem Auto? – Nein, ich laufe.	Do you drive? – No, I walk.
Wir laufen einen Marathon.	We run a marathon.
Ihr tragt dieselben Schuhe.	You wear the same shoes.
Er trägt ihre Taschen.	He carries her bags.
Ich lese viel.	I read a lot.
Lesen Sie Zeitung?	Do you read the newspaper?
Siehst du mich?	Do you see me?
Wir sehen uns morgen!	See you tomorrow!

Sie bricht ihr Versprechen.	She breaks her promise.
Ihr esst zu schnell.	You eat too fast.
Heute Abend essen wir zusammen.	Tonight, we will eat together.
Du sprichst gut deutsch.	You speak German well.
Ihr sprecht zu laut.	You speak to loud.
Er gibt ihr alles, was sie will.	He gives her everything she desires.
Du gibst so schnell nicht auf.	You don't give up so fast.

Of course, there are numerous irregular verbs. Nevertheless, we can categorize them in order to discover a pattern in there irregularity.

a) Verb stem ends on $-d$ or $-t$.

Listen to Track 223

Arbeiten (to work)

1st person singular	ich arbeite	1st person plural	wir arbeiten
2nd person singular	du arbeitest*	2nd person plural	ihr arbeitet*
3rd person singular	er/sie/es arbeitet	3rd person plural	sie/Sie arbeiten

*Here, we insert an additional *e* in front of the regular suffix.

Listen to Track 224

Halten (to hold)

1st person singular	ich halte	1st person plural	wir halten
2nd person singular	du hältst	2nd person plural	ihr haltet
3rd person singular	er/sie/es hält	3rd person plural	sie/Sie halten

QUICK RECAP:

- To form the present simple, we drop the suffix -en and add -e to the end of the verb for ich, -st for du, and -t for er, sie, and es.
- We add -t or -et for ihr.
- There is no change if the subject is wir, sie (they), or Sie.
- Only -t is added for the du-form for verbs that end in -s or esszet.
- For strong verbs, the rule is a -> $ä$ and e -> i or ie in the second and third person singular.
- The present simple is used to express not only the present, but also the future. You would know what it refers to depending on context on a case by case basis.

The wondrous German language reflects a fact of life the great Roman emperor Marcus Aurelius first expressed, "Neither the past nor the future belongs to us. We only have the present."

TIME TO PRACTICE!

Workbook Lesson 12. Present Tense

Exercise 1. Fill in the blanks with the correct verb form.

1. _____ihr morgen ins Training? Wir_____immer! [kommen / kommen]
   – Are you coming to practice tomorrow? We always come!

2. Ich_____in meinem Zimmer und_____für die Schule. [sitzen / lernen]
   – I'm sitting in my room and studying for school.

3. Es_____ihm keinen Spaß. Er____lieber mit seinen Freunden. [machen / spielen]
   – He doesn't enjoy it. He'd rather play with his friends.

4. Meine Frau_____nach Hause und_____das Abendessen. [gehen / kochen]
   – My wife is going home and making dinner.

5. _____du morgen in die Schule? Dann____ich dir dein Buch. [kommen / bringen]
   – Are you coming to school tomorrow? I'll bring your book then.

6. _____du schon zu Hause?_____du zum Essen? [sein / kommen]
   – Are you home? Are you coming to eat?

7. Ich_____ (schwimmen) gern.   – I like swimming.

8. Ich_____Jan und_____25 Jahre alt. [heißen / sein]
   – My name is Jan and I'm 25 years old.

9. Meine Nachbarin_____ (spielen) mit meiner Schwester.
   – My neighbor is playing / plays with my sister.

10. _____ (trinken) du Alkohol?   – Do you drink alcohol?

11. Wir_____ (lachen) sehr laut.   – We laugh very loudly.

12. Meine Mutter _____ (kochen) sehr gern. – My mother loves cooking.

13. Laura _____ (malen) schöne Landschaften.
    – Laura paints beautiful landscapes.

14. Ihr_____ (singen) zu der CD. – You're singing along to the CD.

15. Katja, _____ (lernen) du Mathe?   – Katja, are you studying math?

16. Woher_____ (kommen) Matthias? – Where does Matthias come from?

17. Ich_____ihr immer Briefe, aber sie _____nie zurück. [schreiben / schreiben]
    – I always write her letters, but she never writes back.

18. _____du mir deinen Schlüssel? Ich_____meinen nicht. [geben / finden]
    – Will you give me your key? I can't find mine.
19. Wohin _____ (gehen) wir? – Where are we going?

Exercise 2. Haben or sein? Choose the correct form.

1. Ich_____eine Katze.
2. Er_____klug.
3. _____du Hunger?
4. _____r Schweizer?
5. Wir _____nicht müde.

Exercise 3. Fill in the blanks with the correct verb form.

1. Meine Eltern _____noch im Urlaub, _____aber morgen zurück. [sein / kommen]
   – My parents are still on holiday, but they're coming back tomorrow.
2. Ich_____Äpfel, _____ber keine Tomaten. [mögen / essen]
   – I like apples, but I don't eat tomatoes.
3. Es_____ dunkel und wir _____nach Hause. [werden / gehen]
   – It's getting dark and we're going home.
4. Ihr_____in der Schule und_____ein Diktat. [sein / schreiben]
   – You're in school and you're writing a dictation.
5. Warum_____du noch? _____du nicht, dass die Ampel grün ist? [stehen / sehen]
   – Why are you just sitting there? Don't you see the light is green?

Exercise 4. Enter the correct present tense form for each verb.

1. Ich (kochen) heute das Essen. _____ – I'm making the food today.
2. Das Mädchen (gehen) zur Schule. _____ – The girl is going to school.
3. (lernen) ihr Deutsch? _____ – Are you learning German?
4. Er (wohnen) nicht hier. _____ – He doesn't live here.
5. (Schreiben) du mir eine E-Mail? _____ – Will you email me?
6. Du_____nicht aufstehen? _____du denn keinen Hunger? [wollen / haben]
   – You don't want to get up? Aren't you hungry?
7. Du _____gerne Musik und_____gerne Filme. [hören / sehen]
   – You like listening to music and watching movies.
8. Er_____ (tragen) einen schwarzen Anzug. – He's wearing a black suit.
9. Da_____ (haben) Sie Recht. – You (polite) are right about that.
10. In jedem Mann_____ (stecken) ein Kind. – A child hides in every man.

11. Dieser Wagen _____ (brauchen) doch sicher viel Benzin.

    – This car probably needs a lot of gas.

12. Wo_____ (sein) das Problem? – Where's the problem?

13. Gut, aber_____ (müssen) das alle Leute sehen?

    – Good, but must everyone see that?

14. Wunderbar. Liebe_____ (sein) in jedem Alter schön.

    – Wonderful. Love is beautiful at any age

Exercise 5. Enter the correct present tense form of each verb. Pay attention to irregular verb forms.

1. Der Zug (fahren) in zehn Minuten. _____

2. Du (sprechen) fünf Fremdsprachen. _____

3. Ihr (baden) im See. _____

4. (lesen) er gern Krimis? _____

5. Was (essen) du gerne? _____

6. Das _____ (können) Sie nicht mit mir machen !

7. Das Abitur _____ (können) man auf dem Gymnasium machen.

8. Die langweilige Frisur_____ (stehen) ihr nicht.

9. Mein Bruder_____noch, aber meine Mutter_____schon wach. [schlafen / sein]

10. _____ihr mir heute im Garten helfen. Euer Vater_____keine Zeit. [können / haben]

11. Er _____dem Verkäufer das Geld und_____das Eis. [geben / nehmen]

12. Ich_____,dass es spät_____. (wissen, sein)

13. Er_____seiner Mutter in der Küche_____[müssen / helfen]

Answers:

Exercise 1:

1.Kommt, kommen / 2.sitze, lerne / 3.macht, spielt / 4.geht, kocht / 5.Kommst, bringe / 6.Bist, Kommst / 7.schwimme / 8.heiße, bin / 9.spielt / 10.Trinkst / 11.lachen / 12.kocht / 13.malt / 14.singt / 15.lernst / 16.kommt / 17.schreibe, schreibt / 18.Gibst, finde / 19.gehen /

Exercise 2:

1.Ich habe eine Katze – I have a cat. / 2.Er ist klug – He's smart. / 3.Hast du Hunger? – Are you hungry? / 4.Seid ihr Schweizer? – Are you (pl.) Swiss? / 5.Wir sind nicht müde. – We're not tired.

Exercise 3:

1.sind, kommen / 2.mag, esse / 3.wird, gehen / 4.seid, schreibt / 5.stehst, siehst

Exercise 4:

1.koche / 2.geht / 3.Lernt / 4.wohnt / 5.Schreibst / 6.willst, Hast / 7.hörst, siehst / 8.trägt / 9.haben / 10.steckt / 11.braucht / 12.ist / 13.müssen / 14.ist

Exercise 5:

1.fährt / 2.sprichst / 3.badet / 4.Liest / 5.isst / 6.können / 7.kann / 8.steht / 9.schläft, ist / 10.Könnt, hat / 11.gibt, nimmt / 12.weiß, ist / 13.muss, helfen /

LESSON 13: ADJECTIVE DECLENSION

In German, adjectives are declined (or inflected) according to the case, number, and gender of the noun they precede. Only adjectives that precede nouns are declined. These are called attributive adjectives.

There are three types of declension — **strong, weak, and mixed** — for the adjectives that are declined.

Adjective declension is not as hard as it sounds, trust me! In fact, it is one of the easier things about German grammar. This lesson will explain all about it — keep reading!

Types of Adjectives in German

German has attributive, predicative, and adverbial adjectives. Predicative and adverbial adjectives are not declined. They always have the same form, regardless of the form of the noun they describe.

1. Predicative Adjectives

These are adjectives that follow the verbs *werden, sein,* and *bleiben* (to become, to be, and to stay or to remain).

Listen to Track 225

Example:

Der Mann ist froh.   The man is happy.

2. Adverbial Adjectives

These are adjectives that follow all other verbs. They answer the question of "how" someone does something, which is the definition of an adverb:

Listen to Track 226

Example:

Der Junge tanzt froh herum.   The boy dances around happily.

3. Attributive Adjectives

As mentioned, attributive adjectives precede nouns. More specifically, they come between a definite or indefinite article and a noun. To decline them correctly, we have to know the case, number, and gender of the noun. This is not something to be readily assumed about the German language learner. It is very important to learn the gender of nouns (der, die, das) because it's at the basis of proper use of the language.

Listen to Track 227

Examples:

Er ist ein sehr froher Junge.	He is a very happy boy. (nominative)
Ich habe nie so einen frohen Mann gekannt.	I have never known such a happy man. (accusative)
Die kluge Frau arbeitet viel.	The smart woman works a lot. (nominative – die Frau)
Sie isst den gelben Apfel, er mag den roten.	She eats the yellow apple, he likes the red one. (accusative – den Apfel)

The 3 Types of Declension

Listen to Track 228

The first type is weak declension, where the adjective follows the definite article.

> *Das schöne Haus*   The beautiful house

As there is weak, there is also strong declension. This is where there is no article. There is only the adjective and the noun.

> *Schönes Haus*   Beautiful house

Finally, mixed declension is where we have an indefinite article followed by the adjective.

> *Ein schönes Haus*   A beautiful house

Now, let's get into more detail.

1. Weak declension

Weak declension gets its name because the article and not the adjective carries the case marker. Ex. *der nette Junge* – the article 'der' indicates the masculine case. Likewise with *die nette Frau* and *das nette Kind*. **The weak declension is used after the definite articles (der, die, das)** and any and all of the following pronouns:

Listen to Track 229

- *jener* (that)
- *dieser* (this)
- *derjenige* (that one)
- *welcher* (which)
- *derselbe* (the same)

Or the following quantity indicators (declined):

Listen to Track 230

- *alle* (all)
- *jede/r* (every)
- *manche/r* (some)

Weak declension is the easiest. **We just add −e or −en to the adjective depending on the case, number, and gender.**

Listen to Track 231

Example:

Jeder gute Mensch hilft den anderen.	Every good person helps others.
Der gute Mensch hilft den anderen.	The good person helps others.
Die guten Menschen helfen den anderen.	The good people help others.

Exceptions to the Rule

When the adjective ends in −el or -er, the ending changes to −le or -re.

Listen to Track 232

Example in the nominative

Sensibel – die sensible Person (not 'die sensibele Person')

Sensitive - the sensitive person (not 'the sensitive person')

Dunkel – das dunkle Auto (not 'das dunkele Auto'), der dunkle Wagen

Dark - the dark car (not 'the dark car'), the dark car

Teuer – ein teures Auto (not: 'ein teueres Auto')

Expensive - an expensive car (not: 'an expensive car')

This rule applies for all cases (N, A, D, G).

Example in the accusative:

Listen to Track 233

Ich will diesen dunklen Wagen kaufen (not 'diesen dunkelen Wagen').

I want to buy this dark car (not 'this dark car').

When the adjective itself ends in -e, we don't add a second one.

Example:

Listen to Track 234

leise – ein leises Lied (not ‚ein leisees Lied')

quiet - a quiet song (not 'a quiet song')

Hoch (tall, high) is an irregular adjective. When it is used attributively, we drop the 'c'.

Hoch – ein hohes Gebäube (not ‚ein hoches')

High - a high building (not 'a high')

Weak Adjective Declension Table

Listen to Track 235

Case	Masculine	Feminine	Neuter	Plural
Nominative	*der nette Verkäufer*	*die nette Person*	*das brave Kind*	*die netten Männer/Frauen/Kinder*
Accusative	*den netten Verkäufer*	*die nette Person*	*das brave Kind*	*die netten Männer/Frauen/Kinder*
Dative	*dem netten Verkäufer*	*der netten Person*	*dem braven Kind(e)*	*den netten Männern/Frauen/Kindern*
Genitive	*des netten Verkäufers*	*der netten Person*	*des braven Kindes*	*der netten Männer/Frauen/Kinder*

2. Strong Declension

Listen to Track 236

The strong declension is used when no article precedes the adjective. It is also used when the adjective is preceded by any of these pronouns:

- *etwas* (something)
- *ein bisschen* (a bit)
- *ein wenig* (a little)
- *dessen, deren* (whose)
- *wessen* (whose)
- *etliche, mehrere* (a few more)
- *dergleichen, …* (the same)
- *derlei, …* (such)
- *manch* (some)
- *ein paar* (a couple)

Or by:

- *viele* (many)
- *wenige* (few)
- *einige* (some)
- *wie viel* (how much)
- *viel* (a lot)
- *wenig* (little)

In strong declension, there is no article before the adjective and the adjective is declined to show the case, gender, and number. As you can see, there is a great deal more variation here than with weak declension.

Strong Adjective Declension Table

Listen to Track 237

Case	Masculine	Feminine	Neuter	Plural
Nominative	*netter Mann*	*nette Frau*	*nettes Kind*	*nette Männer/Frauen/Kinder*
Accusative	*netten Mann*	*nette Frau*	*nettes Kind*	*nette Männer/Frauen/Kinder*
Dative	*nettem Mann*	*netter Frau*	*nettem Kind*	*netten Männern/ Frauen/Kindern*
Genitive	*netten Mannes*	*netter Frau*	*netten Kindes*	*netter Männer/ Frauen/Kinder*

Examples:

Listen to Track 238

Das ist der Klang guter Musik. (feminine, genitive)

That's the sound of good music.

Heißer Kaffee schmeckt mir gut. (masculine, nominative)

I like hot coffee. (masculine, nominative)

Sie verkaufen kalte Milch. (feminine, accusative)

They sell cold milk. (feminine, accusative)

Ich esse jeden Tag frisches Brot. (neuter, accusative)

I eat fresh bread every day. (neuter, accusative)

Morgens kaufe ich Milch und frische Brötchen. (plural, dative)

In the morning I buy milk and fresh bread. (plural, dative)

3. Mixed Declension

Our final category is mixed declension, which is used **when the adjective comes after an indefinite article, a possessive pronoun, or 'kein' and its ending**

depends on the case, gender, and number. More specifically, it is used when the adjective is preceded by any of the following:

Listen to Track 239

- An indefinite article (*ein, eine*)
- A possessive pronoun (*mein, dein, sein*)
- The negation *kein/keine* (none)

Mixed Adjective Declension Table

Listen to Track 240

Mixed declension	Masculine	Feminine	Neuter	Plural
Nominative	*ein netter Verkäufer*	*eine nette Person*	*ein nettes Kind*	*keine netten Männer/Frauen/Kinder*
Accusative	*einen netten Verkäufer*	*eine nette Person*	*ein nettes Kind*	*keine netten Männer/Frauen/Kinder*
Dative	*einem netten Verkäufer*	*einer netten Person*	*einem netten Kind*	*keinen netten Männern/Frauen/Kindern*
Genitive	*eines netten Verkäufers*	*einer netten Person*	*eines netten Kindes*	*keiner netten Männer/Frauen/Kinder*

Mental Shortcut: Declension in the Dative and Genitive

Listen to Track 241

It will help to remember that **for all plural nouns and all singular nouns in the dative and genitive cases, the adjective ends in –en where weak or mixed declension** is used **ex.** *die netten Kinder, dem netten Kind, der netten Frau, des netten Mannes.*

In the genitive, the masculine and neuter nouns always take –s or –es at the end. Monosyllabic nouns take –es (*eines netten Kindes*), while nouns of two or more syllables only take –s (*des spannenden Basketballspiels*).

Declension of Two or More Consecutive Adjectives

This is pretty simple. The same type of declension will apply to two or more consecutive adjectives used in the same sentence.

Listen to Track 242

Wir wollen in einem guten billigen Restaurant essen.

We want to eat in a good, cheap restaurant.

In this case we have the dative neuter (das Restaurant), mixed declension. It takes the dative because it answers the question of "where". Another example:

Wir wollen in ein gutes billiges Restaurant gehen.

We want to go to a good, cheap restaurant.

In this example, we have accusative neuter, mixed declension. It is accusative because it answers the question of "where to."

QUICK RECAP

- Adjectives are declined according to the case, number, and gender of the noun they precede. Only attributive adjectives – ones that precede nouns - are declined.
- There are three types of declension – strong, weak, and mixed – for the adjectives that are declined.
- The first type of declension is weak declension, where the adjective follows the definite articles (der, die, das). We just add –e or –en to the adjective depending on the case, number, and gender.
- The second type is strong declension, where there is no article, only the adjective and the noun. The adjective is inflected according to case, number, and gender.
- The third and final type is mixed declension, where the adjective comes after an indefinite article, a possessive pronoun, or 'kein' and its ending depends on the case, gender, and number.
- When the adjective ends in –el or -er, the ending changes to –le or -re.
- When the adjective itself ends in -e, we don't add a second -e.
- For all plural nouns and all singular nouns in the dative and genitive cases, the adjective ends in –en for weak and mixed declension.
- The same type of declension will apply to two or more consecutive adjectives used in the same sentence.

When you learn noun words, always learn their gender! If you don't know the gender or case, you can only hope to get declension right by accident.

TIME TO PRACTICE!

Workbook Lesson 13. Adjective Declension

Exercise 1: Fill in the blanks to enter the right form of the adjective
Nominative

Adjective	Definite Article	Indefinite Article
1. Rot	Die_____Flasche	Eine_____Flasche
2. Süß	der _____Apfel	ein _____Apfel
3. Schön	das _____Lied	ein _____Lied
4. Hoch	der _____Turm	ein _____Turm
5. Dunkel	Die _____Farbe	Eine _____Farbe

Exercise 2: Enter the right form of the adjectives.

Accusative, Dative, Genitive.

1. Wohin soll ich die (neu) _____ Vase stellen?
2. Das Fahrrad gehört dem (klein) _____ Kind.
3. Wer ist der Besitzer des (laut) _____ Hundes?
4. Rolf sitzt auf dem (groß) _____ Stuhl.
5. Aus einem (offen) _____ Fenster schaute eine Frau heraus.
6. Er ist der Sohn (reich) _____ Eltern.
7. Mein Nachbar repariert (defekt) _____ Autos.
8. Hast du die Telefonnummer eines (zuverlässig) _____ Mechanikers?
9. Wir haben ein (spannend) _____ Konzert besucht.
10. Meine Tante hat ein (grün) _____ Auto.

Answers:

Exercise 1: 1. Die rote Flasche, eine rote Flasche / 2. Der süße Apfel, ein süßer Apfel / 3. Das schöne Lied, ein schönes Lied / 4. Der hohe Turm, ein hoher Turm / 5. Die dunkle Farbe, eine dunkle Farbe

Exercise 2: 1. neue / 2. kleinen / 3. lauten / 4. großen / 5. offenen / 6. reicher / 7. defekte / 8. zuverlässigen / 9. spannendes / 10. grünes

LESSON 14: POSSESSIVE PRONOUNS (POSSESSIVPRONOMEN)

Possessive pronouns are words like mine, yours and theirs. In this lesson, we walk through when to use the various forms of German possessive pronouns. Having four cases and genders to work with means there's a lot of endings you'll be working with. To simplify it, we're going to tackle each in bite sized chunks and cover ways you can more easily recall how to put these important pieces of grammar to use.

As the name suggests, possessive pronouns show ownership. Unlike possessive adjectives (my, your, her) they can stand independently. The English possessive pronouns here are matched with their German counterparts:

Listen to Track 243

Mine – *mein*

Yours (sg) – *dein*

His – *sein*

Hers – *ihr*

Its – *sein*

Ours – *unser*

Yours (pl) – *euer*

Theirs – *ihr*

Using these bases, we're going to go through the many potential forms of German possessive pronouns.

Genders and Cases

English and German possessive pronouns work in the same way but have grammatical differences. In German, gender is extended to all nouns rather than just referring to the gender of the speaker (his/her). They also mark neutral and plural genders. You can see what I mean in this table of nominative possessive pronouns:

Listen to Track 244

Nominativ	Ich	Du	Er/Es	Sie (f)	Wir	Ihr	Sie (pl)
maskulinum	*meiner*	*deiner*	*seiner*	*ihrer*	*unserer*	*eurer*	*ihrer*
neutrum	*meins*	*deins*	*seins*	*ihres*	*unseres*	*eures*	*ihres*
femininum/plural	*meine*	*deine*	*seine*	*ihre*	*unsere*	*eure*	*ihre*

Note: The -e is sometimes excluded from *Ihres* to form *Ihrs* in the neuter form.

Listen to Track 245

Examples:

*Das ist **meiner**.*	That is **mine**. (Maskulinum)
*Dieses Buch ist **ihres**.*	This book is **theirs**. (Neutrum)
*Diese Katze ist nicht **seine**.*	This cat is not **his**. (Femininum)
*Diese Bücher sind **deine**.*	These books are **yours**. (Plural)

Notice that the gender of the possessive pronouns matches that of the noun rather than whoever owns it. Thus, **his** in example three is feminine because the noun "cat" is feminine, not masculine because of the pronoun "his".

In addition to gender, you have to account for case when dealing with German possessive pronouns. German also has four cases – a bit more than we're used to in English. These are the nominative, accusative, dative, and genitive. Putting these together with the noun's gender will help you devise the correct form.

Listen to Track 246

Akkusativ	Ich	Du	Er/Es	Sie (f)	Wir	Ihr	Sie (pl)
maskulinum	meinen	deinen	seinen	ihren	unseren	euren	ihren
neutrum	meines	deines	seines	ihres	unseres	eures	ihres
femininum/plural	meine	deine	seine	ihre	unsere	eure	ihre

You'll notice that the only difference between the nominative and the accusative sets is the masculine form. Where in nominative case the possessive pronouns end in -er, here they end in -en, just as with the articles der/den. One good thing about German is that the inflections on words use a relatively consistent system from set to set.

Listen to Track 247

Examples: (nouns included in parentheses to reference gender)

*Hast du **deinen** vergessen (Schlüssel)?*

Did you forget **yours** (keys)? (Maskulinum)

*Es ist für **meines** (Kind).*	It's for **mine** (child). (Neutrum)
*Es liegt in **seiner** (Nähe).*	It's around **his** (neighborhood). (Femininum)
*Habt Ihr **eure** erinnert (Schuhe)?*	Did you remember **yours** (shoes)? (Plural)

The accusative case is used for direct objects as well as with some prepositions (durch, gegen, um, ohne, für, bis, etc). This differs from the nominative which is used for subjects of a sentence. Next, we'll take a look at the dative case. We use the dative with indirect objects and a separate set of prepositions (aus, bei, mit, nach, zu, seit, etc).

Listen to Track 248

Dativ	Ich	Dich	Er/Es	Sie (f)	Wir	Ihr	Sie (pl)
Maskulinum/Neutrum	*meinem*	*deinem*	*seinem*	*ihrem*	*unserem*	*eurem*	*ihrem*
Femininum	*meiner*	*deiner*	*seiner*	*ihrer*	*unserer*	*eurer*	*ihrer*
Plural	*meinen*	*deinen*	*seinen*	*ihren*	*unseren*	*euren*	*ihren*

Here, the -em final for masculine and neuter words enters the scene. We see the same conjugation with them as we would with the article dem. This is also the only instance where the feminine and plural forms diverge.

Listen to Track 249

Examples:

*Du kannst auf **unserem** sitzen (Stuhl).*

You can sit on **ours** (chair). (Maskulinum)

*Ich werde mit **meinem** anrufen (Handy).*

I'll call with **mine** (phone). (Neutrum)

*Sie gibt **ihrer** das Geld (Mutter).*

She gave the money to **hers** (mother). (Femininum)

*Sollen sie in **eure** kommen (Klassen)?*

Should they come to **yours** (classes)? (Plural)

And with this we finally move on to the last case! The genitive is used with possession, some prepositions, and some idioms. The possessive genitive in German is essentially equal to etwas+von+jemand (the something of someone). Unlike the other cases, only possessive adjectives (or dependent possessive pronouns) can be used here. These are words like my, your, her, and their.

Listen to Track 250

Genitiv	Ich	Dich	Er/Es	Sie (f)	Wir	Ihr	Sie (pl)
maskulinum/neutrum	*meines*	*deines*	*seines*	*ihres*	*unseres*	*eures*	*ihres*
femininum/plural	*meiner*	*deiner*	*seiner*	*ihrer*	*unserer*	*eurer*	*ihrer*

There are only two different forms for this one – the masculine/neuter and feminine/plural.

Examples:

Listen to Track 251

*Das ist der Hund **meines** Bruder.*   That is my **brother's** dog. (Maskulinum)

*Wo ist das Spielzeug **unseres** Kindes?*   Where is our **child's** toy? (Neutrum)

*Er kann nicht kommen, wegen **seiner** Frau.*

He cannot come, because of **his** wife. (Femininum)

*Diese sind die Schuhe **ihrer** Schwestern.*   These are her **sisters'** shoes. (Plural)

Knowing this form is particularly important for meaning. For instance, the first sentence might read, "That is the dog, my brother," to someone unfamiliar with this case, which just doesn't make sense. When you know the genitive **meines** indicates the brother's ownership the correct meaning comes through.

How Do I Keep Track of All of These?

Unfortunately, memorization and practice are the best ways to solidify your German possessive pronouns. Luckily, many of these endings come out as a schwa (ə - like the 'a' in sofa) in speech. I've been told by native speakers that by defaulting to this pronunciation, you can generally be understood in conversation.

Writing is a different story. In this context, correct spellings become much more important. In order to help you remember all the various forms, I've included a little trick I learned in one of my own German classes.

Listen to Track 252

	maskulinum	femininum	neutrum	plural
Nominativ	-(e)**r**	-**e**	-(e)**s**	-**e**
Akkusativ	-(e)**n**	-**e**	-(e)**s**	-**e**
Dativ	-(e)**m**	-(e)**r**	-(e)**m**	-(e)**n**
Genitiv	-(e)**s**	-(e)**r**	-(e)**s**	-(e)**r**

The table gathers of all of the endings according to gender and case. When they're organized this way, you get the letters: rese, nese, mrmn, srsr. Looks like a bunch of nonsense, right? But you can turn these into a mnemonic that will stick in your mind. The one I utilize is: **rese** (reesuh) **nese** (neesuh), **Mister Merman, senior senior**. Alternatively, you could try making up your own.

The possessive pronouns used in German depend on gender, number, and case. They are especially important in written materials and exams where your grammar is more likely to be scrutinized. It is good to keep in mind that these inflections are similar to that of other parts of speech (der/einen/wem). So, there is really only a single system to memorize with the use of different bases for different meanings.

QUICK RECAP:

- The gender of the possessive pronouns matches that of the noun rather than whoever owns it.
- The only difference between the nominative and the accusative sets is the masculine form. Where in nominative case the possessive pronouns end in -er, here they end in -en, just as with the articles der/den.
- For the dative, -em is added for masculine and neuter words, -er for feminine, and -en for plural. We see the same conjugation with them as we would with the article dem.
- The genitive is very simple - -es is added for masculine and neuter nouns and -er for feminine and plural ones.

TIME TO PRACTICE!

Workbook Lesson 14. Possessive Pronouns

Exercise 1. Fill in the blanks with the suitable possessive pronoun.

1. _____ Rücken tut weh. – Her back hurts.
2. Ich finde _____ Vorschlag gut. – I find her suggestion good.
3. Hast du von_____ Kuchen gekostet? – Did you try my cake?
4. Er hat_____ Brille vergessen. – He forgot his glasses.
5. Wir sind zu_____ Großeltern gefahren. – We traveled to our grandparents'.
6. Ich habe _____ Freundin gerade eine SMS geschrieben. Hast du _____ angerufen? – I just texted my girlfriend. Did you call yours?
7. Die kleine Lisa hat _____ Lieblingsspielzeug in den Kindergarten mitgenommen. Der kleine Otto hat _____ zu Hause vergessen. – Little Lisa took her favorite toy in the garden. Little Otto forgot his at home.
8. _____ Haus ist groß und dort ist genug Platz für alle. – Their house is big and there's enough room for everyone.
9. _____ Lehrer ist viel besser als _____. – Our teacher is much better than yours (plural).
10. Entlang _____ Hauses wachsen Sonnenblumen. Was wächst um _____ Haus herum? – Sunflowers grow along her house. What grows around yours (singular)?

11. Ich suche _____ Katze. – I'm looking for my cat.

12. Sie füttern gerade _____ Hund. - They're feeding their dog.

13. Mutter spielt mit _____ Bruder. – Mom is playing with my brother.

14. Wer hat _____ Auto gesehen? – Who has seen his car?

15. Ist das _____ Uhr? Ja, das ist _____ Uhr. – Is that your (polite) watch? Yes, that's my watch.

16. _____ Auto hat die gleiche Farbe wie _____ Fahrrad. – His car is the same color as his bike.

17. Du gehst ohne ____ Eltern ins Kino. – You go to the movies without your parents.

18. _____ Eltern spielen mit _____ Katze. – My parents are playing with our cat.

19. Ihr fahrt mit _____ Hund in den Urlaub. – You're going on holiday with your dog.

20. Wir stehen im Keller _____ Hauses. – We're standing in our basement.

21. Das ist die Hütte _____ Hundes. – That's my dog's house.

22. Das ist das Auto _____ Bruders. – That's my brother's car.

23. Wir gehen mit _____ Schwester ein Eis essen. – We're going to grab an ice cream with your (singular) sister.

24. Das ist das Fahrrad _____ Sohnes. – That's their son's bike.

25. Das ist das Auto _____ Vaters. – That's her dad's car.

26. Habt ihr _____ Schlüssel wieder gefunden? – Did you find your keys?

27. Wir haben _____ Lehrer ein schönes Geschenk gemacht. – We gave our teacher a nice present.

28. Ich trinke ein Bier mit dem neuen Freund _____ Schwester. – I'm having a beer with my sister's new boyfriend.

29. Hier ist der neue Freund _____ Tochter. – Here's our daughter's new boyfriend.

30. Ich gehe mit _____ Eltern in ein gutes Restaurant. – I'm going to a good restaurant with my parents.

31. Wir fahren mit dem Auto _____ Eltern in den Urlaub. – We're going on holiday in our parents' car.

32. Das ist das Auto _____ Chefin. – That's my boss's car.

33. Du gibst _____ Sohn einen Kuss. – You gave his son a kiss.

34. In _____ Auto sitzt _____ Vater. – His father's sitting in his car.

Exercise 2. Multiple choice.

1. You and a friend are arguing whether a dog belongs to a man or a woman. You think it is the woman's dog. You say: Das is _____.

   a. Seiner   b. Ihrer   c. Es   d. Sie

2. You've come to pick up a friend from the airport, but they haven't seen the car you drove in before. They want to know if a car they see is yours. They say: Ist das _____?

   a. dein   b. deiner   c. eures   d. deines

3. Someone is asking whom a suitcase belongs to. To say "that's mine" in German, you'd say:

   a. das ist meiner   b. das ist seiner   c. das ist meinem   d. das ist mein.

Exercise 3. Fill in the blanks with the suitable possessive pronoun.

1. Ihr Auto ist kaputt, darum benutzt sie_____

   - Her car is broken, that's why she uses his.

2. Ich habe einen Vorschlag gemacht, aber _____ ist besser.

   – I made a suggestion, but yours (singular) is better.

3. Die Kuchen sind sehr lecker. Hast du schon von_____probiert?

   - The cakes are very tasty. Have you tried mine?

4. Es ist immer schön, die Familie zu sehen. Darum besuchen wir_____ sehr oft.

   - It's always good to see family. That's why we visit ours often.

5. Die kleine Maria hat ihr Spielzeug mit in die Schule genommen. Paul hat _____ im Bus verloren.

   - Little Maria took her toy to school. Paul lost his in the bus.

6. Ich habe meiner Mutter gerade eine Nachricht geschrieben. Hast du_____ auch schon zum Muttertag geschrieben?

   - I just texted my mom. Did you text yours for Mother's Day?

7. Mein Buch ist viel besser als_____ - My book is much better than yours.

8. Entlang _____Hauses ist ein Zaun. - Along his house, there is a fence.

9. Wir füttern gerade unseren Hund. _____ hat schon etwas gefressen.

   - We are feeding our dog. Yours (plural) already ate.

Answers:

Exercise 1:

1.Ihr / 2.ihren / 3.meinem / 4.seine / 5.unseren / 6.meiner, deine / 7.ihr, seines / 8.Ihr / 9.unser, eurer / 10.seines, dein / 11.meine / 12.ihren / 13.meinem / 14.sein / 15.Ihre, meine / 16.Ihre, meine / 17.deine / 18.Meine, unserer / 19.deinem / 20.unseres / 21.meines / 22.meines / 23.deiner / 24.ihres / 25.ihres / 26.eure / 27.unserem / 28.meiner / 29.unserer / 30.meinen / 31.unserer / 32.meiner / 33.seinem / 34.seinem, sein

Exercise 2:

1)B / 2)d / 3)a

Exercise 3:

1.seines / 2.deiner / 3.meinen / 4.unsere / 5.seines / 6.deiner / 7.deines / 8.seines / 9.Eurer

LESSON 15: PERFECT TENSES: PRESENT PERFECT (PERFEKT) AND PAST PERFECT (PLUSQUAMPERFEKT)

The **present perfect**, sometimes just called **perfect tense**, is a very important tense in German. It expresses events or actions that have happened and been completed in the past. Informally and in the spoken language, it is the most popular tense to talk about the past. Unlike the present and imperfect tense, the present perfect has two parts to it. It is formed by using the **auxiliary verbs *haben*** or ***sein*** and the **past participle (Partizip II).**

The **past perfect,** also called the **pluperfect**, expresses past actions that happened before other past events. Once you understand how to form the present perfect, the past perfect will be easy, it follows pretty much the same rules.

Do not worry, if you are not familary with some of these terms. I will talk you through these tenses step by step, so you can start feeling at home in the past. Let's start with the present perfect.

The Present Perfect (Perfekt) in Brief

This tense is mainly reserved for the spoken language, or used in private letters, emails or other informal correspondence. It usually describes a past event that has been completed.

The English equivalent would be: *have seen, have driven,* but also *saw, drove* when talking, rather than writing in German.

It is formed by using either ***haben*** or ***sein* in the present tense + the past participle** of your chosen verb.

So what does this mean in detail?

Auxiliary verbs *haben* and *sein*

Auxiliary verbs can usually not stand on their own. For the present perfect tense *haben* or *sein* are used in conjunction with the **past participle** of the main verb to express the past. *Haben* and *sein* stand in the present tense. Both are irregular and need to be conjugated.

Present tense conjugation of haben/sein:

Listen to Track 253

haben (to have)		sein (to be)	
ich **habe**	wir **haben**	ich **bin**	wir **sind**

du **hast**	ihr **habt**	du **bist**	ihr **seid**
er/sie/es **hat**	sie/Sie **haben**	er/sie/es **ist**	sie/Sie **sind**

The Past Participle

The **past participle** is the second part of the present perfect. Generally it is formed by using the *verb stem* (infinitive without the ending) plus the following:

1. Forming the past participle of regular verbs:

Listen to Track 254

most verbs	**ge-** + verbstem + **-t**	lachen → **ge**lacht	to laugh → laughed
verb stem ends **-d** or **-t**	**ge-** + verbstem + **-et**	arbeiten → **ge**arbeitet	to work → worked
verb ends **-ieren**	verbstem + **-t**	reparieren → *repariert*	to repair → repaired

2. Forming the past participle of irregular verbs:

For irregular verbs the *verb stem* changes, and you have to memorize this form when learning these verbs. The *altered verb stem* is preceded by **ge-**, same as the regular verbs, but ends with **-en.**

Listen to Track 255

ge- + changed verbstem + **-en**	singen → **ge**sungen	to sing → sang
	fahren → **ge**fahren	to drive → driven

3. Forming the past participle of mixed verbs:

Some verbs have a past participle, which combines irregular and regular elements. For these verbs, the verb stem changes, but **ge-** and **-t** are still added, same as regular verbs.

Listen to Track 256

ge- + changed verbstem + **-t**	denken → **ge**dacht	to think → thought
	kennen → **ge**kannt	to know → known

4. Forming the past participle for verbs with prefixes:

Verbs with **separable prefixes** are formed as usual, but the **ge-** is added after the prefix and before the verb.

Listen to Track 257

prefix + **ge-** + verbstem + **-t**	auslachen → *aus**ge**lacht*	to laugh at → laughed at
(or other endings depending on verb)	abstimmen → *ab**ge**stimmt*	To vote on → voted on

For verbs with **inseparable prefixes** and verbs with **more than one prefix**, the **ge-** is omitted.

Listen to Track 258

prefix + verbstem + -t (or other endings depending on verb)	verkaufen → *verkauft* verstehen → *verstanden*	to sell → sold to understand → understood
prefix + prefix + verbstem + -t (or other endings depending on verb)	vorbereiten → vorbereite**t** missverstehen → *missverstanden*	to prepare s.th. → prepared to misunderstand → misunderstood

Now we are familiar with the most important elements of the present perfect tense, we can start applying them.

Using the Present Perfect:

Some verbs form this tense with *haben*, others only with *sein*. A few can be combined with either, depending on the context.

Present perfect with *haben*:

Listen to Track 259

Most verbs form the present perfect with *haben*. They belong to either of these three categories:

Verbs with accusative object:

*Ich **habe** den Film **gesehen.***	I have seen the film./I saw the film.
*Er **hat** Klavier **gespielt.***	He has played piano./He played the piano.

Verbs without object:

*Es **hat geregnet.***	It has rained./It rained.
*Wir **haben gefeiert.***	We have celebrated./We celebrated.

Reflexive verbs:

*Du **hast** dich **sehr geärgert.***

You have been very annoyed./You were very annoyed.

*Ihr **habt** euch **geschämt.***

You have been embarrassed./You were embarrassed.

Present perfect with *sein*:

Listen to Track 260

Verbs that form the present perfect with *sein* are always irregular. The following two categories always use *sein:*

Verbs that imply movement, change of location or time:

*Sie **ist weggegangen**.*	She has gone away./She went away.
*Wir **sind** früh **aufgestanden**.*	We've gotten up early./We got up early.

The verbs *sein, bleiben, werden:*

*Ich **bin** zu Hause **gewesen**.*	I have been at home./I was at home.
*Er **ist** bei der Arbeit **geblieben**.*	He has stayed at work/He stayed at work.

Present perfect with either *haben* or *sein*:

Listen to Track 261

Use *sein,* if the verb indicates movement:

*Ich **bin** nach Hause **gefahren**.*	I have driven home./I drove home.

Use *haben,* if the verb stands with an object:

*Ich **habe** Tim nach Hause **gefahren**.*

I have driven Tom home./I drove Tim home.

Present perfect with modal verbs:

Listen to Track 262

Modal verbs, e.g. *können, mögen, wollen* are always combined with *haben,* though they are rarely used in the present perfect. It is far more common to use them in the imperfect tense. There are two different options of forming the present perfect for modal verbs:

The present perfect is formed as usual, if the modal verb is on its own in the sentence.

*Ich **habe** gestern nicht **gewollt**.*	I did not want (to) yesterday.

But if the modal verb stands together with another main verb, both verbs stand at the end of the sentence in the infinitive form, first the main verb, last the modal:

*Ich **wollte** gestern **lesen**.*	I wanted to read yesterday.

Present perfect with two verbs (not modal verbs):

It is common to use express certain actions in german with two verbs, e.g. *schwimmen gehen.* Here the present perfect is as usual formed with *haben* or *sein* with the second verb as the past participle at the end of the sentence. But the first verb stays in the infinitive and precedes the past participle.

Listen to Track 263

*Wir **sind** Montag **schwimmen gegangen.***	We went swimming on Monday.
*Er **ist spazieren gegangen.***	He went for a stroll.

But there are alway exceptions: *hören, sehen, lassen* do not change into the past participle when used with another verb. They also stay in the infinitive form:

Listen to Track 264

*Ich **habe** dich **singen hören.*** (NOT gehört)	I heard you singing.
*Er **hat** es **kommen sehen.*** (NOT gesehen)	He saw it coming.
*Wir **haben** sie **laufen lassen.*** (NOT gelassen)	We let them go.

Once you are familiar with the rules of the present perfect, the past perfect is simple.

The Past Perfect (Plusquamperfekt):

The past perfect always expresses a past that has happened before another past event or action. It never stands alone, but is always used in relation to other past tenses.

The words **nachdem, bevor, zuvor** often prelude the past perfect.

Listen to Track 265

Imperfect tense	past perfect tense
Er rief uns an,	*nachdem wir bei der Party **angekommen waren**.*
He called us,	after we had arrived at the party.
present perfect tense	**past perfect tense**
Sie hat endlich ihre Kündigung eingereicht.	*Bereits im Jahr davor **hatte** sie schon darüber **gesprochen**.*
She has finally handed in her notice.	She had already talked about it in the previous year.

Forming the past perfect:

It is formed by using either **haben** or **sein in the imperfect tense + the past participle** of your chosen verb. For choosing the right auxiliary verb, forming the past participle, as well as using modal verbs, verbs with prefixes etc., follow exactly the same rules as for the present perfect.

Imperfect tense conjugation of haben/sein:

Listen to Track 266

haben (to have)		**sein** (to be)	
ich **hatte**	wir **hatten**	ich **war**	wir **waren**
du **hattest**	ihr **hattet**	du **warst**	ihr **wart**
er/sie/es **hatte**	sie/Sie **hatten**	er/sie/es **war**	sie/Sie **waren**

Examples:

Listen to Track 267

Ich **hatte** draußen **gewartet**.	I had waited outside.
Du **warst** in die Schule **gegangen**.	You had gone to school.
Wir **waren schwimmen gegangen**.	We had gone to swim.
Sie **hatten** es nicht **gekonnt**.	They had not been able to.
Sie **hatten** es nicht **machen können**.	They had not been able to do it.

QUICK RECAP:

- Follow the same rules when forming the present perfect and past perfect tense. Both tenses consist of two parts, the auxiliary verbs *haben* or *sein* plus the past participle. Only difference is that for the **present perfect** *haben* and *sein* are used in the present tense, and for the **past perfect** they are used in the imperfect tense.

- Therefore you need to memorize the conjugation of *haben* and *sein* well, and familiarize yourself with the past participle.

- The past perfect is only used in relation to other past tenses and expresses a past that has happened prior to another past action or event.

- The present perfect is to go-to past in spoken language and other informal communication. You will hear it a lot in conversation, so start practicing now! Soon you will talk about the past like a native.

TIME TO PRACTICE!

Workbook Lesson 15. Perfect Tenses

Exercise 1. Make sentences using the present perfect tense.

1. Mein Vater_____dich nach Hause_____[bringen] – My father took you home.

2. Wer _____meine Tasche_____? [finden] – Who found my bag?

3. Gestern_____ wir zur Schule_____[gehen] – We went to school yesterday.

4. Letztes Jahr____ch nicht in den Urlaub. [fahren] – I didn't travel on holiday last year.

5. Goethe_____Faust_____[schreiben]. – Goethe wrote Faust.

6. Ich_____diese Aufgabe nicht_____. [lösen] – I didn't solve the problem.

7. Meine Eltern_____mich spielen_____[lassen] – My parents let me play.

8. Meine Eltern_____spät nach Hause _____[kommen] – My parents came home late.

9. Das _____ich Ihnen doch_____[sagen] – I told you that.

10. Er _____ein Buch _____[schreiben] – He wrote a book.

11. Letzte Woche _____ich Tennis _____[spielen] – I played tennis last week.

12. Meine Mutter _____mir den Schlüssel _____. [geben] – My mother gave me the key.

13. Ihr _____es_____ [wissen] – You knew it.

14. Wir _____ immer die besten Freunde _____[sein] – We were always best friends.

15. Du _____die ganze Pizza _____? [essen] – You ate the whole pizza?

16. Ich_____alle Bücher von London_____[lesen] – I have read all of London's books.

17. Wir_____den neuen Film noch nicht_____[sehen]. – We haven't seen the new film yet.

18. Mein Vater war da. Er_____aber nicht lange_____ [bleiben] – My father was there. He didn't stay long.

19. Ich_____ zur Schule gehen_____sollen] - I should have gone to school.

20. Ihr_____unseren Lehrer nicht_____ [mögen] – You didn't like our teacher.

21. Keiner meiner Lehrer_____Müller_____[heißen] – None of my teachers were called Mueller.

22. Ich _____gestern ein Buch_____(lesen). – I read a book yesterday.

23. Max hat das Lied von Rammstein____ (singen). – Max sang the song by Rammstein.

24. Meine Mutter ist mit mir spazieren_____ (gehen). – My mother walked with me.

25. Wir haben uns "Twilight 2" im Kino _____ (anschauen). – We saw Twilight 2 at the movies.

26. Meine Freundin hat mir einen Brief _____ (schreiben). – My girlfriend wrote me a letter.

27. Gestern Abend habe ich meine Hausaufgaben _____ (machen). – I did my homework last night.

28. Ich habe den ganzen Tag am Computer _____ (spielen). – I played computer all day.

29. Meine Eltern sind im Park Rad _____ (fahren). – My parents are riding bikes in the park.

30. Picasso hat viele Bilder _____ (malen). – Picasso painted a lot of pictures.

Exercise 2. Change into the present perfect tense.

1. Im Januar besucht Peter seine Großeltern im Dorf.	In January, Peter had visited his grandparents in the village.
2. Er macht seine Übungen regelmäßig.	He had done his exercises regularly.
3. Der Mechaniker repariert den kaputten Motor.	The mechanic had repaired the damaged engine.
4. Warum schreibt ihr diese Antwort?	Why had you written this answer?
5. Ich schlafe um vierzehn Uhr ein.	I had fallen asleep by 2:00 p.m.
6. Die Sportler laufen um den Sportplatz.	The athletes had run around the sports field.
7. Er beantwortet erst zehn Fragen.	He had only answered ten questions.

Exercise 3. Make sentences in the past perfect tense.

1. Wir_____ einen Hund und eine Katze _____.

2. Du_____keine Zeit_____ .

3. Sie_____bereits vor der Schule_____.

4. _____ ihr gestern meine Mutter_____?

5. Er _____nach Berlin_____.

6. Ich _____gestern meinen Schlüssel_____.

7. Wir_____nach Amerika _____.

8. Du_____nie mit mir spielen _____.

9. Ihr_____damals ohne mich nach Hause_____.

10. Wir _____nicht zu Hause_____.

11. Ihr_____nicht_____, dass wir bereits zu Hause waren.

12. Wer_____meinen Schlüssel_____?

13. Ich_____gerade 18_____, als ich meine Freundin heiratete.

14. Ihr_____zu spät_____.

15. Sie_____Deutsche nicht. Das änderte sich, als sie nach Berlin kam.

16. Ich_____früh_____.

Answers:

Exercise 1:

1.Mein Vater hat dich nach Hause gebracht. / 2.Wer hat meine Tasche gefunden? / 3.Wer hat meine Tasche gefunden? / 4.Letztes Jahr bin ich nicht in den Urlaub gefahren. / 5.Goethe hat Faust geschrieben. / 6.Ich habe diese Aufgabe nicht gelöst. / 7.Meine Eltern haben mich spielen lassen. / 8.Meine Eltern sind spät nach Hause gekommen. / 9.Das habe ich Ihnen doch gesagt. / 10.Er hat ein Buch geschrieben. / 11.Letzte Woche habe ich Tennis gespielt. /12.Meine Mutter hat mir den Schlüssel gegeben. / 13.Ihr habt es gewusst. / 14.Wir sind immer die besten Freunde gewesen. / 15.Du hast die ganze Pizza gegessen? / 16.Ich habe alle Bücher von Jack London gelesen. / 17.Wir haben den neuen Film noch nicht gesehen. / 18.Er ist aber nicht lange geblieben. / 19.Ich sollte zur Schule gehen / Ich habe zur Schule gehen gesollt. / 20.Ihr mochtet unseren Lehrer nicht. / 21.Keiner meiner Lehrer hat Müller geheißen. / 22.Ich habe gestern ein Buch gelesen. / 23.gesungen / 24.gegangen /25. angeschaut / 26.geschrieben / 27.gemacht / 28.gespielt / 29.gefahren / 30.gemalt

Exercise 2:

1.Im Januar hatte Peter seine Großeltern im Dorf besucht. / 2.Er hatte seine Übungen regelmäßig gemacht. / 3.Der Mechaniker hatte den kaputten Motor repariert. / 4.Warum hattet ihr diese Antwort geschrieben? / 5.Ich war um vierzehn Uhr eingeschlafen. / 6.Die Sportler waren um den Sportplatz gelaufen. / 7.Er hatte erst 10 Fragen beantwortet.

Exercise 3:

1. haben / 2. haben / 3. essen / 4. sehen / 5. fahren / 6. vergessen / 7. fliegen / 8. wollen / 9. gehen / 10. sein / 11. wissen / 12. nehmen / 13. warden / 14. kommen / 15. mögen / 16. aufstehen

The grammar term "relative pronouns" may not ring any bells for you. It may sound complicated, but in English, you already know what they are without realizing it!

Don't worry, we're here to make German relative pronouns or Relativepronomen easy!

What is a Relative Pronoun?

A relative pronoun is intended to connect two sentences that contain the same noun or subject. They replace the original noun. In English, our relative pronouns are: who, whose, which, that, whom and where.

Examples:

- "I had lunch with someone who really loves cheesecake." The *'who'* is describing the noun *'someone'*.
- "Does anyone know whose book this is?" *'Whose'* describes *'anyone'*.
- "I want to see the fish that has bright colors." *'that'* describes *'the fish'*.
- "Don't make the meal which makes me sick." *'which' describes 'the meal'*.
- "Do you remember the teacher for whom I worked?" *'Whom' replaces the 'teacher'*.
- "I want to go to that school where I learned how to write." *'Where' describes 'the school'*.

Sounds simple, enough right? But, when you get to the moment, you may be struggling to figure out which relative pronoun to use!

In German, there are two forms of relative pronouns: the definite articles which are *der*, *die*, and *das*, and *welcher* in its declined form.

There are some others, but we'll get to that later! All of the relative pronouns will mean either that, who, whom, whose, or which. But they change according to the case in which they're used.

The definite articles decline exactly the same as when they're used as relative pronouns. But, it can still be a little tricky.

Here's a quick overview

Nominative Case

Listen to Track 268

Masculine	der
Feminine	die

Neuter	*das*
Plural	*die*
Meaning	he/ she/ it/ that/ who/ which

Accusative Case

Listen to Track 269

Masculine	*den*
Feminine	*die*
Neuter	*das*
Plural	*die*
Meaning	he/ she/ it/ that/ who/ which

Dative

Listen to Track 270

Masculine	*dem*
Feminine	*der*
Neuter	*dem*
Plural	*denen*
Meaning	he/ she/ it/ that/ who/ which

Genitive

Listen to Track 271

Masculine	*dessen*
Feminine	*deren*
Neuter	*dessen*
Plural	*deren*
Meaning	whose

1. Der

Der is the masculine pronoun, so it will only be used with "masculine" nouns. It can be used to talk about people or things.

Listen to Track 272

For example, these are masculine nouns:

der Mann (man)

der Computer (computer)

der Käse (cheese)

der Hund (dog)

But, when used as a relative pronoun, der can change from den to dem to dessen, depending on the case in which it's used.

For example, if it's the direct object, it will change to den (Accusative case). If it's the indirect object, it will change to dem (Dative case), and if it's used like 'whose', it will be deren or dessen (Genitive case) .

2. Die

Die is the feminine pronoun, so it will only be used with "feminine" nouns. Examples of feminine nouns are:

Listen to Track 273

die Frau (woman)

die Katze (cat)

die Blume (flower)

die Kleidung (clothes/clothing)

As a relative pronoun, die changes from der to deren, depending on the case. Die is also used for plural nouns, so for example, a masculine noun can be used with die when there's more than one.

Example: *der Mann* (1-man) and *die Manner* (plural-men). So die will change to der only when it's the indirect object (Dative case), and if it's used like 'whose', it will be deren. (Genitive case)

3. Das

Lastly, das is the neutral pronoun, so you will often see it linked to things/objects, but it will also be paired with people too!

Listen to Track 274

das Mädchen (girl)

das Hemd (shirt)

das Kleid (dress)

das Haar (hair)

As a relative pronoun, das changes from dem to dessen, depending on the case. Das will remain the same in the Accusative case, but it will change to dem as the indirect object (Dative case), and dessen if used as the word 'whose' (Genitive case).

4. Welcher

Welcher in German means 'which', but as a relative pronoun, it will translate to 'whom' in the sentence. And it can be used if you don't want to repeat a definite article. For

Listen to Track 275

Example:

- *Das ist die Köchin, <u>die</u> die beste Suppe macht.*

  This is the cook who makes the best soup.

BETTER:

- *Das ist die Köchin, <u>welche</u> die beste Suppe macht.*

  This is the cook who makes the best soup.

Here, you can change the relative pronoun from die to welche if you don't want to repeat the same word. Or it can be used as the word 'whom' or 'whose'.

Welcher will decline the same way as the relative pronouns do except for the Genitive or possessive case. Check it out here:

Nominative Case
Listen to Track 276

Masculine	welcher
Feminine	welche
Neuter	welches
Plural	welche
Meaning	whom

Accusative
Listen to Track 277

Masculine	welchen
Feminine	welche
Neuter	welches
Plural	welche
Meaning	whom

Dative

Listen to Track 278

Masculine	welchem
Feminine	welcher
Neuter	welchem
Plural	welchen
Meaning	whom

Genitive

Listen to Track 279

Masculine	dessen
Feminine	deren
Neuter	dessen
Plural	deren
Meaning	whose/whom

Listen to Track 280

Welcher examples:

- *Wo ist der Anzug, welchen Sie anprobieren wollten?*
  Where's the suit you wanted to try on?

- *Wo ist der Hund, welchem wir den Ball geben wollten?*
  Where is the dog to whom we wanted to give the ball?

- *Wo sind die Schuhe, mit welchen ich joggen wollte?*
  Where are the shoes I wanted to run with?

- *Ich habe einen Neffen, dessen Lieblingsfarbe ist pink!*
  I have a nephew whose favorite colour is pink!

German's Four Cases

But, in order to use the relative pronouns correctly in German, we need to figure out what to do in all the different cases. We know, the cases can be confusing (too confusing, in fact!)

A case in grammar is just about the function of the noun in the sentence, and when its function changes, the verbs and pronouns also change, and the words all connect together differently.

There can be a lot of different parts to remember, so let's try to make it easy for you.

Here's a quick breakdown of the different cases in German and how the relative pronouns change for each case!

1. Nominative case

This case is probably the easiest one to get your head around because the noun is in place of the subject.

Listen to Track 281

Examples:

• *Der Hai frisst die Robbe.*	The shark eats the seal.
• *Die Robbe frisst den Fisch.*	The seal eats the fish.

Here the shark and the seal are the subjects. In the nominative case, the definite articles/relative pronouns will be in their base form.

Relative pronoun example:

Listen to Track 282

Die Kinder, die Fußball spielen, wohnen dort drüben.

The kids who play football live over there.

The relative pronoun here is 'die' which translates to 'who'.

2. Accusative case

Remember: only 'der' words will change in this case. 'Das' and 'die' words remain the same.

The accusative case focuses on when the noun is receiving the action from the verb or the direct object.

Listen to Track 283

Example:

Sie nimmt den Ball. Wir schauen den Film.

She takes the ball. We watch the movie.

Remember: only 'der' words will change in this case. 'Das' and 'die' words remain the same.

Listen to Track 284

Relative pronoun example:

Der Berg, <u>den</u> ich besteigen will, ist der Mount Everest.

The mountain that I want to climb is the Mount Everest.

The relative pronoun here is 'den' which translates to 'that'.

3. Dative case

The Dative case is used to identify the indirect object of the sentence.

Listen to Track 285

Example:

Der Junge gab <u>dem Hund</u> einen Ball. Der Lehrer gab <u>dem Schüler</u> eine gute Note.

The boy gave <u>the dog</u> a ball. The teacher gave <u>the student</u> a good grade.

Here, the dog and the student are receiving the action, so 'das' and 'der' change to 'dem'.

Listen to Track 286

Relative pronoun example:

Wo ist der Kellner, <u>dem</u> ich ein Trinkgeld geben will?

Where is the waiter who I want to tip?

The relative pronoun here is 'dem' which translates to 'who'.

4. Genitive case

The Genitive case is used to show possession.

Listen to Track 287

Example:

Ich lese das Buch <u>dieses Authors</u>. Das ist das Auto <u>meines Vaters</u>.

I'm reading <u>this author's</u> book. That's <u>my father's</u> car.

Here. the person who is possessing the item goes after the thing they are possessing and der and das change to 'des' and die changes to 'der' for both singular and plural nouns.

Relative pronoun example:

Listen to Track 288

Wo ist die Lehrerin, ihre Schüler so gut lesen können?

Where is the teacher whose children read so well?

The relative pronoun here is 'deren' which translates to 'whose'.

Listen to Track 289

Nominative:

Emil, <u>der</u> ein schwarzes Hemd trägt, ist mein Freund.

Emil, who wears a black shirt, is my boyfriend.

Accusative:

Sarah, <u>die</u> nebenan wohnt, ist sehr hübsch.

Sarah, who lives next door, is really beautiful.

Dative:

Das sind meine Freunde, mit denen ich Skat spiele.

Those are my friends with whom I play Skat.

Genitive:

Laura, deren Wohnung sehr schön ist, lebt in Berlin.

Laura, whose flat is really beautiful, lives in Berlin.

Additional Tips and Advice

When constructing a sentence which uses relative pronouns, the conjugated (changed) verb moves to the end of the sentence or last spot in the relative clause.

That can be a bit tricky to remember since English doesn't operate that way. But, once you get into the swing of it with German, you'll know what sounds right!

Listen to Track 290

For example, check out these sentences:

- *Kennen Sie die Bäckerei? Die Bäckerei <u>liegt</u> an der Straßenecke.* changes to: *Kennen Sie die Bäckerei, die an der Straßenecke <u>liegt</u>?*
  Do you know the bakery which is on the corner of the street
- *Ich habe einen Freund, der Fußball spielt.*   I have a friend who plays football.

- *Das ist der Mann, der Tischler ist.* That is the man who is a carpenter.

Extra possibilities for relative pronouns:

Was er mir gesagt hat, war nicht richtig.

What he told me wasn't correct.

Also...

Wo: where (this word does not change its form when its used as a relative pronoun.)

Weiß er, wo die Post ist? Does he know where the post office is?

Was: what

Was er mir gesagt hat, war nicht richtig What he told me wasn't correct.

QUICK RECAP:

- Relative pronouns in German or "relativpronomen" can be a little tricky to learn, but once you know what they are and the cases which change them, you can get it!
- The relative pronouns in German are 'der, die, das, and welcher'.
- These pronouns decline in mostly the same way they would as definite articles. Check the charts above!
- The 4 cases in German are Nominative, Accusative, Dative, and Genitive cases
- Remember, depending on the case (what function the noun has in the sentence), the relative pronoun will change its form!
- And...you can also use 'wo', 'wer', and/or 'was' as relative pronouns: 'where', 'who', and/or 'what'.
- When using a relative pronoun, the verb will go at the end of the sentence or the relative clause such as *Das sind die Freunde, von welchen ich dir erzählt habe.* verb: to have). (These are the friends I told you about.)
- And, don't worry, practice makes perfect! The more practice you do with relative pronouns, the better you will understand relative pronouns and be able to write and use them comfortably!

TIME TO PRACTICE!

Workbook Lesson 16. Relative Pronouns

Exercise 1. Fill in the blanks with the correct relative pronoun.

German	English
1. Die Angestellte, __ mir geholfen hat.	The clerk who helped me.
2. Der Altbau, _____ wir gesehen haben.	The old building which we saw.

3. Die Ärzte, _____ich angerufen habe.	The doctors whom I called.
4. Das Doppelzimmer, _____ ich reserviert habe.	The double room I booked.
5. Die Bäckerei, zu _____ ich immer gehe.	The bakery I always go to.
6. Der Herr, mit _____ ich telefoniert habe.	The gentleman I spoke to on the phone.
7. Der Geschäftsmann, _____ nach Atlanta kommt.	The businessman who is coming to Atlanta.
8. Das Jahr, _____ im nächsten Januar beginnt.	The year that starts next January.
9. Die Idee, _____ Sie hatten.	The idea you had.
10. Die Messen, _____wir besuchen wollen.	The fairs we want to visit.
11. Das Paket, in _____ ich das Geld gefunden habe.	The package, in which I found the money.
12. Die Gespräche, _____ Sie führen.	The talks you lead.
13. Die Türen, durch _____ sie gehen.	The doors, through which they pass.
14. Er lebt von dem Geld, _____ sein Vater ihm gibt.	He lives on the money that his father gives him.
15. Die türkischen Sitten, von _____ sie nichts wusste, gefielen ihr nicht.	She did not like the Turkish customs, of which she knew nothing.
16. Die Probleme, mit _____ ich zu tun habe.	The problems I have to deal with.
17. Wo ist das Handtuch, mit _____ ich mir die Haare getrocknet habe?	Where's the towel I used to dry my hair?
18. Das Kind litt unter einer Hypersensibilität , _____ es nicht beherrschen konnte.	The child suffered from hypersensitivity that he/she could not control.
19. Der Film, _____ uns gezeigt wurde, gab kein realistisches Bild von Deutschland.	The film that was shown to us did not portray Germany realistically.
20. Man hörte den Leuten nicht zu, _____ Meinung abweichend war.	You didn't listen to people whose opinion was different.
21. Das Haus, _____ Läden geschlossen waren, schien verlassen.	The building whose shops were closed seemed abandoned.
22. Das Mädchen, für _____ er sich interessierte, war sportlich gekleidet.	The girl he was interested in was sportily dressed.
23. Die Grundschule, in _____ er nun geht, wird bald geschlossen.	The primary school he goes to will be closed soon.
24. Wir brauchen einen Hund, mit _____ wir abends spazieren gehen können.	We need a dog that we can walk in the evening.
25. Die Fragen, auf _____ du hast antworten müssen, waren die, die der Lehrer uns in der Prüfung gestellt hatte.	The questions you had to answer were the ones the teacher asked us in the exam.
26. Die Katze, _____die Maus gefressen hat.	The cat that ate the mouse.
27. Das ist die Familie, _____ neben uns wohnt.	This is the family that lives next to us.
28. Die Freundin, mit _____ er im Kino war, hat heute angerufen.	The girlfriend, with whom he went to the cinema, called today.

29. Das Haus, _____ wir letztes Jahr verkauft haben, war sehr schön.	The house we sold last year was very nice.
30. Der Mann, _____ im zweiten Stock wohnt.	The man who lives on the second floor.
31. Das sind die Nachbarn, _____ gestern aus dem Urlaub zurückgekommen sind.	These are the neighbors who came back from vacation yesterday.
32. Das ist die Straße, in _____ unser Auto steht.	This is the street our car is in.
33. Ich bedanke mich für deinen Brief, _____ ich heute erhalten habe.	Thank you for your letter, which I received today.
34. Das sind die Freunde, mit _____ wir im Urlaub waren.	These are the friends with whom we went on vacation.
35. Das Mädchen, _____ der große Hund gehört.	The girl who owns the big dog.
36. Der Mann, _____ das schöne Auto gehört.	The man who owns the beautiful car.
37. Das sind die Vögel, _____ ich etwas zu fressen gegeben habe.	These are the birds, to which I gave something to eat.
38. Die Schule, in _____ meine Schwester geht, liegt in Berlin.	The school my sister goes to is in Berlin.
39. Das ist die Universität, an _____ mein Bruder studiert.	This is the university where my brother is studying.
40. Hier ist ein Bild von dem Haus, in _____ ich wohne.	Here is a picture of the house I live in.
41. Ich kenne den Mann, auf _____ du gewartet hast.	I know the man you were waiting for.
42. Wer war der Mann, _____ gerade hier war?	Who was the man who was just here?
43. Es gibt viele Leute, _____ ich helfen möchte.	There are many people whom I want to help.
44. Hier ist die E-Mail, _____ ich heute bekommen habe.	This is the email I received today.
45. Die Arbeit, _____ er geschrieben hat, war sehr gut.	The paper he wrote was very good.

Answers:

Exercise 1.

1. Die / 2. Den / 3. Die / 4. Das / 5. Der / 6. Dem / 7. Der / 8. Das / 9. Das / 10. Die / 11. Die / 12. Dem / 13. Die / 14. Die / 15. Das / 16. Denen / 17. Denen / 18. Dem / 19. Die / 20. Der / 21. Deren / 22. Dessen / 23. Das / 24. die / 25. dem / 26. die / 27. die / 28. die / 29. der / 30. das / 31. die / 32. der/ 33. den / 34. denen / 35. dem / 36. dem / 37. denen / 38. die / 39. der / 40. dem / 41. den / 42. der /43. denen / 44. die / 45. die /

LESSON 17: COMPARATIVE AND SUPERLATIVE ADJECTIVES (KLEIN, KLEINER, AM KLEINSTEN)

All you need to know about the comparative and superlative in German with detailed explanations and in easy to digest format!

Good news for English speakers: The forms of adjectives in German are very similar to those in English. In German, there are three comparative forms: positive (klein – in English *short* or *small*), comparative (kleiner – *shorter* or *smaller*) and superlative (am kleinsten – *the shortest* or *the smallest*).

Listen to Track 291

Example:

Tobias ist so klein wie Tim	Tobias is as short as Tim.
Tobias ist kleiner als Max	Tobias is shorter than Max.
Sebastian ist am kleinsten in der Klasse	Sebastian is the shortest in the class.

The positive form of the adjective is its basic form. It is used with so...wie (as...as) in the comparative expression. Other comparative expressions that exist are genauso ... wie (exactly as...as), fast so ... wie (almost as...as), halb so ... wie (half as...as), nicht so ... wie (not as...as), and doppelt so ... wie (twice as...as).

The comparative is the first form. **We add the ending -er to the adjective and the preposition als (than)**.

Listen to Track 292

Examples:

Friedrich ist reicher als Peter	Friedrich is richer than Peter.
Du bist dicker als ich	You (sg.) are fatter than me.
Tobias ist dünner als Tomas	Tobias is thinner than Tomas.

German comparative forms differ from English ones in that they are never formed with the word mehr (more).

Listen to Track 293

Example:

- Ehrgeizig → ehrgeiziger, not ehrgeizig → mehr ehrgeizig
  Ambitious → more ambitious, not ambitious → more ambitious

Exceptions to the Rule

Listen to Track 294

If the adjective ends in "-er", we drop the last "e" and add "-er":

Example:

    teuer ⊠ teurer   expensive ⊠ more expensive

If the adjective ends in "-el", we drop the last "e" and add "-er":

    flexibel ⊠ flexibler

If the adjective ends in "-e", we just add "-r":

    müde ⊠ müder   tired ⊠ more tired

Monosyllabic adjectives with the vowels "a", "o" and "u" receive an "Umlaut" (¨) + "er" in the comparative and superlative form.

    Klug ⊠ klüger   smart ⊠ smarter

    krank ⊠ kränker   sick ⊠ sicker

Comparative of inferiority

We form the comparative of inferiority with the construction *weniger ADJECTIVE als.*

Listen to Track 295

Example:

Er ist weniger vorsichtig als ich   He is less cautious than me.

Superlative Adjectives

The highest form of comparison is the superlative. These are monosyllabic adjectives ending in –est and two- or more syllable adjectives preceded by 'most' or 'the most' in English. **In German, we put 'am' or the respective form of the definite article (der, die, das, den, dem, or des) in front of the adjective. At the end of the adjective, we add -ste or -ste(n) depending on case and gender.** It's easier than English because the formation is identical for all adjectives no matter how many syllables they have.

Examples:

Listen to Track 296

Ich habe das schnellste Auto gekauft   I bought the fastest car.

Ich bin mit dem langsamsten Flugzeug gereist   I travelled by the slowest plane.

We use the superlative with the structure am + positive adjective + -sten when the adjective is not followed by a noun:

Examples

Listen to Track 297

Meine Tochter ist die intelligenteste in der Klasse

My daughter is the most intelligent in the class.

Welches Haus ist am kleinsten?   Which house is the smallest?

If an adjective has the vowel a, o, or u and only one syllable, we add an "Umlaut" (¨) to the vowel + "-sten" at the end.

klug → am klügsten clever → the smartest

jung ⊠ am jüngsten young → the youngest

When the adjective ends with one of the following consonants: "-t", "-d","-s", "-sch", "-ß", "-x" or "-z", we add an "-e-" between the adjective and the ending "-sten."

süß ⊠ am süßesten   sweet ⊠ the sweetest

One common exception to this rule is:

groß ⊠ am größten   big ⊠ the biggest

The superlative form of adjectives that end with '-s', '-d', '-t', '-ß', '-z', or '-x' is normally with –est at the end.

Listen to Track 298

Example:

heiß – heißer – am heißesten   hot - hotter - hottest

laut – lauter – am lautesten   loud - louder - loudest

Irregular Adjectives

In English, we have irregular adjectives like good – better – best, bad – worse – worst, many – more – most, and little – less - least. Germans have these just like us, but not all irregular English adjective are also irregular in German. Below are the German translations of the above examples:

Listen to Track 299

Examples:

gut – besser – am besten	good - better – best

(also irregular in German)

schlecht – schlechter – am schlechtesten	bad - worse – worst

(not irregular, but we add an −e after the first ‚t' in the superlative)

viel – mehr – am meisten	much - more – most

(also irregular in German)

wenig – weniger – am wenigsten	little - less – least

(not irregular in German)

German has a few other irregular verbs:

Listen to Track 300

hoch	höher	am höchsten	high, higher, highest
nah	näher	am nächsten	close, closer, closest
gern	lieber	am liebsten	To love doing something or 'gladly, more gladly, the most gladly'

In the first two examples, we add a 'c' in front of the 'h'. This is done for reasons related to ease of pronunciation because the second 'h' in *höher* and the 'h' in *näher* are silent.

'Gladly' is an adjective in English , as well in German, and an irregular one at that. '*Ich fahre gern*' translates as 'I love traveling.'

'Der' vs. 'ein' in the Comparative and Superlative

Listen to Track 301

Example:

der kleine Junge/der kleinere Junge/der kleinste Junge

the little boy / the smaller boy / the smallest boy

‚Klein' is a regular adjective, but we add an −e after the −er in the comparative according to the suffix rule in the masculine nominative.

With the indefinite pronoun (a or an), we add −er once for the comparative and another −er according to the suffix rule in the masculine nominative.

ein kleiner Junge/ein kleinerer Junge/der kleinste Junge

the little boy / the smaller boy / the smallest boy

Predicative adjectives (those that come after the verb sein / to be) can form the superlative with the definite article or 'am'. We add the ending '-ste' at the end when using the definite article.

Listen to Track 302

Example:

Diese Sache ist am wesentlichsten. Diese Sache ist die wesentlichste.

This matter is most significant. This is the most significant matter.

QUICK RECAP

To recap, the rule to form comparatives in German is:

We add the ending -er to the adjective and the preposition als (than).

The rule to form superlatives in German is

'Am' or der, die, das, den, dem, or des in front of the adjective. At the end of the adjective, we add -ste or -ste(n) depending on case and gender.

To form the comparative in the accusative case, **we add −er to the end of the adjectives, then −en at the end of masculine nouns:**

Listen to Track 303

Ich sehe den größeren Mann kommen   I see the taller man coming.

We add −er to the end of the adjectives, then −e at the end of feminine and neuter nouns:

Listen to Track 304

Ich sehe die größere Frau kommen   I see the taller woman coming.

Ich sehe das größere Kind kommen   I see the taller child coming.

To form the superlative in the accusative case, **we just add -sten at the end of masculine nouns:**

Listen to Track 305

Ich besuche den reichsten Mann   I visit the richest man.

We add − ste at the end of feminine and neuter nouns:

Listen to Track 306

Ich besuche die reichste Frau	I visit the richest woman.
Ich besuche das reichste Kind	I visit the richest child.

TIME TO PRACTICE!

Workbook Lesson 17. Comparative and Superlative Adjectives

Exercise 1: Fill in the blanks with the correct adjective form.

(groß)

1. Du bist _____ als ich.
2. Er ist fast so _____ wie sein Mitschüler.
3. Sie sind von allen Ihren Freunden _____.

(Langweilig)

4. Ich finde historische Filme _____.
5. Ich denke, sie sind _____ als Action-Filme.
6. Dieser Film ist _____ von allen Filmen, die ich je gesehen habe.

(Warm)

7. Ich möchte wissen, wo auf der Welt es_____ ist.
8. Ist es in Afrika _____ als in Asien?

Exercise 2: Type in the correct adjective form (positive, comparative, superlative).

1. Von allen Mädchen in seiner Klasse ist Anna ____ .(klein)
2. Mein Hund ist genauso ____ wie deiner. (hungrig)
3. Deine neue Frisur mag ich ____ als die alte. (viel)
4. Im Norden ist es ____ als im Süden. (teuer)
5. Wir hatten in letztem Urlaub ____ Wetter als in diesem. (gut)
6. Das ist das ____ Buch, das ich gelesen habe. (traurig)

Answers:

Exercise 1

1. größer / 2. groß / 3. am größten / 4. langweilig / 5. langweiliger / 6. der langweiligste / 7. am wärmsten / 8. wärmer

Exercise 2

1. am kleinsten / 2. hungrig / 3. mehr / 4. teurer / 5. besseres / 6. traurigste

LESSON 18: THE FUTURE TENSES IN GERMAN

Future Tenses in German: What They Are and How to Use Them

Future tenses are necessary to convey future plans, assumptions or promises. In English we achieve this by using *will*, *shall*, or *going to*. There are two future tenses in German, **Future 1** and **Future 2** (also called **Future Perfect**).You will also hear people using the present tense when referring to future events, especially in the spoken German language, which sounds more complicated than it actually is.

So let's explore all possible futures, starting with Future 1, which is the most commonly used Future tense.

1) Forming and Using Future 1

You can easily recognize Future 1, because it always contains the auxiliary verb **werden** in conjunction with a second verb in the infinitive form. It can be translated with *will, shall, going to*. Just on its own, **werden** can also be translated as *to become*.

To form the tense Future 1, simply choose a **personal pronoun** (ich, du, wir etc.), select the matching conjugation of the verb *werden* in the **present tense,** and add the **infinitive** of the verb you want to use at the end. The infinitive is the verb form, that you will find in a dictionary.

Listen to Track 307

Ich werde singen.	I will sing.
Er wird arbeiten.	He will work.
Wir werden tanzen.	We will dance.

So the the only verb you have to conjugate is **werden**!

werden: conjugation in the present tense

Listen to Track 308

ich **werde** reden	I will/shall/am going to read	wir **werden** schreien	We will scream
du **wirst** schreiben	you will write	ihr **werdet** lachen	you will laugh
er/sie/es **wird** essen	he/she/it will eat	sie/Sie **werden** denken	they/you (formal) will think

Listen to Track 309

Examples of Future 1 in action:

*Ich **werde** dich nie **vergessen**.*
I will never forget you.

*Du **wirst** deine Traumfrau **heiraten**.*
You will marry the woman of your dreams!

*In 100 Jahren **werden** wir Siedlungen auf dem Mond **haben**.*
In 100 years we will have settlements on the moon.

*Morgen **wird** er das Auto **waschen**.*
Tomorrow he is going to wash the car.

*Das **wirst** du nicht **weitersagen**!*
You will not tell this to anybody!

Instead of Future 1, you can also use the present tense, if the context of the sentence indicates that you are referring to the future.

2) Using Present Tense to Express the Future:

The use of present tense is slightly more common in spoken German. If you want to express future plans, intentions, or assumptions by using the present tense, you need to create context, for example using temporal or modal adverbs.

Listen to Track 310

***Morgen** bin ich nicht zu Hause.*
Tomorrow I will not be home. Literally: Tomorrow I am not at home.

***Nächste Woche** regnet es.*
Next week it will be raining.

*Das schaffst du **niemals**!*
You will never accomplish this!

The use of the present tense can indicate a greater likelihood of something happening. But the difference is very subtle, and <u>Future 1 and Present tense are used interchangeably</u>. There is no right and wrong here.

Listen to Track 311

Montag regnet es.	Present tense (most likely)
Montag wird es regnen.	Future 1 (possibly)
Both mean: Monday it will rain.	
Ich komme zu deinem Geburtstag.	Present tense (most likely)
Ich werde zu deinem Geburtstag kommen.	Future 1 (possibly)

Both mean: *I will come to your birthday.*

Now that we have covered the most common ways of talking about the future, we will look at Future 2. It is rarely used, but you will come across it occasionally.

3) Forming and Using Future 2:

To form this tense, choose a **personal pronoun** (ich, du, wir etc.), select the matching conjugation of the verb *werden* in the **present tense,** plus the **past participle** of a verb, and add the **infinitive** of **haben** or **sein** at the end.

Listen to Track 312

personal pronoun with werden	past participle	infinitive of haben/sein	
Ich werde den Zug	**verpasst**	**haben.**	I will have missed the train.
Es wird zu spät	**gewesen**	**sein.**	It will have been too late.
Wir werden die Arbeit	**vollbracht**	**haben.**	We will have accomplished the work.

When and why is Future 2 used?

It is used to express a future event, that will happen before another future event and is seen as completed.

Listen to Track 313

Future 2	Future 1
*Ich **werde** den Zug **verpasst haben**,*	*wenn ich nicht am Bahnhof **stehen werde**.*
I will have missed the train,	if I will not stand at the station.
*Du **wirst angekommen sein**,*	*wenn du den Kirchturm **sehen wirst**.*
You will have arrived,	when you will see the church tower.

And just as Future 1 can be replaced with the Present tense, <u>Future 2 can be replaced with the Present Perfect tense (Perfekt)</u>. This is far more commonly used and indicates the same causality of future events.

Listen to Track 314

Present Perfect instead of Future 2	**Present tense** instead of Future 1
*Ich **habe** den Zug **verpasst**,*	*wenn ich nicht am Bahnhof **stehe**.*
I have missed the train,	if I don't stand at the station.
*Du **bist angekommen**,*	*wenn du den Kirchturm **siehst**.*
You have arrived,	when you see the church tower.

Another use for Future 2: Expressing assumptions about past events

Nach unserem letzten Gespräch **wird** sie ihre Meinung **geändert haben**. After our last talk she will have changed her opinion.

Mit eurer Lebenserfahrung **werdet** ihr eine gute Entscheidung **getroffen haben**. With your life experience you will have made a good decision. This is probably the most likely application of Future 2, you will come across.

QUICK RECAP:

Expressing future plans, intentions or assumptions is actually pretty straightforward in German. All you need to do is:

- Learn to conjugate the verb *werden* in the present tense
- combine it with an infinitive, and
- there you are: You have mastered Future 1! Or, with the help of some temporal adverbs, you can just stick to the present tense.

Future 2 is a bit more complicated, and even native speakers do not use it very often. But try to familiarize yourself with it, as it will aid your understanding and appreciation of the language.

TIME TO PRACTICE!

Workbook Lesson 18. The Future Tenses

Exercise 1. Fill in the correct conjugation of the verb werden to form future 1:

1. Er _____ zu spät kommen. (He will arrive late.)
2. Du _____ morgen zur Schule gehen. (You will go to school tomorrow.)
3. Wir _____ das Buch später lesen. (We will read the book later.)
4. Wann _____ ihr in the Urlaub fahren? (When will you go on holiday?)
5. Ich _____ einen Baum pflanzen. (I will plant a tree.)
6. Sie _____ sich im Kino treffen. (They will meet at the movies.)
7. Wann _____ Sie mir eine Nachricht schicken? (When will you send me a message?)
8. Es _____ sich nicht lohnen. (It won't be worth it.)

Exercise 2. Change the following present tense sentences into future 1:

	present tense	future 1
	Lara sieht einen Film.	Lara wird einen Film sehen.
1	Du lernst deutsch.	
2	Die Freunde treffen sich heute abend.	

3	Wir kochen für dich.	
4	Ich freue mich nicht.	
5	Ihr ärgert euch sehr.	
6	Sie arbeiten am Samstag.	
7	Mein Bruder feiert sein Geburtstag.	
8	Es regnet morgen.	
9	Wir vergessen ihn nie.	

Exercise 3. Complete each sentence in future 2, using the verbs in the left hand column:

		conjugated form of *werden* + past participle + infinitive of *haben/sein*
	singen	**Ich** werde gesungen haben.
1	sprechen	**Er**
2	spielen	**Die**
3	ankommen	**Wir**
4	arbeiten	**Anna**
5	aufstehen	**Ihr**
6	schreiben	**Du**
7	studieren	**Wir**
8	gehen	**Die Kollegen**
9	bleiben	**Der Nachbar**

Exercise 4. Fill in the blanks: choose between future 1, future 2 or present tense

1. Morgen _____ wir in die Stadt _____. (Tomorrow we will go into town.)
2. Du _____ den Koffer _____, wenn das Taxi ankommen wird.
   (You will have packed the suitcase, when the taxi arrives.)
3. Wenn ich nicht zuhause sein werde, _____ ich ins Kino _____.
   (If I won't be at home, I will have gone to the cinema.)
4. Seine Lieblingsband _____ heute abend. (His favorite band plays tonight.)
5. Sie _____ sich auf die Prüfung _____.(They will prepare themselves for the exam.)
6. Ihr _____ am Sonntag nicht _____. (You will not work on Sunday.)
7. Wenn er Maja nicht sehen wird, _____ sie es _____.
   (If he won't see Maja, she will have forgotten about it.)
8. Nächste Woche _____ es. (Next week it rains.)
9. Es _____ bald _____. (It will snow soon.)

Answers:

Exercise 1:

1. wird / 2. wirst / 3. werden / 4. werdet / 5. werde / 6. werden / 7. werden / 8. wird

Exercise 2:

1. Du wirst deutsch lernen. / 2. Die Freunde werden sich heute abend treffen. / 3. Wir werden für dich kochen. / 4. Ich werde mich nicht freuen. / 5. Ihr werdet euch sehr ärgern. / 6. Sie werden am Samstag arbeiten. / 7. Mein Bruder wird seinen Geburtstag feiern. / 8. Es wird morgen regnen. / 9. Wir werden ihn nie vergessen.

Exercise 3:

1. Er wird gesprochen haben. / 2. Die Jungen werden gespielt haben. / 3. Wir werden angekommen sein. / 4. Anna wird gearbeitet haben. / 5. Ihr werdet aufgestanden sein. / 6. Du wirst geschrieben haben. / 7. Wir werden studiert haben. / 8. Die Kollegen werden gegangen sein. / 9. Der Nachbar wird geblieben sein.

Exercise: 4:

1. werden , gehen / 2. wirst , gepackt haben / 3. werde , gegangen sein / 4. spielt / 5. werden , vorbereiten / 6. werdet , arbeiten / 7. wird , vergessen haben / 8. regnet / 9. wird , schneien

LESSON 19: REFLEXIVE PRONOUNS

The German language has many different pronouns for every occasion and situation. In English we use them too, but make do with far fewer of them. But don´t be intimidated. It is very likely, that you have come across and even used them already.

Listen to Track 315

The reflexive pronoun in brief:

Reflexive pronouns always refer to the subject of the sentence. They are only used in the *dative* and *accusative* case. They are commonly used in conjunction with reflexive verbs.

Don´t worry if you are not familiar with some of the grammatical terms, we will look at each one in detail.

1. What is a pronoun?

A pronoun is usually specific to subjects or objects (nouns). Pronouns are used to define or even replace the subject of a sentence.

Listen to Track 316

personal pronoun	*Ich sehe einen Film.*	**I** watch a movie.
reflexive pronoun	*Ich sehe* **mich** *im Spiegel.*	I watch **myself** in the mirror.
possessive pronoun	*Das ist* **meiner**.	That is **mine**.
demonstrative pronoun	*Dieser gefällt mir.*	**This** one I like.
relative pronoun	*Der Film,* **den** *ich sehe...*	The film, **that** I watch...
possessive pronoun	**Welcher** *ist dein Hut.*	**Which** one is your hat?

2. What are reflexive verbs?

Before we get to the reflexive pronouns, we have to talk about reflexive verbs, because they are intrinsically linked. In English these are usually verbs combined with words ending in **-self**, or **-selves**.

To bore **oneself**. You amuse **yourself**. They behaved **themselves**.

True reflexive verbs & pronouns:

German has quite a few reflexive verbs compared to English, and some of them can only be used together with a reflexive pronoun. The pronoun is part of the verb.

In this case we call them **true reflexive verbs** and **true reflexive pronouns**. In the infinite form these verbs are always preceded with the word **sich.**

Listen to Track 317

sich beeilen	*Ich beeile <u>mich</u>*	*Ich beeile*
to hurry	I hurry	this is incomplete

Optional reflexive verbs & pronouns:

These are verbs, where the reflexive pronoun is just an optional addition. The verb can also be used without the pronoun, and the pronoun can also be replaced with another word.

Listen to Track 318

malen	**Ich male <u>mich</u>**	**Ich male**	**Ich male den Hund**
to paint	I paint myself	I paint	I paint the dog

This is a list of the most important true reflexive verbs:

Listen to Track 319

physical/emotional	
sich ausruhen	to rest
sich erholen	to recover
sich erkälten	to get a cold
sich krank/gut/schlecht fühlen	to feel sick/good/bad
sich sehnen nach	to long for
sich schämen	to be ashamed, to be embarrassed
sich sorgen um	to be worried about
human interaction	
sich anfreunden	to befriend
sich kümmern um	to look after
sich streiten	to argue
sich verabreden	to arrange to meet
sich verhalten	to act, to behave
sich verstehen	to get along
sich vertragen	to make up
opinion/decision making	
sich einigen auf	to agree on something
sich entscheiden für/gegen	to decide to/against
sich irren	to err

work	
sich bewerben	to apply for
sich eignen für/zu	to be suited for/to
communication/verbal interaction	
sich bedanken bei	to thank someone
sich beklagen	to complain
sich beschweren	to complain
sich erkundigen	to inquire
sich weigern	to refuse
others	
sich befinden	to be located
sich ereignen	to happen

3. German Reflexive pronouns in *dative* and *accusative*:

Good news, if you already know personal pronouns—the reflexive form nearly always closely relates to the personal. Irregular exceptions are 1. Person singular (*er/sie/es* and **sich**) and 2. Person plural (*sie/Sie* and **sich**)

Listen to Track 320

	reflexive pronouns	
	Dative	*Accusative*
ich	*mir*	*mich*
du	*dir*	*dich*
er/sie/es	*sich*	*sich*
wir	*uns*	*uns*
ihr	*euch*	*euch*
sie/Sie	*sich*	*sich*

4. Choosing the correct case and forming sentences

The reflexive pronoun always relates to the <u>subject</u>.

Deciding whether to use the reflexive pronoun in the *dative* or *accusative* case is actually easy.

If you can replace the reflexive pronoun with another word or leave it out, use the *dative*.

If it is a true reflexive pronoun and cannot be replaced with another word, use the *accusative*.

Listen to Track 321

dative		*accusative*
Ich kaufe **mir** ein Eis.	Ich kaufe nichts.	Ich streite **mich**.
I buy myself an ice-cream.	I buy nothing.	I argue.
Du kaufst **dir** ein Fahrrad.	Du kaufst dem Kind ein Fahrrad.	Du streitest **dich** jeden Tag.
You buy yourself a bike.	You buy the child a bike.	You argue every day.
Er kauft **sich** ein Geschenk	Er kauft ein Geschenk.	Er streitet **sich** nicht.
He buys himself a present.	He buys a present.	He does not argue.
Wir kaufen **uns** ein Haus.	Wir kaufen viel.	Wir streiten **uns** mir dir.
We buy ourselves a house.	We buy a lot.	We argue with you.
Ihr kauft **euch** ein Auto.	Ihr kauft ein Auto.	Ihr streitet **euch** ungern.
You buy yourself a car.	You buy a car.	You argue reluctantly.
Sie kaufen **sich** alles.	**Sie** kaufen alles.	Sie streiten **sich** oft.
They buy themselves everything	They buy everything.	They argue often.

5. Oddity: reciprocal verbs and pronouns

To express the correlation between **several people**, **objects,** or **groups**, reciprocal verbs are used. Reciprocal verbs are mostly plural and also use the reflexive pronoun, but here the reflexive pronoun means **each other**.

As with the reflexive verb, there are true reciprocal verbs, exclusively used with a pronoun, and optional ones.

Listen to Track 322

True reciprocal verbs:

> *Die Frauen haben* **sich** *verstanden.*   The women understood each other.

Optional reciprocal verbs:

> *Die Geschwister ähneln* **sich**. (reciprocal)   The siblings look like each other.
> *Das Kind ähnelt der Mutter.* (non-reciprocal)   The child looks like the mother.

QUICK RECAP:

- Reflexive pronouns are always used with reflexive verbs. True reflexive verbs are exclusively used with reflexive pronouns, optional ones with or without.

- If you start learning the infinite forms of reflexive verbs including the word **sich**, you quickly gain more confidence in using them.
- The German reflexive pronoun refers to the subject of the sentence, and can be in the *dative* or *accusative* case. They are easy to mix up, but not difficult to learn.
- Don´t be afraid to make mistakes, and start to enjoy these quirks of the German language.

TIME TO PRACTICE!

Workbook Lesson 19. Reflexive Pronouns

Exercise 1. Put in the correct reflexive pronoun (dative):

1. Ich wasche _____ die Hände.(I wash my hands.)
2. Meine Schwester näht _____ ein neues Kleid. (Meine Schwester sews a new dress for herself.)
3. Wir kochen _____ ein leckeres Mittagessen. (We cook a tasty lunch for ourselves)
4. Sie haben _____ Tee gemacht. (They made tea for themselves)
5. Er hat _____ einen Brief geschrieben. (He wrote you a letter.)
6. Ihr kauft _____ ein neues Sofa. (You buy a new couch for yourselves.)
7. Haben Sie _____ den Podcast auch angehört? (Did you yourself listen to the podcast as well?

Exercise 2. Put in the correct reflexive pronoun (accusative):

1. Wir ärgern _____ über die Verspätung. (We are annoyed about the delay.)
2. Du freust _____ auf deinen Urlaub. (You are looking forward to your holiday.)
3. Ich bewerbe _____ auf den Job. (I apply for the job.)
4. Die Schüler beschwerten _____ über die Hausaufgaben. (The students complained about the homework.)
5. Sie hat _____ mit dem Nachbarn zerstritten. (She fell out with the neighbor.)
6. Ihr habt _____ zum Essen verabredet. (You arranged to meet for food.)
7. Mein Freund konnte _ nicht entscheiden. (My friend could not make a decision.)

> **Fun fact:** Most people are familiar with the fairytales of the brothers Grimm. But did you know that the language-loving brothers also started the first and most comprehensive German dictionary *Das Deutsche Wörterbuch* in 1838?

Exercise 3. Fill in the blanks choosing the correct reflexive pronoun (accusative or dative):

1. Du interessierst _____ für Philosophie. (You are interested in philosophy.)

2. Gefällt _____ dieser Film? (Do you like this movie?)

3. Er fühlt _____ heute nicht so gut. (He does not feel so well today.)

4. Wir haben _____ gedacht, dass du _____ um die Gäste kümmern wirst. (We thought to ourselves, that you will look after the guests.)

5. Die Kinder fürchten _____ vor dem großen Hund. (The children are afraid of the big dog.)

6. Ich kann _____ keine neuen Schuhe leisten, bis ich bezahlt werde. (Cannot afford new shoes until I get paid.)

7. Ich schäme _____, weil ich _____ nicht bei ihm bedankt habe. (I am embarrassed, because I did not thank him.)

8. Sie können _____ nicht an das Gespräch erinnern. (They cannot remember the conversation.)

9. Wir vertrauen _____ vollkommen. (We trust you completely.)

10. Ich zähle bis 10 und ihr versteckt _____. (I count till 10 and you hide yourselves.)

Exercise 4. Identify whether the underlined reflexive pronouns are in dative or accusative. Mark the correct case with x in the columns on the right:

		Dative	Accusative
1	Ich verspreche _dir_, das Geheimnis nicht weiterzuerzählen. (I promise you not to tell the secret.)		
2	Wir freuen _uns_ auf deinen Besuch. (We are looking forward to your visit.)		
3	Er duscht _sich_ jeden morgen vor dem Frühstück. (He showers every morning before breakfast.)		
4	Patrick hilft _mir_, das Auto zu waschen. (Patrick helps me to wash the car.)		
5	Manchmal verstehe ich _mich_ selbst nicht. (Sometimes I don't understand myself.)		
	Sie treffen _sich_ an der Berliner Mauer. (They meet at the Berlin Wall.)		
7	Sie erzählte _euch_ ihre Lebensgeschichte. (She told you her life story.)		
8	Wir können _uns_ diesen Vorfall einfach nicht erklären. (We just cannot explain this incident ourselves.)		
9	Du erkundigst _dich_ nach der genauen Adresse. (You inquire about the exact address.)		

Exercise 5. Decide whether the sentences below need a reflexive pronoun or not. Fill in the reflexive pronoun sich where appropriate:

1. Die Nachbarn mochten _____ nicht besonders. (The neighbors did not like each other very much.)

2. Die Zuschauer mochten _____ den Film. (The audience liked the film.)

3. Die Männer sahen _____ den Zug abfahren. (The men saw the train take off.)

4. Die Kinder sahen _____ in der Schule. (The children saw each other in school.)

5. Die Frauen freundeten _____ bei der Arbeit an. (The women became friends at work.)

6. Lucy und Sascha einigten _____ auf einen Kompromiss. (Lucy and Sascha came to a compromise.

7. Sie erkannten _____ Tom an seiner roten Jacke. (They recognized Tom because of his red jacket.

8. Deine Söhne ähneln _____ fast gar nicht. (Your sons hardly look alike.)

9. Die beiden Parteien verstehen _____ nicht. (Both parties do not understand each other.)

Answers:

Exercise 1:

1. mir / 2. sich / 3. uns / 4. sich / 5. dir / 6. euch / 7. sich

Exercise 2:

1. uns / 2. dich / 3. mich / 4. sich / 5. sich / 6. euch / 7. sich

Exercise 3:

1. dich / 2. dir / 3. sich / 4. uns , dich / 5. sich / 6. mir / 7. mich , mich / 8. Sich / 9. euch / 10. euch

Exercise 4:

1. dative / 2. accusative / 3. accusative / 4. dative / 5. accusative / 6. accusative / 7. dative / 8. dative / 9. accusative

Exercise 5:

1. sich / 2. none / 3. none / 4. sich / 5. sich / 6. sich / 7. none / 8. sich / 9. sich

LESSON 20: PREPOSITIONAL OBJECT (DAS PRÄPOSITIONALOBJEKT)

Some verbs need to be used in conjunction with a preposition. Examples of such verbs in English are: *to believe in, to count on, to wait for, to think of*. The **prepositional object (Präpositionalobjekt)** is an addition to the sentence and follows after the preposition. It consists of either a single word or a group of words. It must <u>always</u> be preceded by a preposition, otherwise it would just be called an object. In German the preposition will also determine the grammatical case of prepositional object.

Sounds complicated? Well, maybe a little. But I will unravel the mysteries of the **German prepositional object** step by step in this article. And in the process you will also brush up on your knowledge of prepositions and declension.

Let's start by looking at verbs that are used with prepositions.

Verbs with Prepositions

As in English there are verbs in the German language, which are used together with a fixed preposition. The preposition is part of the meaning of the verb. Common translations of prepositions on their own do not always apply in this circumstance, so it is best to learn these verbs together with the preposition.

Listen to Track 323

Examples of verbs+preposition:

glauben *an*	lachen *über*	fragen *nach*	warten *auf*
to believe in	to laugh about	to ask about	to wait for

Now let's form a complete sentence.

*Using the **prepositional object:***

Listen to Track 324

subject	verb+*preposition*	**prepositional object**
Ich	frage *nach*	**dem Weg.**
I	ask about	the route.
Die Kinder	lachen *über*	**den Witz.**
The children	laugh about	the joke.

At this point we need to talk about **declension**. In a regular sentence without preposition, the praedikat (the verb) determines which grammatical case the object

155

has. In a sentence with a preposition, it is <u>always</u> the preposition, that determines the grammatical case of the **prepositional object**.

The Prepositional Object in Dative or Accusative

Certain prepositions require a specific case. Verbs that use a fixed preposition require either the **dative** or **accusative** case. You will have to memorize which one uses which case. But with a bit of practice, it will become quite natural.

Common verbs with prepositions using accusative or dative:

Listen to Track 325

verbs+*an* using <u>dative</u>	sentence with *preposition* and **prepositional object**
jemanden erkennen *an*	Ich erkenne ihn *an* **seinem Hut.**
teilnehmen *an*	Wir nehmen *an* **dem Spiel** nicht teil.
to recognize s.o. by	I recognize him by his hat.
to participate in	We do not participate in the game.
verbs+*an* using <u>accusative</u>	sentence with *preposition* and **prepositional object**
denken *an*	Ihr denkt *an* **mich.**
glauben *an*	Ich glaube *an* **die Zukunft.**
to think of	You think of me.
to believe in	I believe in the future.
verbs+*bei* using <u>dative</u>	sentence with *preposition* and **prepositional object**
sich bedanken *bei*	Tina bedankt sich *bei* **ihrer Mutter.**
sich beschweren *bei*	Er beschwert sich *bei* **seinem Chef.**
to thank s.o.	Tina thanks her mother.
to complain to s.o.	He complains to his boss.
verbs+*mit* using <u>dative</u>	sentence with *preposition* and **prepositional object**
anfangen *mit*	Wir haben *mit* **dem Vortrag** schon angefangen.
sich beschäftigen *mit*	Ich beschäftige mich seit langem *mit* **diesem Thema.**
to begin/start with	We have already started with the presentation..
to occupy yourself with	I have been occupying myself with this subject for a long time.
verbs+*nach* using <u>dative</u>	sentence with *preposition* and **prepositional object**
fragen *nach*	Wir fragen *nach* **einer Gehaltserhöhung.**
schmecken *nach*	Das schmeckt *nach* **Vanille.**
to ask for	We ask for a raise.
to taste of/like	This tastes like Vanilla.
verbs+*auf* using <u>accusative</u>	sentence with *preposition* and **prepositional object**

sich freuen *auf*	Du freust dich *auf* **die Geburtstagsparty.**
warten *auf*	Die Leute warten *auf* **den Zug.**
to look forward to	You look forward to the birthday party.
to wait for	The people wait for the train.
Verbs+*für* using <u>accusative</u>	sentence with *preposition* and **prepositional object**
jemanden danken *für*	Ich danke *für* **Ihre Aufmerksamkeit.**
sich eignen *für*	Er ist nicht geeignet *für* **diesen Auftrag.**
to thank s.o. for	I thank you for your attention.
to be suited for	He is not suited for this assignment.
verbs+*gegen* using <u>accusative</u>	sentence with *preposition* and **prepositional object**
protestieren *gegen*	Alle protestieren *gegen* **die neuen Steuererhöhungen.**
stimmen *gegen*	Wer stimmt *gegen* **mich**?
to protest against	Everybody protests against the new tax increases.
to vote against	Who votes against me?
verbs+*in* using <u>accusative</u>	sentence with *preposition* and **prepositional object**
sich verlieben *in*	Sie verliebte sich *in* **ihr Spiegelbild.**
sich verwandeln *in*	Der Prinz verwandelte sich *in* **einen Frosch.**
to fall in love with	She fell in love with her reflection.
to transform into	The prince transformed into a frog.
Verbs+*über* using <u>accusative</u>	sentence with *preposition* and **prepositional object**
sich ärgern *über*	Sie ärgert sich *über* **die Unordnung.**
lachen *über*	Ihr lacht *über* **den lustigen Film.**
klagen *über*	Viele Leute klagen *über* **das schlechte Wetter.**
to be annoyed by	She is annoyed by the mess.
to laugh about	You laugh about the funny film.
to complain about	Many people complain about the bad weather.

You don't have to learn this list by heart! But it gives you an overview of many common verbs used with fixed prepositions, and the correct declension of the prepositional object.

One last thing: Prepositional objects can sometimes be confused with adverbial clauses, both look very similar.

How to Tell Prepositional Objects and Adverbial Clauses Apart?

Because prepositional objects always belong to verbs with fixed prepositions, a question to your sentence must also contain the same preposition:

Liste0n to Track 326

Examples:

Die Kinder lachen *über* **den Witz**.	Wor*über* lachen die Kinder? → prepositional object
The children laugh about the joke.	What do the children laugh about?
BUT	
Die Sonne ist <u>über dem Berg</u>.	Wo ist die Sonne? → adverbial clause
The sun is above the mountain.	Where is the sun?
Ich warte *auf* **den Zug.**	Wor*auf* warte ich? → prepositional object
I wait for the train.	What am I waiting for?
BUT	
Ich warte <u>auf dem Bahnsteig</u>.	Wo warte ich? → adverbial clause
I wait on the platform.	Where do I wait?
Es schmeckt *nach* **Zitrone.**	Wo*nach* schmeckt es? → prepositional object
It tastes like lemon.	What does it taste like?
BUT	
Er geht <u>nach Hause</u>.	Wohin geht er? → adverbial clause
He goes home.	Where is he going?

So ask the questions: **Wor*über*? Wor*auf*? Wo*mit*? Wo*gegen*? Wo*nach*? Wo*für*?** etc. to establish if you have a prepositional object.

QUICK RECAP:

- Remember that prepositional objects are always used in conjunction with verbs that have fixed prepositions. It is best to learn these verbs together with the prepositions, because prepositions on their own often have different meanings.
- Whether the prepositional object is in the dative or accusative case depends usually on the preceding preposition, but occasionally it can be either, depending on the verb they belong to.
- Ask the right questions to determine, if you are dealing with a prepositional object or an adverbial clause.
- Never worry about making mistakes! It is a complex subject. Over time and with some practice you will develop an intuition for making the right choices. But in the meantime use this guide.

TIME TO PRACTICE!

Workbook Lesson 20.Prepositional Object

Exercise 1. Complete the sentence with the prepositional object in <u>dative</u>:

1. Ich frage nach _____. (I ask after your health.)
2. Wir fangen mit _____ am Montag an. (We start with the project on Monday.)
3. Markus erkundigte sich bei _____. (Markus enquired to his father.)
4. Du bedankst dich bei _____. (You thank the audience.)
5. Sie erkannten den Verbrecher an _____.
   (They recognized the criminal by his voice.)
6. Der Küche riecht nach _____. (The Kitchen smells like fresh bread.)

> **Fun Fact:** Germans love bread! There are more than 300 different types. And there are nearly as many words as there is bread referring to the end slice of the loaf: *Eck, Endstück, Gnuscht, Gombel, Kanten, Kipf, Knorpe, Knurz, Knüstchen, Knut, Kopp, Kruste, Renfchen, Rindel, Rungsen, Storzel…* to list just a few of them.

Exercise 2. Complete the sentence with the prepositional object in accusative:

1. Wir entscheiden uns gegen _____. (We decide against the candidate.)
2. Werdet ihr an _____ denken? (Will you think of me?)
3. Ich beschwerte mich über _____. (I complained about the noise.)
4. Er verliebte sich in _____.
   (He fell in love with the woman of his dreams.)
5. Sie eignete sich nicht für _____. (She was not suited for this profession.)
6. Du freust dich auf _____. (You are looking forward to the holiday.)

Exercise 3. Fill in the blanks using the following prepositions:

an / an / auf / bei / für / für / gegen / in / mit / nach / über / über

1. Diese Suppe schmeckt _____ Fisch. (This soup tastes like fish.)
2. Wir warten _____ den Verkäufer. (We are waiting for the salesman.)
3. Ich möchte mich nochmals _____ dir bedanken. (I want to thank you again.)
4. Petra und Jakob lachen _____ die Situation. (Petra and Jakob laugh about the situation)
5. Die Studenten protestieren _____ die Umweltverschmutzung. (The students protest against the pollution of the environment.)
6. Das Mädchen bedankt sich _____ deinen Besuch. (The girl says thanks for your visit.)

7. Du glaubst nicht _____ meine Fähigkeiten. (You do not believe in my capabilities.)

8. Die Kinder beschäftigten sich _____ dem Hund. (The children occupied themselves with the dog.)

9. Wirst du _____ diesem Kurs auch teilnehmen? (Will you also participate in this course?)

10. Sie interessiert sich _____ Geschichte. (She is interested in history.)

11. Er verwandelte sich _____ ein Monster. (He transformed into a monster.)

12. Wir freuen uns _____ die Gehaltserhöhung. (We are happy about the raise.)

Exercise 4. Identify whether the sentence contains a prepositional object or adverbial clause:

		prepositional object	adverbial clause
1	Paula freut sich auf deinen Besuch. (Paula is looking forward to your visit.)		
2	Wir reisen nach Rom. (We travel to Rome.)		
3	Er denkt an die Vergangenheit. (He thinks about the past.)		
4	Ich glaube an die Wahrheit. (I believe in the truth.)		
5	Die Leute warten auf der Treppe. (The people wait on the stairs.)		
6	Du entscheidest dich für das rote Kleid. (You decide on the red dress.)		
7	Im Sommer fahren wir in den Süden von Deutschland. (In the summer we drive to the south of Germany.)		
8	Letzten Sommer habe ich mich in Lukas verliebt. (Last summer I fell in love with Lukas.)		
9	Sie fragten nach einem guten Restaurant. (They ask for a good restaurant.)		

Answers:

Exercise 1:

1. deiner Gesundheit. / 2. dem Projekt. / 3. seinem Vater. / 4. dem Publikum. / 5. seiner Stimme. / 6. frischem Brot

Exercise 2:

1. den Kandidaten. / 2. mich / 3. den Lärm / 4. seine Traumfrau. / 5. diesen Beruf. / 6. den Urlaub

Exercise 3:

1. nach / 2. auf / 3. bei / 4. über / 5. gegen / 6. **für** / 7. an / 8. mit / 9. an / 10. **für** / 11. in / 12. über

Exercise 4:

1. prepositional object / 2. adverbial clause. / 3. prepositional object / 4. prepositional object / 5. adverbial clause. / 6. prepositional object / 7. adverbial clause. / 8. prepositional object / 9. prepositional object

LESSON 21: MODAL VERBS (MODALVERBEN)

German modal verbs (Modalverben) are useful words, which you will encounter regularly in daily life as well as in the written language. You probably know some already. They are used to express the relationship or attitude somebody has to an activity. In English they are verbs such as can, could, ought, must, may, want etc.

Depending on the situation and how you use them, they can have different meanings. But luckily there are only six of them in the German language. But before we look at the details, let's start with some basics.

What Are Modal Verbs?

Modal verbs help you express things such as *purpose, ability, possability, preference, necessity, requests, demands, permission* and *prohibition*. There are six modal verbs: **dürfen, können, müssen, wollen, sollen, mögen**.

Most of the time they are used together with a second verb. This verb usually stands at the end of the sentence in the infinitive form, while the modal verb is conjugated. All modal verbs are irregular, so you will have to learn the conjugation of each.

Listen to Track 327

Ich **darf** das machen.   Er **kann** singen.   Wir **wollen** autofahren.

I am allowed to do this.   He can sing.   We want to drive.

Similar to English, some of the German modal verbs can have multiple meanings depending on context, or if used in a negative statement.

The six modal verbs and their meanings (including negation):
Listen to Track 328

modal verb	meaning	example	
dürfen	permission	Er **darf** in der Küche rauchen.	He is allowed to smoke in the kitchen.
nicht dürfen	prohibition	Er **darf nicht** in der Küche rauchen.	He is not allowed to smoke in the kitchen.
können	possibility	Ich **kann** morgen mithelfen.	I can help out tomorrow.
	ability	Du **kannst** schwimmen.	You are able to swim.
	polite request	**Können** Sie mir helfen?	Can you help me?
	approval	Das **kannst** du ruhig machen.	It is fine for you to do so.

162

nicht können	impossibility inability polite request critique	Ich **kann** morgen **nicht** mithelfen. Du **kannst nicht** schwimmen. **Können** Sie mir **nicht** helfen? Das **kannst** du **nicht** machen!	I cannot help out tomorrow. You are unable to swim. Can you not help me? You cannot do this!
mögen	preference/ inclination	Sie **mag** Eis essen.	She likes to eat ice cream.
nicht mögen	dislike	Sie **mag kein** Eis essen.	She doesn't like to eat ice cream.
müssen	necessity order/demand	Ich **muss** bald schlafen. Du **musst** jetzt gehen!	I need to sleep soon. You have to go now!
nicht müssen	no necessity slackening of a demand	Ich **muss** noch **nicht** schlafen. Ich bin hellwach! Du **musst** noch **nicht** gehen. Es ist noch früh.	I don't need to sleep yet. I am wide awake! You do not have to go yet. It is still early.
sollen	advice/demand a general rule	Ich **soll** mehr Obst essen, sagt mein Arzt. Nach dem Essen **soll** man sich die Zähne putzen.	I should eat more fruit, says my doctor. After food you should brush your teeth.
nicht sollen	moral prohibition	Du **sollst nicht** stehlen.	You should not steal.
wollen	will/intention	Wir **wollen** nach Amerika reisen.	We want to travel to America.
nicht wollen	refusal	Wir **wollen nicht** nach Amerika reisen.	We don't want to travel to America.

Mögen, möchten, wollen: What's the difference?

Watch out for **mögen**! This verb changes its meaning when it is used in the **Konjunktiv II** form: **ich möchte, du möchtest, er/sie/es möchten**... Then it means **wünschen** (*would like* or *to desire*).

It is often used in polite requests or queries. But it all depends on your intention and mood.

Listen to Track 329

Ich **möchte** noch ein Bier bestellen.   I would like to order another beer.

Möchten Sie noch etwas?   Do you desire anything else?

But it is equally correct, but less polite, is:

Ich **will** noch ein Bier bestellen.	I want to order another beer.
Wollen Sie noch etwas?	Do you want anything else?

Though it is very common to use modal verbs in conjunction with another verb in the infinitive, it is not always necessary.

Using Modal Verbs Without Verb Infinitive

Listen to Track 330

In particular **mögen** und **wollen** are often used on their own.

Sie **mag** Erdbeereis.	She likes Strawberry ice cream.
Wir **mögen keine** Großstädte.	We do not like cities.
Ich **will** einen Hund.	I want a dog.
Sie **wollen** mehr Geld.	They want more money.

Other modal verbs can also stand on their own, if it is obvious through the context, what they relate to:

Listen to Track 331

Kommst du vorbei? Nein, ich **kann** heute **nicht** (vorbeikommen).

Are you coming by today? No, I cannot (come by).

Fass das nicht an! Doch, ich **darf** das (anfassen).

Don't touch this! But I will, I am allowed to (ttouch).

And at some point you will surely come across this colloquial expression:

Ich **muss** mal (pinkeln OR zur Toilette gehen).

I have to (pee OR go to the toilet).

Congratulations, you have now mastered the six German modal verbs!

But hang on in there, we are not quite through yet. There are two more verbs, which are not modal verbs as such, but can be used the same way.

Lassen and Brauchen: How to Use Them Like Modal Verbs

Lassen *(to let, to get, to leave)* can be used like a modal verb in the right context, with or without the infinitive.

Listen to Track 332

request	*Lassen Sie den Teller stehen.*	Leave the plate.
order	*Ich **lasse** das Auto reparieren.*	I get the car repaired
permission	*Die Mutter **lässt** das Kind im Garten spielen.*	The Mother lets the child play in the garden.
prohibition	***Lass** das!*	Stop it!
resignation	*Ich **lasse** das besser sein.*	I'd better leave it be.

Brauchen *(to need, use* or *require s.th.)* can be used with the words **nur** and **nicht** like a modal verb. But the verb in the infinitive needs to be preceded by **zu**. In this context brauchen can be translated as *have to,* and *do not have to.*

Listen to Track 333

necessity	*Du **brauchst nur zu** fragen.*	You just have to ask.
no necessity	*Ihr **braucht nicht zu** arbeiten.*	You don't have to work.

QUICK RECAP:

* Modal verbs help you express and understand intentions, abilities, demands, preferences and prohibitions. They can also enable you to be more polite, demanding or rude.

* All modal verbs are irregular. But there are only six of them, plus a couple more which can be used as such.

* They are often combined with another verb in the infinitive, which usually stands at the end of the sentence.

* Modal verbs can have multiple meanings depending on context. Start paying attention to modal verbs when reading or listening to German. And don't worry about getting it wrong. Often the differences are very subtle and there is no single correct way of saying it. Start experimenting---this is where learning a foreign language becomes interesting!

TIME TO PRACTICE!

Workbook Lesson 21. Modal Verbs

Exercise 1. Fill in the blanks using the modal verbs from the list below:

kann / wollen / muss / braucht / darf / mögen / sollst / muss / möchte / lasse

1. Ich habe eine Allergie und _____ keine Nüsse essen.

    (I have an allergy and are not allowed to eat nuts.)

2. Er hat sich den Tag frei genommen. Er _____ dir heute beim Umzug helfen.
   (He took the day off. He can help you with the move today.)

3. Wir lieben Erdbeeren! Wir _____ sie besonders gerne mit Sahne essen.
   (We love strawberries! We like to eat them especially with cream.)

4. Sie haben sich verabredet und _____ in den Zoo gehen.
   (They arranged to meet and want to go to the zoo.)

5. Dein Arzt sagt, du _____ mehr Gemüse essen.
   (Your doctor says, you should eat more vegetables.)

6. Die Abgabefrist ist am Montag. Dann _____ es fertig sein!
   (The deadline is on Monday. Then it has to be ready!)

7. Bleibst du noch ein wenig? Ich _____ noch einen Kaffee bestellen.
   (Are you staying a bit longer? I would like to order another coffee.)

8. Ihr _____ euch nicht zu bedanken. Das habe ich gerne gemacht.
   (You do not have to say thank you. I was happy to do it.)

9. Warum _____ er schon gehen? Es ist noch früh.
   (Why does he have to go already? It is still early.)

10. Ich gehe zum Friseur und _____ mir die Haare schneiden.
    (I go to the hairdresser and get a haircut.)

Exercise 2. Fill in the blanks choosing the correct modal verb:

1. Wir _____ Klavierspielen lernen. (We want to learn to play the piano.)

2. Alle Kinder _____ Schokolade. (All children like chocolate.)

3. Er _____ dir bei den Hausaufgaben helfen. (He can help you with your homework.)

4. Du _____ auf deine Mutter hören! (You should listen to your mother!)

5. Jeden Montag _____ ich die Küche putzen. (Every Monday I have to clean the kitchen.)

6. Tim _____ immer noch nicht autofahren. (Tim is still not able to drive a car.)

7. Hier _____ man nicht parken. (It is not allowed to park here.)

8. Der Hund _____ auf dem Sofa sitzen. (The dog is allowed to sit on the sofa.)

9. Ihr _____ kein Geschenk mitbringen. (You don't have to bring a present.)

10. Ich _____ nicht in die Schule gehen. (I don't want to go to school.)

Fun fact: The German language assimilates foreign words at a rapid pace, especially from English. Though sometimes the original meaning seems to have been lost in translation, e.g. a *Handy* is a mobile phone, *Boxen* are Loudspeakers, a *Talkmaster* is a chat show host, and a *Smoking* is a tuxedo.

Exercise 3. Fill in the blanks choosing the correct modal verbs and other verbs, where appropriate:

1. Ich lerne seit drei Jahren Gitarre und _____ sehr gut _____.
   (I have studied the guitar for three years and can play very well.)

2. Er _____ ein neues Auto, weil sein altes zu klein ist.
   (He wants a new car, because his old one is too small)

3. Sie nimmt Antibiotika, deshalb _____ sie keinen Alkohol _____.
   (She takes antibiotics, therefore she is not allowed to drink alcohol.)

4. Darf ich Ihnen die Rechnung bringen oder _____ Sie noch etwas _____?
   (May I bring you the bill or would you like to order something else?)

5. Bist du allergisch oder _____ du einfach keine Katzen?
   (Are you allergic or you just don't like cats?)

6. Wir _____ morgen früh _____, damit wir den Zug nicht verpassen.
   (We have to get up early, so we don't miss the train.)

7. Ihr _____ nicht zur zur Arbeit zu _____, wenn ihr krank seid.
   (You do not need to go to work, if you are sick.)

8. Nach dem Essen _____ man nicht _____. Warte noch ein wenig!
   (After food one should not swim. Wait a little bit!)

Answers

Exercise 1:

1. darf / 2. kann / 3. **mögen** / 4. wollen / 5. sollst / 6. muss / 7. **möchte** / 8. braucht / 9. muss / 10. lass

Exercise 2:

1. wollen / 2. **mögen** / 3. kann / 4. sollst / 5. muss / 6. kann / 7. darf / 8. darf / 9. **müsst** / 10. will

Exercise 3:

1. kann , spielen / 2. will / 3. darf / trinken / 4. **möchten** , bestellen / 5. magst / 6. **müssen** , aufstehen / 7. braucht , gehen / 8, soll , schwimmen

LESSON 22: HOW TO ASK QUESTIONS IN GERMAN (INTERROGATIVE PRONOUNS)

This time, we will explain how to ask questions in German, including use of the language's (thankfully) few interrogative pronouns. You'll be happy to know this is one of the easier parts of German grammar.

We will clarify question structure and word order using interrogative pronouns like *wo, wer, wie, was*, etc. Are you ready to start? Let's go!

German Questions and Interrogative Adverbs: How are They Used?

To ask a yes/no question in German, you just invert subject and verb order:

Listen to Track 334

Er hat Zeit.	He has time.
Hat er Zeit?	Does he have time?
Ja, er hat Zeit.	Yes, he has time (Yes, he does).
Nein, er hat keine Zeit.	No, he doesn't have time (No, he doesn't).

And that's the essence of 'yes' and 'no' questions in German. Open questions or "W-Fragen" are slightly different. **To ask an open question in German, you will still invert the word order, but you will also add an interrogative adverb at the beginning** (w-question word).

Listen to Track 335

Examples:

Wann kommst du?	When are you coming?
Wo sind Sie geboren?	Where were you born?
Wie geht es Ihnen?	How are you?
Wer ist das?	Who is that?
Wer sind sie?	Who are they?
Wann hast du Zeit?	When do you (will you) have time?
Warum isst du noch?	Why are you still eating?

Interrogative Adverbs

Listen to Track 336

Wer - Who	*Wie* – How
Was – What	*Wie alt* – How old
Welcher – Which	*Wie viel* – How much
Wann – When	*Wie lange* – How long
Warum – Why	*Wie oft* – How often
Wieso – How so, in what way	*Wie teuer* – What does something cost
	Wie weit – How far

Examples:

Listen to Track 337

Was sagen Sie?	What do you say / What are you saying?
Wer hat das gesagt?	Who said that?
Er hat das gesagt.	He said that.
Sie besucht mich.	She visits me.
Wer besucht mich?	Who is visiting me?

As you can see, it's pretty simple. **We just put the question word (interrogative adverb) at the beginning followed by the verb. If there is an auxiliary verb, it comes after the adverb. The main verb, which is conjugated, goes to the end of the question** in keeping with the German word order rule.

Wer means who and can refer to masculine, feminine, neuter, and plural nouns. This form is only used in the nominative. The adverb designates the person carrying out the action. In the above example *Wer besucht mich, wer* is in subject position. The question is to the person performing the action. We also have *wen* (accusative) and *wem* (dative).

Listen to Track 338

Examples:

Ich kenne den Mann.	I know the man.
Wen kenne ich?	Whom do I know?

In this **example**, the interrogative adverb is in the accusative case. It refers to the direct object in the question. The subject is *ich*.

Listen to Track 339

Ich gehe mit dem Mann aus.	I am going out with the man.
Mit wem gehe ich aus?	Who am I going out with?

In this **example**, the interrogative adverb is in the dative case. It refers to the indirect object in the question. The subject is still *ich*.

Welcher means "which" or "what" and comes before a noun. **The inflection depends on case and gender.**

Listen to Track 340

Examples:

Welcher Bus kommt?	Which bus is coming?

In this example, we have the masculine nominative. It is nominative because it is the subject and masculine because it is *der Bus*.

Welchen Bus nimmst du?	Which bus are you taking?

Here, we have the accusative. *Bus* is the direct object in this question.

Welches Auto hast du gekauft?	Which car did you buy?

We have the neuter accusative. *Auto* is the direct object, *das Auto*.

The following table should make everything clear:

Declension of "welcher"
Listen to Track 341

	Masculine	Feminine	Neuter	Plural
Nominative	*welcher*	*welche*	*welches*	*welche*
Accusative	*welchen*	*welche*	*welches*	*welche*
Dative	*welchem*	*welcher*	*welchem*	*welchen*
Genitive	*welches /welchen*	*welcher*	*welches /welchen*	*welcher*

'Wie' means "how", as in:

Wie komme ich zum Flughafen?	How do I get to the airport?

Just like in English, 'wie' is combined with other words to form interrogative adverbs. Below are some commonly used ones:

Wie viel / Wie viele

"Wie viel" means "How much." It is used with uncountable nouns. "Wie viele" means "how many" and is used with countable nouns.

Listen to Track 342

Wie viel Geld hat er?	How much money does he have?
Wie viele Kinder hat er?	How many children does he have?
Wie oft muss man sich die Zähne putzen?	
How often should you brush your teeth?	
Wie lange hast du in den USA gewohnt?	How long did you live in the US?
Wie alt bist du?	How old are you?
Wie weit weg ist dein Haus?	How far away is your house?
Wo wohnst du?	Where do you live?

The particles her and hin are added to wo to form other interrogative adverbs.

Listen to Track 343

Wohin	Where to
Wohin fahren Sie?	Where are you going (to)?

This one is confusing to English speakers because in English, there often isn't a difference between 'where' and 'where to'. However, in German there is a big one, particularly in that 'wohin' takes the accusative case and 'wo' takes the dative. **'Wo' is only used to denote an absence of movement.**

Woher kennst du ihn?	Where do you know him from?
Woher kommt ihr?	Where do you come from?

Wo + Preposition

Finally, prepositions can often bind to 'wo' to form an interrogative adverb. Their use and translation depend on the verb they go with. Let's take the verb *anfangen mit* as an example.

Listen to Track 344

Wir fangen mit der Hausaufgabe an.	We're starting the homework.
Womit fangen wir an?	What are we starting with?

Sich erinnern an - remember

Ich erinnere mich an meine Kindheit.	I remember my childhood.
Woran erinnere ich mich?	What do I remember?

As you can see, when the preposition begins with a vowel, we add an 'r' between 'it' and 'wo'. **The combination of Wo + (r +) Preposition is only used to ask for or about inanimate objects.**

Listen to Track 345

If we want to ask about a person:

Ich erinnere mich an ihn.	I remember him.
An wen erinnere ich mich?	Who(m) do I remember?

The case depends on the verb. *Erinnern an* goes with the accusative.

Gehen zu – go to
Listen to Track 346

Ich gehe zum Arzt.	I'm going to the doctor.
Zu wem gehe ich?	To who(m) am I going?

Gehören zu – belong to
Listen to Track 347

Die Schuhe gehören mir.	The shoes belong to me.
Wem gehören die Schuhe?	Who do the shoes belong to?

Das Schwimmbad gehört zum Haus.

The pool belongs to (comes with) the house.

Wozu gehört das Schwimmbad?	What does the pool come with?

Denken an – think about
Listen to Track 348

Ich denke an meine Probleme.	I am thinking about my problems.
Woran denke ich?	What am I thinking about?
Ich denke ständig an meine Frau.	I think about my wife all the time.
An wen denke ich ständig?	Who do I think about all the time?

Helfen bei – help with
Listen to Track 349

Wobei können wir helfen?	What can we help with?

Liegen in – consists in, is the essence of something
Listen to Track 350

Was ist das Wesentliche der Sache?

What does the matter consist of (what is the essence of the matter)?

Sprechen über – speak about
Listen to Track 351

Worüber habt ihr gesprochen?	What did you talk about?
Über wen habt ihr gesprochen?	Who did you talk about?

QUICK RECAP:

- To ask a yes/no question in German, you just invert the subject and verb order.
- To ask an open question in German, you will still invert the word order, but you will also add an interrogative pronoun at the beginning.
- We put the question word (interrogative adverb) at the beginning followed by the verb. If there is an auxiliary verb, it comes after the adverb. The main verb, which is conjugated, goes to the end of the question.
- **Wer** means who and can refer to masculine, feminine, neuter, and plural nouns.
- Some adverbs, like **welcher**, are inflected. The inflection depends on case and gender. **Welcher** means 'which' and is followed by a noun.
- "**Wie viel**" means "How much?". It is used with uncountable nouns. "**Wie viele**" means "how many?" and is used with countable nouns.
- **Wo** is only used to denote an absence of movement. The particles **her** and **hin** are added to **wo** to form **wohin** and **woher** (where to and where from), both of which denote movement in a given direction.
- Finally, **prepositions** can often bind to **wo** to form an interrogative adverb. This combination is only used to ask for or about inanimate objects.

TIME TO PRACTICE!

Workbook Lesson 22. How to Ask Questions in German

Exercise 1: Fill in the blanks with the correct word or words.

1. _____ kommt er? Aus Berlin.
2. _____macht er? Er bastelt.
3. _____ ist das? Das ist Herr Flick.
4. _____ wohnt er? In Hamburg.

5. _____ ist das? Es kostet 2 Euro.

6. _____ arbeitet sie? Weil sie Geld braucht.

7. _____ fahren sie? Nach Paris.

8. _____ Kinder hat sie? Sie hat fünf Kinder.

9. _____ Geld hat er? Nur 100 Euro.

10. _____ sind sie? Sie sind die Familie Beier.

11. _____ ist er von Beruf? Er ist Bäcker.

12. _____ gehst du? In die Schule.

13. _____ weißt du die Antwort nicht? Weil ich nicht studiert habe.

Answers:

Exercise 1

1. Woher / 2. Was / 3. Wer / 4. Wo / 5. Wie teuer / 6. Warum, wieso / 7. Wohin / 8. Wie viele / 9. Wie viel / 10. Wer / 11. Was / 12. Wohin / 13. Warum, wieso

LESSON 23: THE KONJUNKTIV MOODS

German has two subjunctive forms, the Konjunktiv I and Konjunktiv II. German language learners learn the second form at level B1 (lower intermediate) and the first form at level B2 (upper intermediate), although exact language level designations can vary according to the system.

Konjunktiv I

Konjunktiv I is used to express hypothetic or unrealistic hopes and wishes, conditional clauses, unreal statements, and tentative or polite statements or questions.

Listen to Track 352

Examples:

Ich wünschte, dass ich schon im Urlaub wäre.

(I wish I were already on vacation.)

Wenn ich schon im Urlaub wäre, würde ich jeden Tag an den Strand gehen.

(If I were already on vacation, I would go to the beach every day.)

Wärst du so nett, mit mir in den Supermarkt zu gehen?

(Would you be so kind as to come with me to the supermarket?)

There are two Konjunktiv II forms. One expresses situations in the present and the other expresses situations in the past. They also differ based on the verb type. In the present, **weak verbs typically take würde as an auxiliary and go at the end of the clause or sentence in the infinitive:**

Listen to Track 353

Ich würde dir ein Geschenk schicken.	I would send you a present.

Schicken is a weak verb: its three forms are schicken – schickte – geschickt. Depending on the subject, only the auxiliary is conjugated:

Du würdest mir ein Geschenk schicken	You would send me a present.
Sie würden uns ein Geschenk schicken	They would send us a present.

As you can see, only the auxiliary ending changes. With strong verbs, it is a little more complicated. Let's take the verb *'tun'* as an example.

Tust du das?	Do you / will you do that?

This is not a hypothetical question. If we want to ask someone if they would (hypothetically) do something, we need to change the verb form. The past simple of tun is tat. We add an –e and an umlaut:

Ich würde   I would do...

For the du form, we also need to add –st at the end:

Du würdest   You would do...

To make a question:

Würdest du das?   What would you?

So this is the rule for strong (irregular) verbs in Konjunktiv II: **we add an umlaut to the past simple of verbs with a stem vowel of a, o, or u, an –e at the end, and then the ending depending on the subject. If the vowel is i or e, we just add an –e at the end, and then the ending depending on the subject.**

Listen to Track 354

Examples:

finden (past simple fand) – er fände	find (past simple found) - he would find
gehen (ging) – wir gingen	go (went) - we went
kommen (kam) – ihr kämet	come (came) - you would come
gießen (goss) – wir gössen	pour (pour) – we would pour

Modal Verbs

The form of modal verbs in KII is the same as the past simple. The only difference is the modal verbs with umlauts in the present tense keep them.

Listen to Track 355

Examples

Ich könnte, wenn ich wollte   I could if I wanted to.

Ich hätte keine Zeit, wenn ich das alles machen müsste.

I wouldn't have time if I had to do it all.

Ich hätte keine Zeit, wenn ich das alles machen sollte.

I wouldn't have time if I had to do all that.

The table below can further clarify the Konjunktiv II in the present:

Listen to Track 356

	Konjunktiv II (present)		
	finden	sein	haben
Ich	*ich fände*	*ich wäre*	*ich hätte*
Du	*du fändest*	*du wär(e)st*	*du hättest*
Er, sie, es	*er fände*	*er wäre*	*er hätte*
Wir	*wir fänden*	*wir wären*	*wir hätten*
Ihr	*ihr fändet*	*ihr wär(e)t*	*ihr hättet*
Sie, sie	*sie fänden*	*sie wären*	*sie hätten*

Sometimes, würde + infinitive is used for strong verbs too in spoken German.

Konjunktiv II to Express Situations in the Past

As mentioned, this mood **can express a situation in the past. To do this, we use the subjunctive forms of sein/haben and the past participle**.

Listen to Track 357

Example:

Du wärst gegangen/er hätte gesagt

You (sg.) would have gone, he would have said

Ich hätte gefunden / ihr wäret gekommen

I would have found, you (pl.) would have come.

The Konjunktiv I

The Konjunktiv I is mainly used for indirect speech, which is when someone communicates what has been said by someone else.

Listen to Track 358

- Er: *Ich bin 35 Jahre alt*
  He says: "I am 35 years old" (Direct speech)

  Er sagt, er sei 35 Jahre alt
  He says (that) he is 35 years old (Indirect speech)

- *Sie: Ich habe Hunger*
  She says: "I'm hungry" (Direct speech)

  Sie sagt, dass sie Hunger habe
  She says that she's hungry (Indirect speech)

The clause with Konkunktiv I ("sie habe Hunger") goes with a main clause in the Indicative ("sie sagt").

Listen to Track 359

The verbs used most often with indirect speech are:

- *fragen*   to ask
- *erzählen*   to narrate, to tell
- *hören*   to hear
- *versprechen*   to promise
- *sagen*   to say, to tell
- *lesen*   to read
- *vermuten*   to assume, to suppose

Indirect speech without "Konjunktiv I"

If you use the particle "dass", it is correct if the subordinate clause is in the indicative instead of Konjunktiv I:

Listen to Track 360

Konjunktiv I Correct	*Er sagt, er sei 35 Jahre alt* He says he is 35 years old
Konjunktiv I + dass Correct	*Sie sagt, dass sie Hunger habe* She says that she is hungry
Indikativ + dass Correct	*Sie sagt, dass sie Hunger hat* She says that she is hungry

If the Konjunktiv I is the same in the Indikativ, which is not uncommon, the Konjunktiv II can be used instead of Konjunktiv I for indirect speech.

Conjugation of Konjunktiv I

The Konjunktiv I is used in the present, the perfect, and the future tense.

Conjugation of weak verbs

As an example, let's conjugate the verb *fragen* (to ask):

Listen to Track 361

	Indikativ	Konjunktiv I
ich	*frag -e*	*frag -e*
du	*frag -st*	*frag -est*

er/sie/es	frag -t	frag -e
wir	frag -en	frag -en
ihr	frag -t	frag -et
sie	frag -en	frag -en

In Konjunktiv I, the persons ich, wir and sie are the same as the Indikativ. The forms du and ihr can also be the same as the indicative depending on the verb stem (for example, if the stem ends with -d, such as reden). Only the forms er, sie, es are always different. It is the same for weak and strong verbs.

Conjugation of strong verbs

Let's look at the verb *sehen* (to see):

Listen to Track 362

	Indikativ	Konjunktiv I
ich	seh-e	seh-e
du	sieh -st	seh -est
er/sie/es	sieh -t	seh -e
wir	seh-en	seh-en
ihr	seh-t	seh-et
sie	seh-en	seh-en

Auxiliary verbs "sein" and "haben" in Konjunktiv I

The conjugation of the Konjunktiv I of the verb sein ('to be') has quite a few specifics: Sei is the form for ich, er, sie, es (with the "-e" ending). The conjugation of haben is regular.

Listen to Track 363

	sein	haben
ich	sei	habe
du	seist / seiest	hab-est
er/sie/es	sei	hab-e
wir	sei-en	hab-en
ihr	sei-et	hab-et
sie	sei-en	hab-en

Conjugation of Modal Verbs

Listen to Track 364

	Indicative - wollen	Wollen in KI	Indicative - können	Können in KI
ich	will	wolle	kann	Könne
du	willst	wollest	kannst	Könnest
er/sie/es	will	wolle	kann	Könne
wir	wollen	wollen	können	können
ihr	Wollt	wollet	könnt	Könnet
Sie / sie	wollen	wollen	können	können

As you can see, **there is no difference between the indicative and the KI for the first and third person plural and the polite 'you' for conjugation of modal verbs.**

For the first person and third person singular, an –e is added to the end of the verb stem. –est is added to the end of the verb stem for the second person singular and –et is added to the end of the verb stem for the second person plural.

Conjugation of Verbs in Perfekt

In the "Konjunktiv I", the Perfekt is constructed with the verb haben or sein in the present + the third form of the verb (Participle II).

Listen to Track 365

	Indikativ	Konjunktiv I
ich	habe gefragt	habe gefragt
du	hast gefragt	habest gefragt
er/sie/es	hat gefragt	habe gefragt
wir	haben gefragt	haben gefragt
ihr	habt gefragt	habet gefragt
sie	haben gefragt	haben gefragt

Conjugations of Verbs in the Future Tense

In the future tense, the Konjunktiv I is formed with the verb werden in the present + the infinitive. We add –st at the end for du. *Werden* is conjugated in the same way for ich, er, sie, es.

Listen to Track 366

	Indikativ	Konjunktiv I
ich	werde fragen	werde fragen

du	wirst fragen	werdest fragen
er/sie/es	wird fragen	werde fragen
wir	werden fragen	werden fragen
ihr	werdet fragen	werdet fragen
sie	werden fragen	werden fragen

Example:

Er sagt, er werde fragen.   He says he will ask.

QUICK RECAP:

- The first of the two Konjunktiv II forms expresses situations in the present and the second expresses situations in the past.

- In the present, weak verbs typically take würde as an auxiliary and go at the end of the clause or sentence in the infinitive.

- For strong verbs in Konjunktiv II, we add an umlaut to the past simple of verbs with a stem vowel of a, o, or u, an –e at the end followed by the ending depending on the subject.

- If the vowel is i or e, we just add an –e at the end, and then the ending depending on the subject.

- To express a situation in the past using Konjunktiv II, we use the subjunctive forms of sein/haben and the past participle.

- In the "Konjunktiv I", the Perfekt is constructed with the verb haben or sein in the present and the third form of the verb (Participle II).

- In the future tense, the Konjunktiv I is formed with the verb werden in the present and the infinitive.

With that, we come to the end of our lesson on the German subjunctive. It is very commonly used and makes the difference between expressing real and hypothetical circumstances. This wouldn't be possible to express without this form and the language would suffer a great deal as a result because language is all about being able to appreciate the complexity of nuance.

TIME TO PRACTICE!

Workbook Lesson 23. The Subjunctive Moods

Exercise 1. Konkunktiv II - Fill in the blanks with the correct form of the verb in brackets.

1. Wenn diese Mutter strenger ____ (sein), ____ (sein) ihre Kinder nicht so verwöhnt.

2. Wenn die Eltern nicht immer nur ihren Frieden haben _____ (wollen), _____ (können) die Kinder mehr Zeit mit ihnen verbringen.

3. Wenn die Eltern mehr Zeit _____ (haben), _____ (werden) sie sich besser um ihre Kinder kümmern.

4. Wenn die Kinder die Regeln besser _____ kennen), _____ (werden) sich die Eltern nicht so oft ärgern.

5. Wenn die Kinder netter _____ (sein), _____ (werden) sie sich in der Schule besser verhalten.(wären, würden)

6. Kinder _____ (dürfen) nicht immer alles machen, was sie wollen.(dürften)

7. Ich finde, dass er strenger mit seinem Kind sein _____ (sollen).

Exercise 2. Konkunktiv I – Fill in the blanks with the correct form of the verb in brackets.

1. Das Mädchen sagt, die Mutter _____ (arbeiten) in einem Restaurant.

2. Sie sagt, der Vater _____ (sein) schon seit ein paar Jahren weg.

3. Ihr behauptet, er ____ (geben) jeden Monat tausend Euro von seinem Gehalt ab.

4. Das Mädchen sagt, es _____ (geben) andere Geschwister.

5. Es wird vermutet, sie ____ (wissen) nicht, wohin sie mit dem Kind gehen können.

6. Ihr sagt, die Älteste _____ (bekomme) ein Kind.

7. Wir haben gefragt, ob die Kinder noch in die Schule _____.

Answers:

Exercise 1: 1. wäre, wären / 2. wollten, könnten / 3. hätten, würden / 4. kannten, würden / 5. wären, würden / 6.dürften / 7. Sollte

Exercise 2: 1. arbeite / 2. sei / 3. gebe / 4. gebe / 5. wissen / 6. bekommen / 7. gehen, answer also gehen

LESSON 24: THE IMPERATIVE

The German Imperative

Like in English, the German imperative is used to express a command or order. The imperative is one of three grammar moods in German, the other two being the indicative and the subjunctive. In this lesson, we'll take a look at how the German imperative is formed, see some examples, and take some quizzes. Ready? Let's begin!

A Quick Background on the German Imperative

The imperative conjugation is very easy to understand. To start off, there are only three forms – the second person singular (**du**), the second person plural (**ihr**), and the polite you-form (**Sie**) There is also the first person plural form (**wir**), which translates to *let us* and is conjugated the same way as the polite you-form.

Listen to Track 367

Examples of conjugation in the second person singular:

Trink einen Saft!	Drink some juice!
Warte doch mal!	Wait a little / a bit!
Steh (e) um 7 Uhr auf!	Get up at 7:00!

Let's look at how regular verbs are conjugated in the imperative:

Listen to Track 368

Person	Conjugation of trinken	English translation	Conjugation of warten	English translation	Conjugation of aufstehen	English translation
1st person singular (ich)	---		---		---	
2nd person singular (du)	*Trink* (optional –e at the end)	drink	*Wart-e*	Wait	*Steh* (optional –e at the end) auf	Get up, stand up
3rd person singular	---					
1st person plural	*trink-en wir*	let's drink	*Wart-en wir*	Let's wait	*Steh-en wir auf*	Let's get up

2nd person plural	*trink-t*	Drink (said to more than one person)	*Wartet*	Wait (said to more than one person)	*Steht auf*	Get up (said to more than one person)
Polite you- *form* (Sie)	*trink-en Sie*	Drink	*Wart-en Sie*	Wait	*Steh-en Sie auf*	Get up, stand up

Rule to Form the Imperative: Regular Verbs

To form the imperative for regular verbs, we just drop the suffix. You can add an –e after the verb stem when conjugating in the du-form, but you don't have to. Native German speakers do it when it sounds better to them. **It's only mandatory when the stem ends in –t or –d:**

Listen to Track 369

Arbeite Work!   *Rede*!   Talk!

There is no imperative for modal verbs or for *I, he, she, it, or they*. It should be obvious why that is. If you want to say a third person should do something, you can use the verb *lassen*.

Listen to Track 370

Lass ihn gehen   Let him go   *Lass sie fahren*   Let them drive

In this case, you are still directing your order to a second person, i.e. using the du-form of *lassen*.

In the ihr-form, we add –t or –et to the stem depending on the last letter of the stem. We add –et when it is –t or –d.

Listen to Track 371

Arbeitet!   Work!   *Redet*!   Talk!

Wartet!   Wait!   *Fragt*!   Ask!

In the Sie-form, we just add – en to the stem to give an order, following by 'Sie':

Listen to Track 372

Arbeiten Sie bitte!   Please work!   *Reden Sie (bitte)!*   Talk!

Warten Sie (bitte)!   Wait!   *Fragen Sie (bitte)!*   Ask!

The same for the wir-form:

Listen to Track 373

Arbeiten wir!	Let's work!	*Reden wir!*	Let's talk!
Warten wir!	Let's wait!	*Fragen wir!*	Let's ask!

The original forms of the imperative, which are the 2nd person singular (du) and plural (ihr) forms, do not have a subject.

Person	Conjugation	Translation
Du	*Frag (e)*	Ask
Ihr	*Frag - t*	Ask

For separable prefix (trennbar) verbs, the prefix goes to the end of the sentence or clause as with imperative sentences and questions.

Listen to Track 374

Example:

    Mach die Tür auf!   Open the door!

Rule to Form the Imperative: Irregular Verbs

Listen to Track 375

Infinitive	Present 2nd person singular	Present 2nd person plural	Imperative 2nd person singular	Imperative 2nd person plural	English translation
Nehmen	*nimm - st*	*nehm-t*	*nimm*	*nehmt*	take
Geben	*gib-st*	*geb-t*	*gib*	*gebt*	give
Empfehlen	*empfiehl - st*	*empfehl-t*	*empfiehl*	*empfehlt*	recommend
Fahren	*fähr-st*	*fahr-t*	*fahr (e)*	*fahrt*	drive

As you know, there are *three types of irregular verbs in the present tense.* The first one is where the vowel *changes from e to i* in the second and third person singular:

1. E changes to I in the second and third person singular

Listen to Track 376

Ich gebe	I give
Du gibst	You give
Er/ sie / es gibt	He / she / there is
Wir / sie / Sie geben	We / she / you give
Ihr gebt	You give

In the du-form imperative, the vowel still changes, but nothing is added at the end of the stem:

Gib mir das Geld!   Give me the money!

In the ihr-form imperative, the vowel does not change and nothing is added at the end of the stem:

Gebt mir das Geld!

2. E changes to IE in the second and third person singular

Listen to Track 377

Ich lese	I read
Du liest	You read
Er/ sie / es liest	He / she / it reads
Wir / sie / Sie lesen	We / they / you read
Ihr lest	You read

In the du-form imperative, the vowel still changes, but nothing is added at the end of the stem:

Lies den Text!   Read the text!

In the ihr-form imperative, the vowel does not change and nothing is added at the end of the stem:

Lest den Text!   Read the text!

3. A changes to Ä in the second and third person singular

Listen to Track 378

Ich fahre	I drive
Du fährst	You drive
Er/ sie / es fährt	He / she / it drives
Wir / sie / Sie fahren	We / she / you drive
Ihr fahrt	You drive

The vowel changes neither in the du- nor the ihr-form of the imperative. In other words, the umlaut is dropped in the du-form when conjugating the imperative.

Fahr (e) langsamer! (du)	Drive slower! (you)
Fahrt langsamer! (ihr)	Drive slower! (her)

The Sie-form of all imperatives is conjugated the same way for regular and irregular verbs.

Verbs ending in "-rn" or "-ln"

You always add an "-e" in the du-imperative to verbs ending in "-rn" or "-ln":

Listen to Track 379.a

Infinitive	Du-imperative	Ihr-imperative	English translation
ändern	ändere	ändert	Change
lächeln	läch(e)le	lächelt	Smile

Imperative with sein, haben, and warden

Listen to Track 379.b

Infinitive	Du-imperative	Ihr-imperative	Sie-imperative	English translation
sein	sei	seid	seien Sie	be
haben	hab (e)	habt	haben Sie	have
werden	werde	werdet	werden Sie	become

There is no rule for these 3 in the du and ihr-forms. They need to be memorized.

Sounding Polite

Sometimes, command forms can sound impolite. You can add bitte or doch mal to soften your tone.

Listen to Track 380

Komm bitte!   Please come!

Hilf mir doch mal!   Come on, help me!

The Imperative in Negative Sentences

Listen to Track 381

You only need to add 'nicht' to build a negative phrase.

Trink nicht so viel!   Don't drink so much!

QUICK RECAP:

- **To form the imperative for regular verbs**, we simply drop the suffix. You can add an –e after the verb stem when conjugating in the du-form. It's mandatory when the stem ends in –t or –d.
  - In the ihr-form, we add –t or –et to the stem depending on the last letter of the stem. We add –et when it is –t or –d.

○ In the Sie-form, we just add – en to the stem to give an order, following by 'Sie':

○ For separable prefix verbs, the prefix goes to the end of the sentence or clause as with imperative sentences and questions.

- **For irregular verbs** that change from *e to i* or from *e to ie* in the second and third person singular in the present tense, the vowel will still change in the du-form imperative. In the ihr-form imperative, the vowel does not change. Nothing is added at the end of the stem in both cases.

  ○ For irregular verbs that change from *a to ä* in the second and third person singular in the present tense, the vowel changes neither in the du- nor the ihr-form of the imperative. In other words, the umlaut is dropped in the du-form when conjugating the imperative in verbs like *fahren* and *laufen*, which become *du fährst* and *du läufst* in the present tense, indicative mood.

  ○ The Sie-form of all imperatives is conjugated the same way for regular and irregular verbs.

  ○ You always add an "-e" in the du-imperative to verbs ending in "-rn" or "-ln".

TIME TO PRACTICE!

Workbook Lesson 24. The Imperative

Exercise 1. Construct the imperative for the 2nd person plural (ihr).

1. (sein/höflich) _____
2. (schließen/die Tür) _____
3. (laufen/nicht so schnell) _____
4. (sich ein Bonbon nehmen) _____

Exercise 2. Construct the imperative for the polite you-form (Sie)

1. (unterschreiben/hier) _____
2. (zeigen/mir/Ihren Ausweis) _____
3. (sich hinten anstellen) _____

Exercise 3. Construct the imperative for the 2nd person singular (du).

1. (arbeiten/nicht so viel) _____
2. (fragen/die Frau) _____
3. (lesen/langsamer) _____
4. Was haben sie getan? Sag mir bitte! _____! [sprechen]
5. _____ das Geld! [nehmen]

Exercise 4. Fill in the blanks with the correct imperative form of the verb

1. _____ unser Schlafzimmer auf ! /aufräumen (wir)
2. _____ ins Museum! / gehen (du)
3. Ihr wollt schon gehen?_____ doch noch etwas länger. [bleiben]
4. _____ den Tannenbaum ! / schmücken (ihr)
5. Hier habt ihr den Text. Bitte_____ ihn! [lesen]
6. _____ glücklich! / sein (Sie)
7. _____einen Schal ! / tragen (du)
8. _____ nett! /sein (ihr)
9. _____ eine Tour! / machen (Sie)
10. Dein Bruder langweilt sich. _____ doch bitte mit ihm. [spielen]
11. _____doch bitte mal wieder an. / anrufen [du]
12. Das tut weh. _____ bitte _____! [aufhören]
13. Warum bleiben wir immer noch? _____ ! [fahren]
14. Ich habe den Schlüssel verloren._____ mir bitte euren. [geben]
15. Was hast du dort? _____ - es mir! [geben]
16. Essen. _____ [gehen / kommen]

Answers:
Exercise 1

1. Seid höflich / 2. Schließt die Tür. / 3. Lauft nicht so schnell / 4. Nehmt euch ein Bonbon

Exercise 2

1. Unterschreiben Sie hier / 2. Zeigen Sie mir Ihren Ausweis / 3. Stellen Sie sich hinten an

Exercise 3

1. Arbeite nicht so viel / 2. Frag die Frau / 3. Lies langsamer / 4. Sprich / 5.Nimm

Exercise 4

1. Räumen wir / 2. Geh / 3. bleibt / 4. Schmückt / 5. lest / 6. Seien / 7. Trag / 8. Seid / 9. Machen Sie / 10. spiel / 11. Ruf / 12. hör bitte auf / 13. Fahre / 14. gebt / 15. gib / 16. geh, komm

LESSON 25: REFLEXIVE VERBS

In German, reflexive verbs are used to describe an action done by and for one and the same person. Only certain verbs can form reflexive clauses. These verbs are very rare in English, but quite common in German. This lesson will look at how German reflexive verbs are used, the most important rules, word order, and negation of reflexive verbs. We have plenty of examples to make everything clear to you. Are you ready? Let's go!

An Easy Illustration of German Reflexive Verbs

Listen to Track 382

The infinitive of reflexive verbs is preceded by the pronoun "sich" (*sich ärgern, sich streiten, sich verlassen auf, sich interessieren, sich bewerben, sich entscheiden,* etc.). In English, reflexive verbs include the use of pronouns such as 'myself', 'yourself', 'himself', and so on.

Example:

> *Ich sehe mich im Spiegel an.*   I see myself in the mirror.

Other common reflexive verbs are *sich bedanken* (to thank), *sich beeilen* (to hurry up), *sich befinden* (to find oneself in / be located in a particular place), *sich eignen* (to agree), *sich entspannen* (to relax), *sich erkälten* (to get a cold), *sich schämen* (to feel embarrassed about something), *sich verspäten* (to be late), *sich weigern* (to refuse), and *sich Sorgen machen* (to worry, to fret).

Only one of these is reflexive in English too (*sich befinden* / to find oneself in). It may seem like a lot of learn at first – but only at first.

In German, **reflexive verb pronouns can take one of two (or both) cases depending on use. They can be in the accusative or in the dative.** Most take the accusative. Some verbs are sometimes in the accusative and sometimes in the dative. So what does it depend on?

Before we answer that question, let's look at the pronouns:

Listen to Track 383.a

Personal pronoun	Reflexive pronoun in the accusative	Reflexive pronoun in the dative
Ich	*mich*	*mir*
Du	*dich*	*dir*

Er / sie / es	sich	sich
Wir	uns	uns
Ihr	euch	euch
Sie, sie	sich	sich

Examples in the accusative:
Listen to Track 383.b

Ich freue mich über meine neue Wohnung.	I am happy about my new flat.
Ich ärgere mich immer über dich.	I always get mad about you.
Wir streiten uns sehr oft.	We argue very often.
Ich kämme mich.	I comb.
Ich wasche mich.	I wash.
Ich bewege mich.	I move (physically).
Ich setze mich auf den Stuhl.	I sit down / am sitting down on the chair.
Du triffst dich jeden Freitag mit deiner Freundin.	
You meet (as in ‚see') your girlfriend every Friday.	

Examples in the dative:
Listen to Track 384

Ich kaufe mir eine Wohnung	I am buying myself a flat.
Ich kämme mir die Haare.	I comb my hair.
Ich wasche mir die Hände.	I wash my hands.
Ich ziehe mir die Hose an.	I put my pants on.
Ich ziehe mir die Bluse aus.	I take my blouse off.
But! *Ich ziehe* **mich** *an*	I am getting dressed;
Ich ziehe **mich** *aus*	I am getting undressed.

See how we answered the above question? **Verbs like sich kämmen, sich waschen, sich anziehen, and sich ausziehen can take the dative or the accusative. In the sentence 'Ich kämme mir die Haare', there is a direct object, which is die Haare (my hair). Likewise with all the rest that are in dative. If there is no direct object, the pronoun takes the accusative ('ich kämme mich').**

If you can't remember the direct object rule or have trouble identifying the direct object, we may have an easier way for you to remember: **If an item of clothing or a body part is named, the pronoun takes the dative:**

Listen to Track 385

Ich putze mir die Zähne.   I brush my teeth (dative)

But if a body part or item of clothing is not named, the pronoun takes the accusative, as in '*Ich wasche mich.*'

As you can see from the table above, **the pronoun forms differ only in the first and second personal singular (mich** and **mir, dich** and **dir).** In the first person plural, for example, there is no difference in the pronoun:

Listen to Track 386

Wir kämmen uns die Haare.   We comb our hair.

Wir kämmen uns.   We comb.

Reflexive Verbs in the Negative

To negate reflexive verbs, we put ‚nicht' after the verb:

Listen to Track 387

Sie kümmern sich nicht um uns.   They don't care / worry about us.

If an auxiliary or modal verb is used, nicht goes after the verb too:

Listen to Track 388

Sie sollten sich nicht um uns kümmern   They shouldn't worry about us.

If the actor is not the same as the object of action, no reflexive pronoun is used:

Example:

Listen to Track 389

Die Friseurin schneidet sich die Haare.

The hairdresser cuts her hair.

Die Friseurin schneidet dem Kunden die Haare.

The hairdresser cuts the client's hair.

In the second example, the subject (hairdresser) is not the object of action. The client is the object. So, no reflexive pronoun is used with **schneiden** (to cut).

Some verbs can have totally different meanings when you use them as reflexive verbs. Below are some typical examples:

Listen to Track 390

	Meaning	Example
Verlassen	rely on, trust (reflexive)	*Wir können uns auf dich verlassen.*
	leave (not reflexive)	*Du hast mich verlassen.*
aufhalten	to stay (reflexive)	*Ich halte mich gerade in der Hauptstadt auf.*
	Keep, delay (not reflexive)	*Sie haben Ihre Lehrerin aufgehalten.*
umziehen	to change clothes (reflexive)	*Das Kind hat sich umgezogen.*
	To move (not reflexive)	*Ich bin in eine neue Stadt umgezogen.*
verlaufen	get lost (reflexive)	*Ihr habt euch verlaufen.*
	transpire/go (not reflexive)	*Die Vorstellungsgespräche verlaufen immer gut.* *Die Zeit ist schnell vergangen.*
ausziehen	To take off clothes or shoes (reflexive) To move out of a place	*Ich ziehe mir die Hose aus.* *Ich ziehe aus der Wohnung aus.*

Word Order

In a main clause, the reflexive pronoun comes right after the main verb.

Example:

Listen to Track 391

Sie ruhen sich morgens aus.   They rest in the morning.

Er hat sich die Haare gewaschen.   He washed his hair.

The object comes between the reflexive pronoun and the verb when the object of the verb is a pronoun itself:

Listen to Track 392

Example:

Ich putze mir die Zähne. → Ich putze sie mir.

I brush my teeth. → I clean them.

The conjugated verb comes at the end of a dependent clause. The reflexive pronoun comes after the subject.

Example:

Ich teile dir mit, wenn ich ausziehe.   I will let you know when I move out.

QUICK RECAP:

- Reflexive verb pronouns can take the accusative or the dative case.
- If there is a direct object in the sentence, they tend to take the dative.
- If there is no direct object, the pronoun takes the accusative.
- If an item of clothing or a body part is named, the pronoun takes the dative.
- The pronoun forms differ only in the first and second personal singular (mich and mir, dich and dir).
- To negate reflexive verbs, we put ‚nicht‘ after the verb.
- If an auxiliary or modal verb is used, nicht goes after the verb too.
- In a main clause, the reflexive pronoun comes right after the main verb.

Reflexive verbs and pronouns are particularly difficult to native English speakers because these are extremely rare in English. We wouldn't say "I shower myself" or "I shave myself", but we *would* say "Ich dusche mich, ich rasiere mich."

TIME TO PRACTICE!

Workbook Lesson 25. Reflexive Verbs

Exercise 1. Fill in the blanks with the correct reflexive verb to complete the sentences.

1. Wenn ihr keine Mäntel anzieht, werdet ihr_____.
2. Er _____ die Haare.
3. Du musst_____.
4. Ich_____ um eine Stelle.
5. Wir haben_____.
6. Sie haben_____.

Exercise 2. Fill in the blanks with the correct reflexive verb and identify if it's Accusative or Dative?

Example: Ich habe _____ (_____) versteckt. < Answer: mich (Akkusativ) >

1. Wäschst du _____ (_____) die Haare?
2. Ich habe _____ (_____) versteckt.
3. Dreh _____ (_____) nicht um!
4. Ich ziehe _____ (_____) schnell einen Mantel an.
5. Hast du_____ schon etwas zum Trinken bestellt?

Exercise 3. Make sentences. Do we need to use reflexive pronouns in these?

1a. **aufhalten** (present)

    (ich/in Berlin)_____

1b. (ihr/eine Bekanntin)_____

2a. **verlassen** (present perfect)_____

    (?/wann/er/das Land)_____

2b. (er/auf das Versprechen)_____

Exercise 4. Fill in the blanks.

1.   Ich_____,damit ich den Zug in Innsbruck erreiche. [sich beeilen]

2.   Ich_____, dass Sie im August kommen. [sich freuen]

3.   Wir_____auf eure Party. [sich freuen]

4.   Wir_____an den Tisch. [sich setzen]

5.   Wir_____im Park erkältet. [sich haben]

6.   Wir_____ Dienstagabend einen Film_____. [sich ansehen]

7.   Ich_____um einen Job bei Siemens. [sich bewerben]

8.   Wir_____in den Ferien. [sich erholen]

9.   Unsere Kinder_____selbst die Schuhe_____. [sich anziehen]

10. Eure Freunde_____den Wettbewerb_____. [sich anschauen]

11. Meine Tante_____zum Fest einladen. [sich nicht lassen]

12. Er_____für das neueste Buch. [sich interessieren]

13. Du_____für alte Gebäude. [sich interessieren]

14. Er_____für die schwarze Jacke entscheiden. [sich nicht können]

Answers:

Exercise 1:

1. sich erkälten / 2. sich kämmen / 3. sich schämen; nicht / 4. sich bewerben / 5. sich verlaufen; uns verlaufen / 6. sich bemühen; sich bemüh

Exercise 2:

1. dir, Dativ / 2. mich, Akkusativ / 3. dich, Akkusativ / 4. mir, Dativ / 5. dir, Dativ

Exercise 3:

1a. Ich halte mich in Berlin auf, reflexive pronoun is used

1b. Ihr haltet eine Bekannte auf, no reflexive pronoun is used

2a. Wann hat er das Land verlassen? No reflexive pronoun is used

2b. Er hat sich auf das Versprechen verlassen, reflexive pronoun is used

Exercise 4:

1.Ich beeile mich / 2.Ich freue mich / 3.Wir freuen uns /4.Wir setzen uns / 5.Wir haben uns / 6.Wir sehen uns Dienstagabend einen Film an. / 7.Ich bewerbe mich / 8.Wir erholen uns / 9.Unsere Kinder ziehen sich selbst die Schuhe an. / 10.Unsere Kinder ziehen sich selbst die Schuhe an. / 11.lässt sich nicht 12.interessiert sich / 13.interessierst dich / 14.Er könnte sich nicht

LESSON 26: THE PASSIVE VOICE IN GERMAN

German has the active and the passive voice just like English, the Aktiv and Passiv. This lesson will explain the differences between the active and the passive voice, the different forms of the passive, and how to build a clause and sentence in the passive voice.

Introduction to the Passive Voice in German

In the active voice, the person or thing (agent) carrying out a given action is the subject. In the passive voice, the subject is either unknown or becomes the object.

Listen to Track 393

Examples:

Autos werden hergestellt.   Cars are (being) manufactured.

In this example, the subject is unknown. In other words, we don't know who is manufacturing the cars. That changes with the next example:

Autos werden von BMW hergestellt.   Cars are (being) manufactured by BMW.

In active voice, the sentence would be *BMW stellt Autos her*.

Types of Passive

There are two types of passive in German: the Vorgangspassiv (process passive) and the Zustandspassiv (static passive). Below is an example of the first:

Listen to Track 394

Das Konto wird eröffnet.   The account is (being) opened.

And the second:

Das Konto ist eröffnet.   The account is opened.

Passive Voice in the Present Tense

Before we get to the grammar rule, which is pretty straightforward anyway, what is the difference between the two? When the process passive is used, it implies a regular, recurrent action. On the other hand, the static passive implies a one-time or at least an irregular action. In the above example, it would be better to use the process passive because accounts are being opened around the world on a daily basis.

So, about the rule: **To form a clause or sentence in the process passive, we use a conjugated form of werden and the past participle of the main verb. To form a clause or sentence in the static passive, we use a conjugated form of sein and the past participle of the main verb.**

Listen to Track 395

Let's see a few more examples in the process passive:

Das Buch wird gelesen.	The book is being read.
Das Haus wird repariert.	The house is being repaired.

And in the static:

Listen to Track 396

Das Buch ist gelesen.	The book is read.
Das Haus ist repariert.	The house is repaired.

Comparison of Active and Passive Voice in the Present Tense

Listen to Track 397

Active Voice	Passive Voice
ich massiere	*ich werde massiert*
I massage	I am being massaged.

Passive Voice in the Past Simple

The rule to build a clause or sentence in the passive in the past tense is very similar to the present. **To form a clause or sentence in the process passive in the past tense, we use a conjugated form of wurden and the past participle of the main verb. To form a clause or sentence in the static passive, we use a conjugated form of war and the past participle of the main verb.**

Listen to Track 398

Active voice	Process Passive	Static Passive
Ihr massiertet	*Ihr wurdet massiert*	*Ihr wurdet massiert worden*
You massaged	You were (being) massaged	You were massaged.

Prepositions with the Passive Voice

The prepositions von and durch are used with the passive voice. Both come before the agent. Von indicates the person or animal that caused the action and always takes the dative. Durch is used to indicate the means and always takes the accusative.

Listen to Track 399

Examples:

Die Firma wurde von meinem Vater gegründet.

The company was founded by my father.

Die Bibliothek wird durch Spenden finanziert.

The company is funded by donations.

Passive Voice in the Perfect Tense

What if we want to say something **has been done** in German? You probably want to know because this tense is really common in English. It's just as common in German.

Rule: **To form a clause or sentence in the process passive perfect, we use a conjugated form of 'sein', the past participle of the main verb, and worden. The second two go at the end of the clause or sentence.**

Listen to Track 400

Example:

Das Haus ist von meinen Eltern repariert worden.

The house has been repaired by my parents.

We might also want to say something **had been done.** This is the past perfect in English. **In German, the past perfect passive is almost the same as the present perfect passive. We just replace the conjugated form of sein with war:**

Das Haus war von meinen Eltern repariert worden.

The house had been repaired by my parents.

Passive Voice in the Perfect Tenses
Listen to Track 401

Present Perfect Active	Present Perfect Passive	Past Perfect Active	Past Perfect Passive
Sie hat die Arbeit gemacht.	*Die Arbeit ist von ihr gemacht worden.*	*Sie hatte die Arbeit gemacht.*	*Die Arbeit war von ihr gemacht worden.*
She has done the work.	The work has been done by her.	She had done the work.	The work had been done by her.

Passive Voice in the Future Tenses

It's also possible to use the passive voice in the future tense, although rare. We use a conjugated form of warden, the past participle of the main verb, and werden again.

Future I
Listen to Track 402

Active voice	Passive voice
ich werde massieren I will massage	*ich werde massiert werden* I will be massaged

Future II
Listen to Track 403

Active voice	Passive voice
ich werde massiert haben I will have massaged	*ich werde massiert worden sein* I will have been massaged.

When you change a sentence from active to passive voice, the accusative becomes the nominative (the subject) and the nominative becomes dative if 'von' (by) is used, which always takes the dative. If durch is used, it becomes accusative. Of course, this is important mainly for masculine nouns:

Listen to Track 404

Active voice: *Der Mann trinkt einen Wein.*   The man is drinking a wine.

Passive voice: *Ein Wein wird vom Mann getrunken.*   A man drinks a wine.

But not only for masculine nouns:

Listen to Track 405

Active voice: *Die Frau trinkt einen Wein.*   The woman is drinking a wine.

Passive voice: *Ein Wein wird von der Frau getrunken.*   A woman drinks a wine.

When is It *not* Possible to Use the Passive?

You can't use the possessive with:

- Reflexive verbs
- Verbs like *haben, bekommen, erhalten, kriegen* etc. that indicate possession (more on this coming up)
- The construction *es gibt*

- Modal verbs

You also can't use the passive if the accusative is one of the subject's body parts or a piece of clothing that belongs to the subject.

The Passive with Modal Verbs

While you can't use the passive with modal verbs on their own, you can when a full verb is also involved. In this case, the full verb takes the passive voice.

Listen to Track 406

Example:

Active voice: *Sie müssen die Arbeit machen.*	They have to do the work.
Passive voice: *Die Arbeit muss von ihnen gemacht werden.*	The work has to be done by them.

Use with Modals in the Past Tense

Listen to Track 407

Active voice: *Sie mussten die Arbeit machen.*	They had to do the work.
Passive voice: *Die Arbeit musste von ihnen gemacht werden.*	The work had to be done by them.

It gets a bit harder with the perfect tenses. Somewhat needlessly, as this form translates the same way as the past tense in English:

Listen to Track 408

Active voice: *Sie haben die Arbeit machen müssen.*	They had to do the work.
Passive voice: *Die Arbeit hat von ihnen gemacht werden müssen.*	The work had to be done by them.

Forms That Have the Same Meaning as the Passive

Clauses formed with the pronoun 'man' as subject are not true passives, but they have the same meaning. In English, 'man' translated as "one", as in "One must always be careful." It's also used to refer to assumptions as to what people do.

Example:

Listen to Track 409

Was trinkt man in China?   What does one drink in China?

Was macht man zum Abnehmen?

What does one do to lose weight? (in the sense of what people in general do to lose weight)

Verbs Indicating Possession in the Passive Voice

This construction is formed with the verbs *kriegen, bekommen,* or *erhalten,* which serve not as main verbs, but as auxiliaries. The dative object becomes the subject:

Listen to Track 410

Example:

Active voice: *Sie schicken uns heute das Geld.*

They are sending us the money today.

Passive voice: *Wir erhalten heute (von ihnen) das Geld geschickt.*

We receive the money (from them) today.

QUICK RECAP:

- To form a clause or sentence in the process passive, we use a conjugated form of *werden* and the past participle of the main verb. To form a clause or sentence in the static passive, we use a conjugated form of *sein* and the past participle of the main verb.

- To form a clause or sentence in the process passive in the past tense, we use a conjugated form of *wurden* and the past participle of the main verb. To form a clause or sentence in the static passive, we use a conjugated form of war and the past participle of the main verb.

- To form a clause or sentence in the passive perfect present, we use a conjugated form of 'sein', the past participle of the main verb, and worden. The second two go at the end of the clause or sentence.

- The past perfect passive is almost the same as the present perfect passive. We just replace the conjugated form of sein with war.

- When a sentence changes from active to passive voice, the accusative becomes the nominative. The nominative becomes dative if 'von' (by) is used, which always takes the dative. If durch is used, it becomes accusative.

- If you use the passive with a modal verb and a full verb, only the full verb takes the passive. Its past participle is then used.

- Clauses formed with the pronoun 'man' as subject are not true passives, but they have the same meaning.

TIME TO PRACTICE!

Workbook Lesson 26. The Passive Voice in German

Exercise 1. Fill in the blanks with the correct words to form a sentence with a passive voice in the present tense.

1. Ich liebe meinen Hund. Mein Hund _____ von mir _____.
2. Er liest ein Buch. Das Buch _____ von ihm _____.
3. Mein Mann isst ein Ei. Ein Ei _____ von ihm _____.
4. Wir fahren das Auto in die Garage. Das Auto wird von _____ in die Garage _____.
5. Ihr öffnet die Tür. Die Tür wird _____ euch _____.
6. Ich koche die Suppe. Die Suppe _____ _____.
7. Ein Mann fragt mich nach dem Weg. Ich _____ von einem Mann nach dem Weg _____.
8. Ich nehme den Schlüssel. Der Schlüssel _____.
9. Du gießt die Blumen. Die Blumen _____.
10. Ich sehe dich. Du _____ von mir _____.

Exercise 2. Fill in the blanks with the correct words to form a sentence with a passive voice in the past tense.

1. Er spielte Klavier. Klavier _____ von ihm _____.
2. Meine Mutter fragte mich. Ich _____ von meiner Mutter _____
3. Ich schrieb den Brief. Der Brief _____ von mir _____.
4. Wir reparierten unser Auto. Unser Auto _____ von uns _____.
5. Ich lernte das Alphabet. Das Alphabet _____.
6. Ich fütterte meine Katze. Meine Katze wurde _____ mir _____.
7. Sie machten selbst ihre Hausaufgaben. Ihre Hausaufgaben wurde von _____ selbst _____.

Exercise 3: Love a good challenge? Try the 7 above in the perfect passive! The first 4 should be in the present, and the last 3 in the past.

1. _____.
2. _____.
3. _____.
4. _____.
5. _____.

6. _____ .

7. _____ .

Answers:

Exercise 1:

1. wird, geliebt / 2. wird, gelesen / 3. wird, gegessen / 4. uns, gefahren / 5. von, geöffnet / 6. wird von mir gekocht / 7. werde, gefragt / 8. wird von mir genommen / 9. werden von dir gegossen / 10. wirst, gesehen

Exercise 2:

1. wurde, gespielt / 2. wurde, gefragt / 3. wurde, geschrieben / 4. wurde, repariert / 5. wurde von mir gelernt / 6. von, gefüttert / 7. ihnen, gemacht

Exercise 3:

1. Klavier ist von ihm gespielt worden. / 2. Ich bin von meiner Mutter gefragt worden. / 3. Ein Brief ist von mir geschrieben worden. / 4. Unser Auto ist von uns repariert worden. / 5. Das Alphabet war von mir gelernt worden. / 6. Meine Katze war von mir gefüttert worden. / 7. Ihre Hausaufgaben waren von ihnen selbst gemacht worden.

LESSON 27: DATIVE VERBS IN GERMAN

This lesson will look at the dative verbs in German. These verbs require the dative case for objects. We list the most common dative verbs and explain how to make sentences using them. We also recap the rules and end with exercises for you to practice what you've learned. Let's start!

Quick Clarification on Dative Verbs

German cases determine the rules for adjective endings, when and which personal pronouns to use, and types of articles. **The object of dative verbs is always in the dative case regardless of the tense**. True dative verbs, of which there are only around 50 in German, take a dative object without one in the accusative. First, a quick review of dative pronouns and articles:

Dative Personal Pronouns

Listen to Track 411

Pronoun	Dative
ich	mir
du	dir
er	ihm
sie	ihr
es	ihm
wir	uns
ihr	euch
sie	ihnen
Sie	Ihnen

Dative Articles

Listen to Track 412

Article Type	Masculine	Feminine	Neuter	Plural
Definite Articles	dem	der	dem	den
Indefinite Articles	einem	einer	einem	none

Most dative verbs take *haben* in the perfect tense.

Listen to Track 413

Examples:

danken	to thank	*Wir danken dir für die Hilfe.* We thank you for your help.
antworten	to answer	*Sie antworten mir so bald wie möglich.* They (will) answer me as soon as possible.
raten	to advise	*Sie hat ihr geraten, zu Hause zu bleiben.* She advised her to stay home.
helfen	to help	*Kann ich Ihnen helfen?* Can I help you (polite you-form)?

When we use dative verbs, we answer by responding, help by helping, and give thanks by thanking. The object is implied and no preposition is used.

Below are some common dative verbs. **The object of the verb takes the dative case, marked by either a dative pronoun or a dative article**.

Listen to Track 414

Dative Verb	English translation	Example sentence in German	Example translation
weh tun	to hurt	*Das hat ihr wirklich wehgetan.*	That really hurt her.
passen	to fit	*Der Mantel passt ihm gut.*	The coat fits him well.
gehören	to belong to	*Die Halskette gehört dir.*	The necklace belongs to you.
gefallen	to like	*Die Pizza schmeckt mir nicht.*	I don't like the pizza.
gratulieren	to congratuate	*Wir gratulieren Ihnen zum Abschluss.*	We congratulate you on your graduation.
helfen	to help	*Ich habe deinem Mann geholfen.*	I helped your husband.
antworten	to answer	*Sie haben mir nicht geantwortet.*	You didn't answer me.
Schenken	To gift	*Ich schenke ihr Blumen.*	I gift her flowers.
passieren	to happen to	*Ist das den Kindern passiert?*	Did that happen to the children?

Listen to Track 415

Other verbs that take the dative include *ähneln* (to look like), *befehlen* (to order, command), *begegnen* (to come across, to face), *bleiben* (to stay, remain), *dienen* (to serve, to be used for), *erlauben* (allow), *fehlen* (to lack, to miss), *folgen* (follow), *gelingen* (to succeed, to work out), *genügen* and *reichen* (to be enough), *nützen* (to be of use), *vertrauen* (to trust), *zuhören* (to listen), and *zustimmen* (to agree).

Listen to Track 416

Examples:

Dieses Bild ähnelt dem Foto, das du mir gezeigt hast.

This picture looks like the photo you showed me.

Der König befiehlt seinem Volk, Steuern zu zahlen.

The king orders his people to pay taxes.

Der Sportler ist dem Tod begegnet.

The athlete faced death.

Diese Geräte dienen unserer Arbeit.

These devices serve our work. (in the sense of helping us do it better)

Warum ist mir in diesem Haus nichts erlaubt?

Why am I not allowed to do anything in this house?

Es fehlt den Nachbarn an Geld und anderen Mitteln.

The neighbors lack money and other resources.

Der Fremde ist mir den ganzen Tag gefolgt.

The stranger followed me (around) all day.

Der Kuchen ist meinem Mann nicht gelungen.

My husband failed with the cake.

Because '*gelingen*' can be translated as 'to succeed', the literal translation of '*der Kuchen ist meinem Mann nicht gelungen*' could be 'the cake was my husband not successful.' The subject of the German sentence is *Kuchen*, but the subject of the English sentence is 'husband'. The literal translation obviously leaves something to be desired as we wouldn't say something like that in English.

This is one of the problems with German dative verbs – the word order is counterintuitive to English speakers. With practice, it will get easier, and you'll start to understand how to use them correctly.

More examples of sentences using German dative verbs:

Listen to Track 417

Das Geld reicht der Familie nicht.	The money is not enough for the family.
Was nützt mir das?	Of what use is that to me?
Kannst du deinem Kollegen vertrauen?	Can you trust your coworker?

Kollege is a member of the N- declension (in German N-Deklination) category of nouns. All of these nouns take an –n at the end in all cases except the nominative. To switch the subject and object around:

Kann dein Kollege dir vertrauen?	Can your coworker trust you?

Bitte hören Sie dem Gespräch zu und antworten Sie auf die Fragen!

Please listen to the conversation and answer the questions!

Ich stimme deiner Meinung zu.

I agree with your opinion (with what you're saying).

Most dative verbs take a direct object, which is used in the dative case. They are relatively easy to translate. Just ask yourself whom you believe, are helping, are following, are thanking, or are answering. The answer to those questions is in the dative.

QUICK RECAP:

- The object of dative verbs is always in the dative case regardless of the tense.
- When we use dative verbs, we answer by responding, help by helping, and give thanks by thanking. The object is implied and no preposition is used.
- The object of the verb takes the dative case, marked by either a dative pronoun or a dative article.

TIME TO PRACTICE!

Workbook Lesson 27. Dative Verbs in German

Exercise 1. Fill in the blanks with the correct dative verbs.

1. Der Junge hat_____(seine Freundin) geantwortet. (seiner Freundin)
2. Wir danken_____(ihr) für die Hilfe. (euch)
3. Ich glaube_____(mein Chef) nicht. Er lügt! (meinem Chef)
4. Hast du_____(deine Mutter) geholfen? (deiner Mutter)
5. Gehört die Jacke_____(Sie)?
6. Antwortet sie_____(seine Freundin)?

7. Glaubst du_____(sie - singular)?

8. Die Lehrerin hilft_____(die Schüler).

9. Diese Taschen gehören_____(wir) nicht.

Exercise 2. Translate these sentences to German.

1. Why are you (plural) following me? _____

2. How can I help you (singular)? _____

3. Can you (du-form) advise me? _____

4. Please (du-form) congratulate them on their graduation. _____
_____

5. He can't order me!_____

6. Did they thank him for the money?_____

Answers:

Exercise 1:

1. euch erkälten / 2. kämmt sich / 3. dich nicht **schämen** / 4. bewerbe mich / 5. (Ihnen) / 6. (seiner Freundin) / 7. (ihr) / 8. (den Schülern) / 9. (uns)

Exercise 2:

1. Warum folgt ihr mir? / 2. Wie kann ich dir helfen? / 3. Kannst du mir einen Rat geben? / 4. Bitte gratuliere ihnen zum Abschluss. / 5. Er kann mir nicht befehlen! / 6. Haben sie ihm für das Geld gedankt?

LESSON 28: PRESENT PARTICIPLES AND GERUNDS

All About the German Present Participle and Gerund: What They Are and How to Use Them

The **German present participle** and the **German gerund** can seem confusing for the English speakers, mostly because in the English language they both look the same. Both are formed by adding the ending *-ing* to the verb form, e.g. *exciting*, *smoking*.

In German they look different from each other, but the rules on how to form and use either of them are very straightforward for a change. Once you understand what is what, you will never mix them up again!

It is also good to remember that besides the **present participle (Partizip I)**, there is also the **past participle (Partizip II)**, so don't confuse these two terms.

But in this lesson we will focus on the present participle.

So what is it exactly?

Understanding the Present Participle

Forming the present participle is very simple. Just use the infinitive form of any verb and add a *-d* at the end.

Listen to Track 418

infinitive	*present participle*	
sprechen	***sprechend***	speaking
lesen	***lesend***	reading
bellen	***bellend***	barking
tanzen	***tanzend***	dancing

And that's all there is to it! Now let's look at what it is used for.

Applications of the present participle

There are three ways the present participle can be used: As an **adjective**, an **adverb** or a **noun**. There are a few things to consider for each application.

1. Present participle as adjective

As an adjective it stands before a noun and has to follow the same rules of *declension* as all adjectives. Adjectives provide more information about the nouns they relate to.

Listen to Track 419

present participle	used as an *adjective* in a sentence	
weinend	Das *weinende* Kind stand vor der Tür.	The crying child stood in front of the door.
lesend	Der *lesende* Mann sieht entspannt aus.	The man, who is reading, looks relaxed.
spielend	Ich sehe die *spielenden* Hunde.	I see the playing dogs.

2. Present participle as adverb

As an adverb it usually follows after the verb; it *does not require declension* and therefore remains always unchanged. Adverbs provide more information about the verb they relate to.

Listen to Track 420

present participle	used as an *adverb* in a sentence	
weinend	Das Kind stand *weinend* vor der Tür.	The child stood crying in front of the door.
lesend	Der Mann entspannt sich *lesend* im Zug.	The man relaxes reading on the train.
spielend	Die Hunde laufen *spielend* im Park herum.	The dogs run around playing in the park.

3. Present participle as noun

As a noun the present participle needs to be *capitalized* and is subject to *declension* as all nouns in German. You basically omit the original noun and replace it with the present participle, when it is obvious through the context to whom you are referring.

Listen to Track 421

present participle	used as a *noun* in a sentence	
weinend	Der *Weinende* stand vor der Tür. Wir trösten die *Weinenden*.	The crying (boy, neighbor...) stood in front of the door. We comfort the crying (people, children, men, women...).
lesend	Der *Lesende* sieht entspannt aus. Die Brille des *Lesenden* fiel runter.	The reader (person who is reading) looks relaxed. The reader's glasses fell.
spielend	Die *Spielenden* da drüben kenne ich nicht. Der Regen machte dem *Spielenden* nichts aus.	The (dogs, children, athletes...) playing over there I do not know. The rain does not bother the playing (dog, boy, athlete...)

You can relax now, this was the hard part. The German gerund is less demanding.

Understanding the German Gerund

A Gerund is essentially a verb used as a **noun**. In German you just use the *infinitive* verb form as is, and *capitalize* it. And it follows the same rules of *declension* as all nouns.

But at least you don't have to worry about the grammatical gender too much, because gerunds are always *neutral*. Usually the gerund is preceded by the definite article, but sometimes, when speaking in general terms, it can be omitted.

For the plural form, the gerund stays exactly the same, no endings or umlaut are being added.

Listen to Track 422

infinitive	used as *gerund* in a sentence	
rauchen	**Das *Rauchen* ist hier verboten**	(The) smoking is not allowed here.
feiern	Wir freuen uns aufs (auf **das**) *Feiern.*	We are looking forward to celebrating.
aufstehen	Nach **dem** *Aufstehen* trinkt er Kaffee.	After getting up he drinks coffee.
laufen	*Laufen* ist gut für dich.	Running is good for you.
lernen	Deutsch *Lernen* ist nicht schwer.	Learning German is not hard.
reisen	**Die *Reisen*** sind schon geplant. (plural)	The trips are already planned.

German gerunds are also commonly used on signage prohibiting something in combination with the word *verboten* (prohibited, forbidden):

Listen to Track 423

Parken verboten	Parking is not allowed
Betreten verboten	No access
Ballspielen verboten	Ball games are not allowed
Essen und Trinken verboten	Food and drink is not allowed
Anfassen verboten	Do not touch
Mitführen von Hunden verboten	Accompanying dogs are not allowed and so on...

Hopefully this helps you to stay out of trouble in Germany, because now you should be able to recognize what not to do!

QUICK RECAP

- The German present participle and the gerund are both derived from the infinite verb form. In contrast to English they are distinct from each other.

- The present participle is just the infinitive+*d* at the end. You can use it as an adjective, adverb or noun.
- The gerund is simply the infinitive and is used as a noun. Therefore it must be capitalized.
- Using either of them is pretty straightforward, but you might like to brush up on your declension.
- Now you have not only learned the present participle and gerund, but, if you already have some verbs in your vocabulary, you have instantly gained a whole load of new adjectives, adverbs and nouns.

TIME TO PRACTICE!

Workbook Lesson 28. Present Participles and Gerunds

Exercise 1. Fill in the blanks using the present participle of the verbs in brackets:

1. Der _____ Mann stieg in den Zug. (lachen)
2. Ich gebe den _____ Leuten eine Flasche Wein. (essen)
3. Wir gehen _____ in die Schule. (singen)
4. Die Hunde laufen _____ hinter dem Auto her. (bellen)
5. Die neue Kollegin sitzt am Tisch. Es ist die _____ da drüben. (lesen)
6. Du sitzt immer _____ vor dem Fernseher. (schlafen)
7. Die _____ Frau steht auf dem Balkon. (rauchen)
8. Das Wartezimmer ist überfüllt. Die _____ stehen schon vor der Tür. (warten)
9. Annika schaute _____ aus dem Fenster. (träumen)
10. Die _____ Nachbarn riefen die Polizei. (streiten)

Exercise 2. Fill in the blanks matching the correct present participle of the words provided:

1. schreibende / schreibend / Schreibende /schreibenden
   a) Lisa sitzt _____ in der Schule.
   b) Der _____ hörte mich nicht.
   c) Der _____ Junge ist mein Bruder.
   d) Der Lehrer beaufsichtigte die _____ Schüler.
2. protestierende / Protestierenden / protestierenden / protestierend
   a) Die _____ Arbeiter standen vor der Fabrik.
   b) Wir gehen _____ aus dem Raum.

c) Der _____ Student wurde vom Campus verwiesen.

d) Die _____ verlangen bessere Bedingungen.

3. schimpfend / schimpfend / Schimpfende / schimpfende

a) Die _____ hat ihre Tasche verloren.

b) Sie geht _____ aus dem Haus.

c) Meine Mutter jagt die Katze _____ aus der Küche.

d) Der _____ Mann war schuld an dem Unfall.

> **Fun fact:** Johann Wolfgang von Goethe might be one of the most famous German writers, but he certainly did put in the hours. It took him 60 years to complete his masterpiece *Faust*, which explains why it is difficult to place it within a single literary epoch.

Exercise 3. Fill in the blanks using the present participle:

1. Die _____ treffen sich in der Bücherei.
   (The studying (people...) meet in the library.)
2. Das _____ Mädchen erreichte die Baumspitze.
   (The climbing girl reached the tree top.)
3. Wir verbrachten die Nacht _____ auf der Party.
   (We spent the night dancing at the party.)
4. Die _____ Kinder haben die Zeit vergessen.
   (The playing children forgot the time.)
5. Ich beobachtete die _____ Vögel im Garten.
   (I watched the singing birds in the garden.)
6. Die Suppe stand _____ auf dem Herd.
   (The soup stood cooking on the stove.)
7. Der _____ konzentriert sich auf seinen Pinselstrich.
   (The painting (person...) concentrates on his brushstroke.)
8. Du verbringst deinen Urlaub am Strand _____.
   (You spend your holiday laying on the beach.)

Exercise 4. Fill in the blanks using the gerund, including the article where appropriate:

1. Im Restaurant ist _____ verboten. (In the restaurant smoking is prohibited.)
2. Mir macht _____ am meisten Spass. (I enjoy swimming the most.)
3. Meiner Tochter fällt _____ leicht. (My daughter finds the reading easy.)

4. Ich verbiete dir _____ auf der Straße. (I prohibit you (the) playing on the street.)

5. Er hasst _____ des Hundes. (He hates the (dog's) barking.)

6. Wir freuen uns schon auf _____. (We already look forward to the eating.)

7. Sie interessieren sich für _____ von Antiquitäten. (they are interested in the collection of antiques.)

8. _____ ist besonders wichtig für gestresste Menschen. (Sleeping is especially important for stressed people.)

Answers

Exercise 1:

1. lachende / 2. essenden / 3. singend / 4. bellend / 5. Lesende / 6. schlafend / 7. rauchende / 8. Wartenden / 9. träumend / 10. streitenden

Exercise 2:

1. a) schreibend b) Schreibende c) schreibende d) schreibenden

2. a) protestierenden b) protestierend c) protestierende d) Protestierenden

3. a) Schimpfende b) schimpfend c) schimpfend d) schimpfende

Exercise 3:

1. Studierenden / 2. kletternde / 3. tanzend / 4. spielenden / 5. singenden / 6. kochend / 7. Malende / 8. liegend

Exercise 4:

1. Rauchen / 2. Schwimmen / 3. das Lesen / 4. das Spielen / 5. das Bellen / 6. das Essen / 7. das Sammeln / 8. Schlafen

LESSON 29: GERMAN CONJUNCTIONS

I was late because I fell asleep.

I want to come, but I'm too tired.

The work was too hard, so he couldn't finish.

What do these sentences have in common? They are held together by "because", "but", and "so." Words like these let us make long, complex sentences. They are called **conjunctions.**

The Main Types of Conjunctions in German

The two main categories of German conjunctions are coordinating conjunctions and subordinating conjunctions. There are also compound conjunctions, which we will also cover near the end of this lesson.

Coordinating conjunctions do not affect the position of the verb. In other words, the verb takes second position when they are used, as it typically does.

Below is a list of the coordinating conjunctions in German.

Listen to Track 424

und	and
oder	or
denn	because
aber	but
sondern	but (as in rather)
beziehungsweise	or, more precisely

Coordinating conjunctions connect two sentences of equal importance into one.

Listen to Track 425

Examples:

→ *aber, sondern, denn, und, oder*

Sie ist sehr klug, aber sie ist leider faul.

She is very smart, but she's unfortunately lazy.

Er ist nicht nur der beste Koch der Welt, sondern [er] schreibt auch Kochbücher.

He is not only the best cook in the world, but he writes cookbooks as well.

Wir konnten nicht ins Büro gehen, denn das Kind war krank.

We couldn't go to work because the child was sick.

Er zeichnet und singt gern.

He likes drawing and singing.

Ich sehe abends fern oder (ich) schlafe ein.

In the evening, I watch TV or fall asleep.

(Ich) can be omitted, that's why it is in brackets. However, you don't have to omit it.

Tips:

- There is always negation before the word "*sondern*".
- *Aber* can be preceded by negation, but it doesn't have to be.
- You use "*sondern*" where you'd use "*instead* or *but rather*" in English. That's the difference between "*sondern*" and "*aber*".
- Both "*denn*" and "*weil*" mean '*because*', but they require a different word order. 'Weil' is a subordinating conjunction. When it is used, the verb in the clause or sentence beginning with '*weil*' goes to the end. You can't start a sentence with "*denn*".
- "We can conclude that word order remains standard – SVO - with coordinating conjunctions like '*denn*', '*und*', '*aber*', '*beziehungsweise*', '*oder*', and '*sondern*'.

Subordinating Conjunctions
Listen to Track 426

The verb goes to the end of the subordinate clause with subordinating conjunctions. Here is a shortened list:

bis	until
bevor	before
dass	that
nachdem	after
damit	so that
ob	whether, if
seitdem	since

obwohl	although
sobald	as soon as
soweit	insofar as
sofern	provided that
wo	where
während	while
wenn	if, when
weil	because
wie	how

Examples:

Listen to Track 427

Woran denkst du, bevor du einschläfst?

What do you think about before you fall asleep?

Ich warte, bis du endlich kommst.

I will wait until you finally come.

Ich bin der Meinung, dass er nicht kommt.

I believe that he will not come.

Ich spare, damit ich ein Auto kaufen kann.

I am saving money so that I can buy a car.

Wir haben gegessen, nachdem wir nach Hause gekommen waren.

We ate after we got home.

Note: Do not confuse *nachdem* with *nach*. *Nach* is a preposition, not a conjunction.

Sie haben mich gefragt, ob ich Ihnen Geld leihen würde.

You asked me if I would lend you money.

Note: Do not confuse *ob* and *wenn*. *Wenn* can also be translated as 'if', but only in conditionals, as in:

Listen to Track 428

Wenn ich früh aufstehe, arbeite ich mehr.

When I get up early, I work more.

Sie wollen Kinder, obwohl sie nicht genug verdienen.

They want children even though they don't earn enough.

Ich lasse es Sie wissen, sobald ich es selber weiß.

I'll let you know as soon as I do (meaning as soon as I myself find out).

Er war Astronaut, soweit ich mich erinnern kann.

He was an astronaut as far as I remember.

Meine Eltern haben sich kennengelernt, während sie studierten.

My parents met while they were studying.

Während can also be used as a preposition meaning '*during*', in which case it precedes a noun in genitive:

Listen to Track 429

Während seines Studiums haben sie sich kennengelernt.

They met during their studies.

I mentioned '*weil*' and '*denn*' earlier. They both mean '*because*', only the word order is different.

Listen to Track 430

Er arbeitet nicht, weil er krank ist.

He's not working / doesn't work because he is ill.

Er arbeitet nicht, denn er ist krank.

He's not working / doesn't work because he is ill.

Wenn du möchtest, kannst du hier bleiben.

If you want, you can stay here.

Wenn ich mich ausruhe, bekomme ich bessere Ideen.

If I rest, I get better ideas.

Conjunctional Adverbs

Word order is inverted, and the verb comes after the conjunctional adverb. Here is a list of these:

Listen to Track 431

deshalb	that's why
dann	then
deswegen	due to that
ferner	in addition
folglich	as a result
genauso	exactly as...as
inzwischen	in the meantime
jedoch	but
schließlich	ultimately, at the end
seitdem	since then
später	later
trotzdem	despite that
vorher	prior, in advance

Examples:

Listen to Track 432

Ich bin müde, deshalb will ich schlafen.   I'm tired, that's why I want to sleep.

Ich bin müde. Trotzdem gehe ich aus.   I'm tired. Despite that, I'm going out.

(*Trotzdem* can only be used to begin a sentence.)

Ihr wart verärgert , jedoch zeigtet ihr es nicht.

You were angry, but you didn't show it.

Ich komme nach Hause, dann dusche ich.

I come home, and then I shower.

Compound Conjunctions

Compound conjunctions are formed by 2 words and always go together in a sentence.

Listen to Track 433

entweder ... oder   either... or

Entweder kommst du jetzt oder du bleibst zu Hause.

You either come now or stay home.

Der Rock ist entweder blau oder schwarz. The skirt is either blue or black.

weder noch   neither... nor

Er hat weder eine Stelle noch Geld. He has neither a job nor money.

Zwar...aber   though or while... but (also)

Zwar ist er unser Chef, aber er ist auch ein guter Mensch.

Though he is our boss, he is also a good person.

Einerseits...andererseits   on one hand...on the other hand

Einerseits will ich ins Kino gehen, andererseits habe ich keine Zeit.

On one hand, I want to go to the cinema; on the other hand I have no time.

Nicht nur...sondern auch   Not only... but also

Meine Nachbarn sind nicht nur nett, sondern auch reich.

My neighbors are not only nice, but also rich.

anstatt ... zu   instead of

QUICK RECAP:

• Sentence word order depends on the type of conjunction used. If a coordinating conjunction is used, the verb takes second position as usual.

• If a conjunctional adverb is used, word order is inverted, and the verb comes after the conjunctional adverb.

• With subordinating conjunctions like *obwohl*, the verb goes to the end of the subordinate clause.

It would not be an exaggeration to say one could not utter a single meaningful sentence without using conjunctions. The trick is to make a list of the most commonly used conjunctions and memorize the word order rule for each.

TIME TO PRACTICE!

Workbook Lesson 29. German Conjunctions

Exercise 1. Fill in the blanks with a correct conjunction. Sometimes, there is more than one right answer.

1. _____ sie ins Kino gehen, gehe ich mit ihnen. – When they go to the movies, I go with them.

2. Sag mir,_____sie ins Kino gehen. – Let me know if they are going to the movies.
3. Ich möchte gern wissen, _____ er das Leben genießt. – I'd like to know if he enjoys life.
4. _____du Lust hast, machen wir eine Radtour. – If you want, we can go on a cycling tour.
5. Der Papa ist zufrieden, _____ ich gute Noten habe. – Dad is happy if/when I have good grades.
6. Ich möchte wissen, _____du bald fertig bist. – I'd like to know if you'll be done soon.
7. Weißt du, _____ sie mitkommt? – Do you know if/when she's coming?

Exercise 2. Fill in the blanks using one of the following conjunctions:

entweder...oder

weder...noch

nicht nur..., sondern auch

sowohl...als auch

je ....,desto

mal....,mal

1. _____gehen wir ins Kino, _____ wir besuchen unsere Freunde.
2. Ich gehe_____heute_____ morgen ins Kino.
3. Ich kann _____ Französisch,_____ Deutsch.
4. Wir machen Gymnastik_____morgens,_____ abends.
5. _____ mehr ich trainiere,_____ besser werde ich.
6. _____ ich, _____ mein Freund spielen heute Fußball.
7. Ich mag_____ Fleisch, _____ Fisch.
8. _____ ist er zu Hause, _____ im Kino.
9. _____ öfter wir üben, _____ besser spielen wir.
10. Der Tee ist kalt,_____ der Kuchen schmeckt_____ nicht
11. Ich spreche mit meinem Sohn_____ Russisch, _____ Französisch.
12. _____ ich_____ meine Eltern kennen diese Stadt.
13. Ich lese_____ gern Krimis, _____ historische Romane.

14. Mein Cousin wohnt_____ bei den Eltern_____ im Studentenwohnheim.

15. Er kommt _____ um 6_____ um 7 Uhr nach Hause.

16. _____länger ich in Frankreich wohne, _____ besser spreche ich Französisch.

17. _____ich_____ meine Frau können Ihnen diese Stadt zeigen.

18. Er bekommt _____ eine Fünf, _____ eine Drei.

19. _____ nehmen wir mein Auto_____wir bestellen ein Taxi.

20. Hier studieren_____Deutsche_____Ausländer.

Exercise 3. Multiple choice.

1. Which word could you use as a conjunction in the sentence 'He's staying home because it's raining'?

   a) den   b) sondern   c) weil   d) oder   e) a and b   f) a and c

2. Which of these conjunctions means 'but'?

   a) denn   b) oder   c) aber   d) sondern   e) c and d   f) c and b

3. Which of these words means 'as if'?

   a) ob   b) als ob   c) als   d) wenn   e) als wenn

4. Which is the correct translation of this sentence: Ich fahre Auto oder ich fahre Rad?

   a) I drive and I cycle   b) I go hiking or I cycle   c) I cycle, but I also drive
   d) I drive or I cycle

5. Which phrase would you use to complete the following sentence so that it means that you don't have any siblings: ich habe ... Brüder ... Schwestern

   a) sowohl ... als auch   b) entweder ... oder   c) weder ... noch

6. Which of these sentences is not correct?

   a) Ich gehe nicht ins Kino, weil ich spiele Tennis.

   b) Ich gehe nicht ins Kino, denn ich Tennis spiele.

   c) Ich gehe nicht ins Theater, weil ich Tennis spiele.

   d) Da ich Tennis spiele, gehe ich ins Kino nicht.

   e) Ich gehe ins Kino nicht, wenn ich spiele Tennis.

   f) No right answer

7. What is the correct way to complete this sentence: Wir besichtigen das Museum, ...?

   a) ...während wir sind in Berlin

   b) ...während wir in Berlin sind

   c) ...während wir in Berlin

8. Which of these reflects the meaning of the following sentence accurately? 'Although it was short, the concert was really good'.

   a) Obwohl es kurz war, war das Konzert wirklich gut.

   b) Das Konzert war kurz. Trotzdem war es wirklich gut.

   c) Das Konzert war kurz, jedoch war es wirklich gut.

   d) All of the above

9. Which of these sentences is correct?

   a) Nachdem wir uns erholt haben, sehen wir fern.

   b) Nachdem wir haben uns erholt, hören wir Musik.

   c) Nachdem wir uns erholt haben, wir hören Musik.

Exercise 4. Fill in the blanks with the correct conjunction.

1. Er kommt zu Besuch, _____er die Aufgaben erledigt hat. - He's coming to visit after he's completed his homework.

2. Es gibt immer viel Zeit, _____der Film beginnt. - There is always lots of time before the film begins.

3. Nero spielte seine Flöte _____Rom brannte. - Nero played his flute while Rome burned.

4. Es dauert noch 20 Minuten_____Sie fertig sind. - It'll be another 20 minutes until you're finished.

5. Ich habe euch oft gesehen,_____ich hier bin. - I've seen you often since I've been here.

6. _____ich nach London fahre, esse ich nichts. - When I go to London, I eat nothing.

7. _____ ich jünger war, hatte ich keine Haustiere. - When I was younger, I didn't have any pets.

8. Ich habe gelacht, _____ich weinen wollte. - I laughed although I wanted to cry.

9. Ich weiß nicht, _____die Show beginnt. - I don't know when the show starts.

10. _____der Wind weht, bin ich glücklich. - As long as the wind blows, I'm happy.

11. Sie hat mir einen Blick zugeworfen, _____sie mich niemals gesehen hätte. - She threw me a look as if she had never seen me before.

12. Ruf mich bitte an, ____du zu Hause bist. - Please call me as soon as you're home.

13. Ich darf keine Muscheln essen,_____ ich bin allergisch. - I'm not allowed to eat mussels because I'm allergic.

14. Er konnte die Halskette nicht kaufen, _____er nicht genug Geld hatte. - He couldn't buy the necklace as he didn't have enough money.

15. Ich bin mir nicht sicher, _____ich morgen einkaufen gehen kann. - I'm not sure if I can go shopping tomorrow.

16. Sie spart Geld, _____sie im Großhandel einkauft. - She saves money by shopping wholesale.

17. Er macht das Licht an, ___er besser sieht. - He turns on the light so he sees better.

18. Hier ist meine Handynummer,_____sie sich verlaufen. - Here is my mobile number in case they get lost.

19. Er schweigt, _____er nicht lachen kann. – He stays silent so that he can't laugh.

20. Macht die Fenster leise zu, _____die Kinder nicht aufwachen. - Close the windows quietly so the children don't wake up.

21. Wir glauben, _____ihre Antwort falsch ist. - We think that their answer is wrong.

Answers:

Exercise 1:

1.wenn / 2.ob / 3.ob / 4.wenn / 5.wenn / 6.ob / 7.ob

Exercise 2:

1.entweder...oder / 2.weder...noch, sowohl...als auch / 3.nicht nur...sondern auch / 4.nicht nur...sondern auch / 5.je...desto / 6.nicht nur...sondern auch / 7.nicht nur...sondern auch / 8.mal...mal, entweder...oder 9.je...desto / 10.und...auch / 11.mal...mal / 12.weder...noch / 13.nicht nur...sondern auch / 14.weder...noch 15.entweder...oder / 16.je...desto / 17.sowohl...als auch / 18.mal...mal / 19.Entweder...oder / 20.nicht nur...sondern auch

Exercise 3:

1)f / 2)e / 3)b / 4)d / 5)c / 6)f / 7)b / 8)d / 9)a

Exercise 4:

1.nachdem / 2.bevor / 3.während / 4.bis / 5.seitdem / 6.Wenn / 7.als / 8.obwohl / 9.wann / 10.solange / 11.als ob / 12.sobald / 13.denn / 14.da / 15.ob / 16.indem / 17.damit / 18.falls / 19.sodass / 20.damit / 21.dass

LESSON 30: ADVERBS

Adverbs are words that modify the meaning of a verb, an adjective, or another adverb. They do not undergo declension (do not change). This lesson will discuss the types of adverbs in German, how they are used, and the word order use governing them. We will end with exercises to practice what you've learned. Are you ready? Let's go!

Types of Adverbs

In German, we have **adverbs of frequency, temporal adverbs, adverbs of place, adverbs of manner, pronoun adverbs, question word adverbs, modal adverbs, and causal adverbs.**

Adverbs of frequency are those that answer the question of, "How often". The main ones are listed in the table below:

Listen to Track 434

Adverb	Translation
immer	always
häufig	frequently
meistens	most of the time
ab und zu	once in a while
oft	often
selten	rarely
manchmal	sometimes
nie	never
fast nie	almost never

There are also adverbs of fixed frequency. They are used to express that something happens at fixed intervals. Examples of these are *morgens* (in the morning), *abends* (in the evening), *montags* (on Mondays, also *dienstags, mittwochs*, etc), *monatlich* (monthly), *jährlich* (annually), and so on.

Temporal adverbs

As the name suggests, temporal adverbs are used to refer to time. They answer the question of 'When'. **The temporal adverbs referring to the day are listed below:**

Listen to Track 435

Adverb	Translation
heute	today
gestern	yesterday
morgen	tomorrow
übermorgen	the day after tomorrow
Vorgestern	the day before yesterday

There are also so-called subjective temporal adverbs. Here are some examples:

Listen to Track 436

Adverb	Translation
jetzt	now
früher	earlier
später	later
sofort, gleich	immediately
damals	then
dann	after/then
bald	soon

The adverb *gerade* translates as *right now, at the moment, or just*. However, it is rarely translated literally. When it is used, it translates to the present continuous in English:

Listen to Track 437

Ich komme gerade   I was just coming, I am coming now.

Adverbs of Place

Adverbs of place answer the question 'Where'. Below are some examples:

Listen to Track 438

Adverb	Meaning
oben	up
unten	down
links	on the left
rechts	on the right
vorn (e)	in front
hinter	behind
hier	here

da, dort	there
innen	inside
außen	outside
nirgends	nowhere
überall	everywhere

You've probably come across a lot of words starting with "hin" and "her" in German. These particles indicate the direction of movement based on the position of the speaker.

Heraus

If I am outside my office and my coworker is still inside and I want her to come out:

Listen to Track 439

Kommen Sie bitte heraus! or *Bitte kommen Sie heraus!*   Please come out!

Hinein

If my coworker and I are outside the office and I want her to go inside, for example to get some documents she left behind:

Listen to Track 440

Gehen Sie bitte hinein!   Please go in!

Hinaus

If we are both in the office and I want to tell her to go out and grab us something to eat or some coffee:

Listen to Track 441

Gehen Sie bitte hinaus!   Please go out!

Herein

Finally, if I am in the office and she is outside, but the boss says her lunch break is over, I'd call her and say:

Listen to Track 442

Kommen Sie (wieder) herein!   Come (back) in!

Other adverbs that indicate movement include *aufwärts / abwärts* (upwards / downwards) and *vorwärts / rückwärts* (forwards /backwards).

Adverbs of Manner

Adverbs of manner are used to express how people do things. They answer the question of 'how'.

Listen to Track 443

Adverb	Meaning
erstens	firstly
zweitens	secondly
außerdem	in addition
auch	also
ebenfalls	as well

Pronoun Adverbs

Pronoun adverbs are the combination of a pronoun and a preposition. They only refer to inanimate objects. The most common ones are those beginning with 'da'. For example:

Listen to Track 444

Ich denke nie daran.   I never think about that.

Because the verb and preposition are *denken an* (think about), we connect the preposition 'an' with 'da'. When the preposition starts with a vowel, we put an 'r' between it and 'da'.

Er kann nicht mehr darauf warten.   He can't wait for that anymore.

The verb and preposition are *warten auf* (wait for). We connect 'auf' with 'da' the same way.

Sie sind nicht sehr gut darin.   They aren't very good at that.

This comes from *gut in* – good at. We connect in with 'da'.

Dafür habe ich keine Zeit.   I don't have time for that.

We have '*Zeit haben für*' (to have time for). The adverb comes from *für* and *da* – for that.

Question word adverbs

Also called interrogative adverbs, **these are the words used to form questions.** The table below lists the most common ones:

Listen to Track 445

• *Wie* (how) • *Wie viel* (how much/ many) • *Wie alt* (how old) • *Wie oft* (how often) • *Wie lange* (how long) • *Wie weit* (how far)	• *Wann* (when) • *Warum* (why) • *Wieso* (why)	• *Wo* (where) • *Worauf* (where upon) • *Woran* (whereof) • *Woraus* (what from) • *Womit* (whereby)	• *Worüber* (what about) • *Worum* (what about) • *Wozu* (what for) • *Wohin* (where to) • *Woher* (from where)

Please note that for the adverbs in the third and fourth column, the translations given are not the only possible ones. As with pronoun adverbs, **they are derived from a verb or adjective with wo preceding them:**

Listen to Track 446

Woran denkst du?	What are you thinking about?
Worauf kann er nicht mehr warten?	What can't he wait for anymore?
Worin bist du gut?	What are you good at?
Wofür hast du keine Zeit?	What don't you have time for?

Modal Adverbs

Modal adverbs answer the questions "How" or "How much". Below are some common ones:

Listen to Track 447

Modal adverb	Translation	Example	Example translation
Gut	well	Mir geht es gut.	I'm doing well
Schlecht	bad	Mir geht es schlecht.	I'm doing badly.
Gern (e)	To like doing something, to do it with pleasure	Ich fahre gerne Ich esse gerne Pizza	I like driving I like eating pizza
So	like this / so	Das geht so.	It goes like this
Schnell	fast, quickly	Mein Computer ist schnell	My computer works fast.
Langsam	slowly	Du arbeitest langsam.	You work slowly.

Causal adverbs

Our final category of adverbs **indicates the origin or reason for an action. They answer the question of "why".** The most common ones are *darum,* *deshalb, daher, and deswegen* (therefore, for this reason, that's why) and *folglich* (thus, as a consequence). They are used to link two sentences.

Listen to Track 448

Ich will mehr Geld haben, deshalb arbeite ich mehr.

I want (to have) more money, that's why I am working more.

When the adverb is placed at the beginning of a sentence, the subject is moved to third place. This is in keeping with the rule that the verb must come second.

Other Adverbs

Other adverbs include limiting adverbs such as *wenigstens* (at least), *nur, and lediglich* (only) and adverbs of quantity such as *sehr* (very), *genug* (enough), and *kaum* (barely, hardly).

Adverbs in the Comparative and Superlative

Some adverbs can form comparatives and superlatives like adjectives:

Listen to Track 449

Adverb	Comparative	Superlative
bald	*eher*	*am ehesten*
soon	sooner	the soonest
Viel	*Mehr*	*Am meisten*
A lot, many	More	The most
Oft, häufig	Öfter, häufiger	*am öftesten, am häufigsten*
often	more often	the most often
wohl	*wohler*	*am wohlsten*
well	better	the best

Word Order

In general, adverbs are placed near the word they are making reference to. They can be placed at the beginning of the sentence or clause to add emphasis:

Listen to Track 450

Dort ist der Unfall passiert.   That's where the accident occurred.

Der Unfall ist dort passiert.   The accident occurred there.

In the first sentence, the location is perceived as more important than the accident itself. Maybe accidents happen at that place often. In the second sentence, the emphasis is on the accident.

Adverbs of manner usually come after the verb, which they make reference to. They come right before the past participle in the perfect tense.

Listen to Track 451

Example:

Der Unfall ist heute passiert.	The accident occurred today.
Sie haben gestern gespielt.	They played yesterday.

When there is more than one adverb in a sentence or clause, the rule to follow is: temporal, causal, modal, local or TeKaMoLo.

Listen to Track 452

Example:

Es gab keinen Stau. Ich bin gestern deshalb schnell dort angekommen.

There was no traffic jam. Therefore, I got there fast yesterday.

It's also correct to say,

Deshalb war ich schnell da (dort).	So I got there quickly.

Pronoun objects like me, you, him, her etc. come before adverbs in a sentence.

Listen to Track 453

Diese Schuhe sind schön. Du hast sie vorgestern ziemlich billig gekauft.

These shoes are nice. You bought them quite cheaply yesterday.

QUICK RECAP:

- In German, there are adverbs of frequency, temporal adverbs, adverbs of place, adverbs of manner, pronoun adverbs, question word adverbs, modal adverbs, and causal adverbs.
  - Adverbs of frequency are those that answer the question of, "How often".
  - Temporal adverbs are used to refer to time. They answer the question of 'When'.
  - Adverbs of place answer the question 'Where'.

- ○ Adverbs of manner are used to express how people do things. They answer the question of 'how'
- ○ Pronoun adverbs are the combination of a pronoun and a preposition. The most common ones begin with 'da' followed by the preposition.
- ○ Question word adverbs are used to form questions. They are the German words for 'where, how, why, who', etc. Others begin with 'wo' followed by a preposition, as with pronoun adverbs.
- ○ Modal adverbs answer the questions "How" or "How much".
- ○ Causal adverbs indicate the origin or reason for an action. They answer the question of "why".
- In general, adverbs are placed near the word they are making reference to. They can be placed at the beginning of the sentence or clause to add emphasis:
- 3. Adverbs of manner usually come after the verb, which they make reference to. They come right before the past participle in the perfect tense.
- When there is more than one adverb in a sentence or clause, the rule to follow for word order is: temporal, causal, modal, and local or **TeKaMoLo**.

TIME TO PRACTICE!

Workbook Lesson 30. Adverbs

Exercises 1. Here, you practice what you've learned. There can be more than one right answer!

1. Fahren Sie erst nach_____, dann_____ und Sie sind da.
2. Das Auto ist nicht _____ es ist_____.
3. Der Film war_____gut.
4. Wir haben_____gegessen. Wir sind nicht mehr hungrig.
5. Er würde sie _____wiedersehen.
6. Ich habe keine Zeit._____ kann ich nicht kommen.
7. Du rufst_____deine Oma an.
8. Ich gehe nach _____und dann wieder nach_____ .
9. _____ist es schmutzig. Wir müssen mal wieder putzen.

Exercises 2. Select the adverbs in the following sentences. In some sentences, there is more than one.

1. Wir spielen oft draußen hinter dem Haus. – We often play outside behind the house.
2. Da gibt es eine große Wiese und dahinter fängt gleich der Wald an. – There is a big meadow there and the woods start right behind it.

3. Dort ist es auch ein altes Baumhaus, das jetzt uns gehört. – There is an old tree house there too, which is ours now.

4. Unten am See kann man sogar baden, aber das Wasser ist meistens kalt. – You can bathe down by the lake, but the water is usually cold.

5. Hoffentlich ist es morgen schön, denn mein Freund will kommen. – Hopefully it will be nice tomorrow, because my friend wants to come.

6. Dann könnten wir aufs Baumhaus klettern und von oben die Leute beobachten. – Then, we could climb up in the tree house and watch the people from above.

7. Das machen wir immer. – We always do that.

8. Vielleicht kommst du auch? – Maybe you'll come too?

Exercises 3. Fill in the table with the adverbs you selected above.

Adverbs of place	
Adverbs of time	
Adverbs of frequency	
Other adverbs	

Exercises 4. Fill in the blanks with the correct adverb listed below.

Schnell   langsam   klein groß kurz lang heiß kalt

1. Heute muss alles_____gehen, weil Gäste kommen. – Everything has to happen quickly today, because guests are coming.

2. Wir haben_____eingekauft, aber trotzdem etwas vergessen. – We shopped in bulk, but we still forgot something.

3. Die Zwiebel muss noch_____geschnitten werden. – The onion must be cut in small pieces.

4. Die Nudeln dürfen nicht zu_____kochen, sonst haben sie keinen Biss. – The noodles shouldn't be cooked for too long because they have no bite.

5. Ich hoffe, dass du das Fleisch nur _____angebraten hast. – I hope you fried the meat only briefly.

6. Das Essen sollte_____serviert werden und alle sollen es gleichzeitig bekommen. – The food should be served hot and everyone should get it at the same time.

7. Wir möchten unseren Kaffee nicht_____trinken. – We don't want to drink our coffee cold.

8. Wir möchten_____essen und genießen. – We want to eat slowly and enjoy our meal.

Exercises 5. Adjective or adverb? Fill in the blanks.

Kurzfristig   kurz   genau   schwer   ausführlich   lang

1. Zum Glück habe ich einen_____Termin bekommen. – Luckily, I got an appointment soon.

2. Wenn_____ein Termin frei wird, sagen wir Ihnen Bescheid. – If an appointment becomes available soon, we'll confirm.

3. Die Patientin ist_____gestürzt und hat sich verletzt. – The patient had a severe fall and hurt herself.

4. Sie hat sich noch nicht von ihrem_____Sturz erholt. – She hasn't recovered from her severe fall yet.

5. Der Arzt hat uns die Untersuchung_____erklärt. – The doctor gave an exact explanation of the exam.

6. Wir haben den Arzt um eine_____Erklärung der Untersuchung gebeten. – We asked the doctor for an exact explanation of the exam.

7. Wir haben ein _____Gespräch über die Therapie geführt. – We had an in-depth discussion of the treatment.

8. Die Therapie wurde_____besprochen. – The treatment was discussed in depth.

9. Manchmal müssen Patienten_____warten, bis sie an der Reihe sind. – Sometimes patients have to wait for their turn for a long time.

10. Die _____Warterei beim Arzt kann sehr anstrengend sein. – The long waiting at the doctor's can be very stressful.

11. Ich muss_____beim Arzt anrufen, weil ich ein Rezept brauche. – I have to give the doctor a quick call because I need a prescription.

12. Für ein Rezept genügt ein_____Anruf. – A quick call is enough for a prescription.

Exercises 6. Match the questions and answers.

1. Wann hast du Zeit?	a. Abends bin ich öfter noch im Büro. Ruf vorher an.
2. Wie sieht es am Sonntag aus?	b. Ich habe immer Zeit.
3. Hast du Samstag frei?	c. Dienstags kann ich nie.
4. Wann könnten wir uns mal treffen?	d. Nein, samstags muss ich meistens arbeiten.
5. Wie ist es mit Dienstag?	e. Sonntags bin ich selten zu Hause.
6. Und Freitag?	f. Vielleicht mal mittags. Manchmal kann ich eine längere Mittagspause machen.

| 7. Kann ich abends mal bei dir vorbeikommen? | g. Freitags gehe ich zum Tennisspielen. |
| 8. Du jast ja nie Zeit | h. Ich weiß. Das wurde mir oft gesagt. |

Exercises 7. Match the sentences.

1. Hier wohne ich.	a. Oben im zweiten Stock sind die Schlafzimmer.
2. Ich sitze immer vorne im Auto.	b. Da wohnst du.
3. Unten im Keller ist der Hobbyraum.	c.Und ein bisschen weiter weg ein Restaurant.
4. Links in der Küche steht der Kühlschrank.	d. Rechts haben wir den Herd.
5. Nebenan gibt es ein Cafe.	e. Meine Schwester sitzt gerne hinten.

Answers:

Exercise 1:

1. rechts...links or vice versa / 2. hier, da /3. she / 4. Gerade / 5. gern, heute, morgen, etc. / 6. daher, deshalb, etc. / 7. täglich, wöchentlich / 8. oben...unten or rechts...links / 9. überall

Exercises 2:

1.draußen / 2.dahinter / 3.dort, auch, jetzt / 4.unten, moistens / 5.hoffentlich, morgen / 6.dann, von oben / 7.immer / 8.vielleicht, auch

Exercises 3:

Adverbs of place	Von oben, unten, dort, dahinter, draußen
Adverbs of time	Dann, morgen, jetzt
Adverbs of frequency	Immer, meistens,
Other adverbs	Vielleicht, auch, hoffentlich,

Exercises 4:

1.schnell / 2.groß / 3.Klein / 4.lang / 5.kurz / 6.heiß / 7.kalt / 8.langsam

Exercises 5:

1.kurzfristigen, adjective / 2.kurzfristig, adverb / 3.schwer, adverb / 4.schweren, adjective / 5.genau, adverb / 6.genau, adverb / 7.ausführliches, adjective / 8.ausführlich, adverb / 9.lange, adverb / 10.lange, adjective / 11.kurz, adverb / 12.kurzer, adjective

Exercises 6:

1)b / 2)e / 3)d / 4)f / 5)c / 6)g / 7)a / 8)h

English Translation

1. When do you have time?	a. In the evening, I am often in the office. Call me in advance.
2. How do things look on Sunday?	b. I always have time.
3. Do you have Saturday off?	c. It's never possible on Tuesdays.
4. When could we meet?	d. No, I usually have to work Saturdays.
5. How about Tuesday?	e. I'm rarely home on Sundays.
6. And Friday?	f. Maybe at noon. Sometimes I can take a longer lunch break.
7. Can I see you in the evening?	G. I go to play tennis on Fridays.
8. You really don't ever have time!	H. I know. I've been told that many times.

Exercises 7:

1)b /2)e / 3)a / 4)d / 5)c

English Translation

1. I live here.	a. The bedrooms are up on the second floor.
2. I always sit in the front of the car.	b. You live there.
3. The hobby room is in the basement.	c. And a little further down, a restaurant.
4. The refrigerator is on the left in the kitchen.	d. We have the stove on the right.
5. There is a cafe next door.	e. My sister likes to sit in the back.

CONCLUSION

Learning grammar is never an easy task so if you were able to finish all the lessons in this book by consistently learning everyday, kudos to you. You did an amazing job and you should be very happy with your achievement.

If you were not able to follow the daily schedules recommended, don't despair. The important thing is you made use of this book to build a solid foundation for your German grammar. We at My Daily German hope that you will continue to keep learning everyday.

Even just an hour a day or less would go a long way. It could be just listening to a 30-minute German podcast, watching a German movie or TV series, writing to a friend in German, talking to a native German speaker, changing your social media settings to German or reading the news in German... the list goes on.

If you wish to further your studies in German language, we have other books available at My Daily German and on Amazon. Please feel free to browse the different titles. The books such as German Short Stories will help improve your reading and listening skills as well as solidify the knowledge you learned in this grammar book.

You can also follow us on <u>Facebook</u> where we post our new articles on German grammar and culture as well as other updates.

Thank you so much for using this book. It has been a great 30 days (or more) with you. We wish you the best of luck on your German studies.

Frederic Bibard

Founder, My Daily German

AUDIO DOWNLOAD INSTRUCTIONS

Copy and paste this link into your browser:

- https://www.mydailygerman.com/download-audio-grammar
- Click on the book cover. It will take you to a Dropbox folder containing each individual file. (If you're not familiar with what Dropbox is or how it works, don't panic, it just a storage facility.)
- Click the DOWNLOAD button in the Dropbox folder located in the upper right portion of your screen. A box may pop up asking you to sign in to Dropbox. Simply click, "No thanks, continue to download" under the sign in boxes. (If you have a Dropbox account, you can choose to save it to your own Dropbox so you have access anywhere via the internet.)
- The files you have downloaded will be saved in a .zip file. Note: This is large file. Don't try opening it until your browser tells you that it has completed the download successfully (usually a few minutes on a broadband connection but if your connection is unreliable, it could take 10 to 20 minutes).
- The files will be in your "downloads" folder unless you have changed your settings. Extract them from the folder and save them to your computer or copy to your preferred devices, *et voilà !* You can now listen to the audio anytime, anywhere.

IMPORTANT: If you have trouble to download the audio. Do not hesitate to contact us at contact@mydailygerman.com

Made in the USA
Middletown, DE
25 March 2021